JAPANESE MONOGRAPH
NO. 155

RECORD OF OPERATIONS AGAINST SOVIET RUSSIA

ON NORTHERN AND WESTERN FRONTS OF MANCHURIA, AND IN NORTHERN KOREA

(AUGUST 1945)

PREPARED BY
MILITARY HISTORY SECTION
HEADQUARTERS, ARMY FORCES FAR EAST

DISTRIBUTED BY
OFFICE OF THE CHIEF OF MILITARY HISTORY
DEPARTMENT OF THE ARMY

This monograph may not be reproduced
without the permission of the Office
Chief of Military History

Monograph No. 155

Editor's Preface

This is the last in a series of three monographs covering Japanese military activities in Manchuria from January 1943 to the end of World War II hostilities, prepared by former commanders and staff officers of the Kwantung Army. The first (No. 138) deals with Kwantung Army's wartime vigil throughout Manchuria in preparation for operations. The second (No. 154) deals with actual military operations against Soviet forces on the eastern front. This monograph, No. 155, covers operations in the northern and western parts of Manchuria and also in northern Korea.

Like No. 154, this monograph is actually a collection of closely related sub-monographs, each a separate--but by no means complete--study in itself. In preparing these accounts each author relied principally upon notes supplemented by what he could best recall from the past or--more properly--on what impressed him most. Such reliance has not in every case brought forth complete details of tactical operations so much as a picture as seen by the participant from his particular vantage point. (The name of each contributor is given in the first footnote to each sub-monograph).

Since the preparation of the original monograph (in Japanese) in 1950, and its translation by ATIS in 1951, some new information has become available, mainly from repatriates interviewed by the First Demobilization Bureau; this information had been incorporated into the edited version. Because of the condition of the original English translation, the editor's task has amounted to one of re-writing.

The major components of Kwantung Army whose story is told in this monograph are the Third Area Army (Thirtieth Army and Forty-fourth Army) and the Fourth Army, plus the Thirty-fourth Army in northern Korea. The division-by-division account presented in Monographs 154 and 155 requires the reader to labor through two volumes to get a complete picture of operations. To give the reader a broad picture, therefore, the editor has prepared the following summary, (which unfortunately could not be included in the earlier monographs) which he feels may be useful to the reader as an introduction:

> On 9 August 1945, the USSR, in fulfillment of a secret agreement reached at Yalta to enter the war against Japan within three months after the surrender of Germany,

Note: Representative Fraction on maps is not to be used. Graphic Scale can be used to measure distance on the sketches.

i

but in violation of her Neutrality Pact with Japan--
which although abrogated had one more year to run--
attacked Japan's armed forces in Manchuria, Korea,
Sakhalin, and the Kurile Islands simultaneously.

The attack on Manchuria was carried out by the Soviet's
Far East General Army, commanded by Marshal A.M.
Vassilievsky. The army launched its invasion along
the 4,000 kilometer front with three principal drives.
From the east came General Meretskov's 1st Far East
Area Army which attacked Japan's First Area Army and
headed for Harbin and Chilin. From the north came
General Prukaev's 2d Far East Area Army which attacked
Japan's Fourth Army; one thrust from the direction of
Blagoveshchensk headed for Tsitsihar, the other, starting at Khabarovsk and advancing up the Sungari River,
headed for Harbin. The third drive came from the west:
Marshal Malinovsky's Zabaikal Army, supported by cavalry
units of the Outer Mongolia Army, drove towards Hsinking
(Changchun) the capital, and Mukden, while one spearhead
made a dash towards Peiping. Each of the Soviet drives
was supported by strong armored units whereas the only
armored units the Kwantung Army had were two ill-equipped
tank brigades.

The Soviet land offensive was supported by two fleets.
The Pacific fleet, based at Vladivostok and consisting of one cruiser, eight destroyers, ninety submarines,
and sixty torpedo boats, moved to disrupt Kwantung Army's
maritime transportation. On the 11th this naval force
supported amphibious landings at Najin, and on the 14th
at Chongjin, both on the northeast coast of Korea. The
other naval force employed was the Amur River Fleet
which consisted of twenty gunboats and forty armed river
patrol boats; this force supported the river crossings
of the 2d Far East Area Army.

The ability of Kwantung Army elements to counter the
Soviet invasion was perhaps at its lowest ebb since
1941. Almost every one of its first-class divisions
had been transferred to other theaters of war--prin-
cipally the Pacific. To replace them, hastily organized
divisions, formed largely from recruits who had previously been deferred from military service, were
deployed in areas formerly garrisoned by much larger
and stronger forces and at fortifications which had been
stripped of many of their weapons.

By early 1945 Kwantung Army had so little strength left that it was directed by Imperial General Headquarters to create "the semblance of strength" in order to deceive Soviet intelligence. One of the strategems adopted in this connection was to refer to a division as an "army."

Aside from its weak strength and its "false front" Kwantung Army's desperation was revealed by its abandonment of a holding plan and the adoption of a delaying plan, by its shortages of weapons of all types (and the use of bamboo spears as substitutes for rifles), by the lack of tanks and antitank weapons, and by the fact that it had to resort to the use of suicide squads to stop Soviet tanks. In the months from early 1943 to August 1945, Manchuria which had been regarded as the granary, the arsenal, and the manpower reservoir of the Japanese Army, had been divested of much of these resources, and the Kwantung Army, once the most vigorous of Japanese forces, had had so much of its strength sapped that it had become a shadow of its former self and could no longer be considered an effective fighting force. The loss of effectiveness had not been accompanied, however, by an equal loss of morale, for although the Soviet Army accomplished its objective of defeating the Kwantung Army it did not do so in a true military sense, since the Kwantung Army--much of it still intact--did not surrender because of military necessity but at the command of the Japanese emperor.

Map scales used in this monograph, as well as orthographic usages generally conform to those adopted for its predecessors Nos. 138 and 154. Also, as in those earlier monographs, research assistance was provided the editor by ex-colonel Muraji Yano, who at the editor's request also compiled several lists which did not appear in the original manuscript. These have been added as appendices.

The reader seeking additional information on Kwantung Army and the military aspects of Manchuria by Japanese writers may find the following studies helpful: Monograph No. 77, which covers the 1941-1943 period in detail, and Monograph No. 151, which covers air operations. In addition, a series of approximately thirteen studies on the military aspects of Manchuria should prove valuable; now being edited by the Military History Section of Headquarters, Army Forces, Far East, these studies should be available by 1956.

September 1954

Monograph No 155

TABLE OF CONTENTS

Kwantung Army Commanders in Captivity   Frontispiece
Editor's Preface   i

Monograph No 155-A

	Page
CHAPTER I Third Area Army and Thirtieth Army	
Third Area Army	1
Estimate of Enemy Situation and Kwantung Army's Operational Plan	3
Organization and Staff of Thirtieth Army Headquarters	6
Construction of Positions and Defense of Cities	8
Thirtieth Army Headquarters at the Beginning of Hostilities	9
Progress of Operations	11
The Thirtieth Army Headquarters at Hsinking	13
The Revolt of the Manchukuoan Army	15
End of Hostilities	16
Transfer to Kungchuling	16
Disarmament	17

Maps

		Following page
No 1	Third Area Army Operational Zone, May – June 1945	3
No 2	Plan of Thirtieth Army Three Defense Lines, June 1945	5
No 3	Deployment of Major Units of Third Area Army 8 August 1945	10
No 4	Thirtieth Army Operations, 9 – 15 August 1945	11

Chart

No 1	Third Area Army Major Components, Before and During Operations	3

Monograph No 155-B

CHAPTER II   The 39th Division

	Page
Transfer from China to Manchuria	18
Opening of Hostilities	20
End of Hostilities	26
The Soviet Occupation	28
Civil Affairs	31

Maps

		Following page
No 1	Intial Deployment of 39th Division, 8 August 1945	19
No 2	Final Deployment of 39th Division 15 August 1945	24

Charts

No 1	Organic Structure of Infantry Divisions in Manchuria, A-Type (Trianglar) Division	19
No 2	Organic Structure of Infantry Divisions in Manchuria, B-Type (Square) Division	19

Monograph No 155-C

CHAPTER III   The 148th Division

	Page
Organization	32
Training	33
Mission and Operational Planning	34
Outbreak of Hostilities	36
Post-War Situation	43

Map

		Following page
No 1	Defense Plan of Hsinking City, 148th Division and 133d Mixed Brigade, 13 August 1945	40

Charts

No 1	Command and Staff of the 148th Division on 5 August 1945	32
No 2	Personnel and Equipment of 148th Division	32

Monograph No 155-D

CHAPTER IV The 138th Division

	Page
Organization	47
Equipment	49
Deployment and Fighting Effectiveness	50
Opening of Hostilities	51
Termination of Hostilities	53
Disarmament	55
Attitude of Soviet Army toward the Japanese Army	56
Transfer from Hsintun to the Mukden Internment Camp	57
Civil Affairs	58
The Manchurian Army Police	59
Manchurian People	60

Map		Following page
No 1	138th Division Deployment, July - August 1945	50

Monograph No 155-E

CHAPTER V The 125th Division

	Page
Organization	62
Transfer of Division to Tunghua	65
Reorganization	67
Opening of Hostilities	69
Termination of Hostilities	71
Civil Affairs	76

Maps		Following page
No 1	125th Division Disposition in Northern Manchuria February - May 1945	64
No 2	125th Division Deployment in the Tunghua Area July - August 1945	66

Monograph No 155-F

CHAPTER VI The Forty-fourth Army

	Page
Origin of Forty-fourth Army Headquarters	78
Disposition of Units Assigned to the Army	82
Units under the Direct Command of the Army	84

vi

	Page
Operational Preparations	85
"Defense" Mission (Public Peace and Order)	86
Fortifications	89
Transportation	91
Communications	92
Training	93
Intelligence	95
Investigation of Military Topography and Geography	96
Organization of New Units	97
Estimate of Soviet Strength	99
Opening of Hostilities	101
Disposition at Termination of War	110
Casualties	111
Situation at the Termination of War	112
Civil Affairs	122
Manchurians, Koreans, and White Russians	125

Maps — Following page

No 1	Forty-fourth Army Defense Area, July – August 1945	86
No 2	Defense of Forty-fourth Army Zone, 9 – 15 August 1945	91

Sketch — Page

No 1	Wire Communications used by Forty-fourth Army End of July 1945	92

Monograph No 155-G

CHAPTER VII   The 63d Division

	Page
Organization	128
Transfer to Manchuria	130
Training	132
Combat Effectiveness	133
Outbreak of Hostilities	134
Disarmament	135

Map — Following page

No 1	63d Division Deployment, 9 – 15 August 1945	131

Monograph No 155-H

	Page
CHAPTER VIII The 117th Division	
Transfer from China to Manchuria	137
Outbreak of Hostilities	138
End of Hostilities	140

Maps — Following page

No 1   Deployment of 117th Division,
         5 - 9 August 1945 — 138
No 2   Redeployment of 117th Division,
         10 - 19 August 1945 — 140

Monograph No 155-I

	Page
CHAPTER IX The 108th Division in Jehol	
Organization	142
Disposition	144
The Southwest Defense Command and Operations Against the Eighth Route Army	147
Status of Preparations for Operations against the USSR	150
Opening of Hostilities	154
Assembly of Division along the Fouhsin-Chinhsien Line	157
Situation in the Jehol Area	160
Post-disarmament Period	161
The Situation at Chinhsien and at Jehol	164
Japanese Residents, Families, and Land Development Groups	164
Manchukuoan Government Agencies, Army, and Police	165

Maps — Following page

No 1   Situation of Elements of 108th Division,
         8 August 1945 — 149
No 2   Final Disposition of 108th Division,
         9 - 15 August 1945 — 154

Sketch — Page

No 1   Signal Communications Used by 108th Division
         End of July 1945 — 152

Monograph No 155-J

	Page
CHAPTER X The 136th Division	
Organization	166
Opening of Hostilities	167
End of Hostilities	170

Map	Following page
No 1 Defense Plan of Mukden, 136th Division 9 - 15 August 1945	168

Monograph No 155-K

	Page
CHAPTER XI The Fourth Army	
Assumption of Responsibility for Northern Manchuria	172
Geographical Characteristics	173
The Defense Plan	174
Fortifications	175
Intelligence	176
Training	178
Reorganization	178
Status of Preparations	179
Outbreak of Hostilities	180
Situation in Forward Areas	183
Termination of Hostilities	186
Civil Affairs	188

Maps	Following page
No 1 Fourth Army Operational Zone, 8 August 1945	173
No 2 Progress of Operations, Fourth Army 9 - 15 August 1945	180

Sketch	Page
No 1 Signal Communications of Fourth Army 9 August 1945	175

Monograph No 155-L

	Page
CHAPTER XII The 123d Division	

	Page
Organization	192
Training	192
Operational Preparations	195
New Operational Plan	197
Fortifications in the Sunwu Area	199
Status of Preparations	201
Situation at the Outbreak of Hostilities	202
Intelligence Estimate	204
Opening of Hostilities	205
Losses	215
Post-Hostilities Situation	216
Civil Affairs	217

Map	Following page
No 1 Progress of Operations, 123d Division 9 - 15 August 1945	197

Monograph No 155-M

CHAPTER XIII The 135th Independent Mixed Brigade

	Page
Organization	219
Outbreak of Hostilities	220
Progress of Operations	221
Casualties	224

Map	Following page
No 1 Progress of Operations, 135th Mixed Brigade 9 - 17 August 1945	221

Monograph No 155-N

CHAPTER XIV The 149th Division

	Page
Organization	226
Operational Preparations	228
Opening of Hostilities	229
Situation at the End of the War	232
Civil Affairs	235

Map	Following page
No 1 Deployment of Elements of 149th Division 9 August 1945	227

Monograph No 155-O

CHAPTER XV   The Thirty-fourth Army Headquarters

	Page
Transfer from China to Korea	237
Operational Preparations	239
End of the War and Negotiations with the Soviets	243
Civil Affairs	247

Map	Following page
No 1 Deployment of Thirty-fourth Army 9 August 1945	239

Monograph No 155-P

CHAPTER XVI   The 137th Division

	Page
Organization	248
Situation Immediately Prior to Hostilities	249
End of the War and Negotiations with the Soviets	251
Assembly in Pyongyang	251

Map	Following page
No 1 137th Division Deployment, 9 August 1945	249

Monograph No 155-Q

CHAPTER XVII   The Nanam Divisional District Unit

	Page
Organization and Missions	257
Assignment and Missions	260
Opening of Hostilities	261
End of Hostilities	264

Maps	Following page
No 1 Deployment of Nanam Divisional District Unit 9 August 1945	258

		Following page
No 2	Progress of Operations, Nanam Divisional District Unit 13 - 18 August 1945	261

Table

		Page
No 1	Actual strength of Kwantung Army Components at Outbreak of Hostilities (August 1945) and KIA Estimates	266

Appendicies

No I	Major Tactical Ground Units of Japanese Army Up to 1945	268
No II	Conditions in USSR Internment Camps for Japanese POWs	274

No III	List of Commanders in Kwantung Army
	  a Early 1943
	  b Early 1944
	  c 31 July 1945
		277

No IV	Chart 1 Japanese Casualties	280
	Chart 2 Figures on Japanese Repatriates	281
INDEX		282

Monograph No 155-A

CHAPTER I

Third Area Army and Thirtieth Army[1]

Third Area Army[2]

In May 1945, Kwantung Army decided to modify the boundaries of the three major military sub-divisions of Manchuria, and to alter the disposition of subordinate commands. Retaining the same number of military sub-divisions, it expanded the eastern front zone of the First Area Army, gave Fourth Army responsibility for northern Manchuria, and moved Third Area Army southward to assume control of southcentral and southwestern Manchuria.

This redisposition, made pursuant to the abandonment of the holding operational plan and the concurrent adoption of the delaying operational plan, gave Third Area Army responsibility for the following provinces: Jehol, Chinchou, Antung, Fengtien, Tunghua, West Hsingan, South Hsingan, Chilin, and the southern parts of East Hsingan and Lungchiang. By these changes, Kwantung Army, while retaining the three military sub-divisions of the country, indicated

---

1. Most of the information in this chapter relative to Thirtieth Army Headquarters was furnished by Lieutenant Colonel Masahiko Kuwa, operations staff officer of that headquarters.
2. No separate monograph on Third Area Army Headquarters has been prepared. Most of its top ranking officers are still in Soviet custody. The information relative to this headquarters was compiled from several sources, including the monographs on the Thirtieth and Forty-fourth Armies. (See also Monograph No 138).

the ascending importance of southcentral and southwestern Manchuria, since prior to this time this area had been under the jurisdiction of the Kwantung Defense Army which, as "a peace and order" force, was neither prepared nor equipped for military operations.

The new zone assigned to Third Area Army gave it a common boundary with Outer Mongolia, Inner Mongolia, and China. Each of these countries was a potential base from which the enemy could attack: Outer Mongolia was under Soviet control; Inner Mongolia, though under Japanese control, was not well defended and could be easily overrun by the Outer Mongolian Army of the Soviets; China was already being used as a base of operations by the Chinese Nationalist forces as well as the Chinese Communist forces, and the latter could be expected to intensify their activities in the event the Soviets attacked Manchuria.

Upon assuming control of its new zone, Third Area Army was given only one major subordinate command--the Kwantung Defense Army which subsequently (on 5 June) was converted to a tactical command and redesignated the Forty-fourth Army. Third Area Army assigned Forty-fourth Army the western part of its zone (excluding Jehol Province), from the border of Outer and Inner Mongolia eastward to the approaches of the Hsinking-Mukden railway. It retained under its direct control the southwestern and eastern parts of its zone. In the southwestern part, principally in Jehol Province, the 108th Division was deployed; in the eastern part, several inherited units

were deployed and several divisions were being newly organized.
(See Map No 1)

The vacuum in the eastern sector of Third Area Army's zone clearly indicated the need for an additional army headquarters, particularly in view of the fact that Kwantung Army planned to make its last stand in this sector. Kwantung Army had recognized this while planning the redisposition of its commands pursuant to its adoption of the delaying operational plan.

Although not formally authorized to organize Thirtieth Army until late July, Kwantung Army Headquarters, assuming that authorization would be granted, included it in all its planning. Meanwhile, it instructed Third Area Army Headquarters to initiate operational preparations which would later become the responsibility of the new army headquarters.

By the time hostilities began Third Area Army had, besides its two army headquarters, nine divisions and five brigades. (See Chart No 1)

Estimate of Enemy Situation and Kwantung Army's Operational Plan

On 14 June, Kwantung Army Headquarters held a meeting at Hsinking with commanders of its major subordinate commands and gave them the following estimate of the enemy situation:

> Soviet forces are expected to start the invasion of Manchuria in concert with the imminent U.S. landing on the Japanese homeland or southern Korea. The invasion is expected to begin before mid-winter, but not earlier than September.

Headquarters also summarized for the assembled commanders the instructions it had received from General Yoshijiro Umezu, Chief of the Army General Staff, during the Dairen Conference of 4 June[3], at which the concept of the delaying plan had received formal approval. Indicating that it had had time to complete only a rough outline of an operational plan, Headquarters announced its decision to disseminate this rough outline in view of the rapidly changing war situation. The objectives of this plan, insofar as they pertained to Third Area Army, were:

> To <u>exhaust</u> the invading Soviet forces by carrying out harassing operations in the area between the western border and the Dairen-Hsinking Railway, but to avoid a major engagement; then to withdraw to the Tunghua area and destroy the enemy in the area east of the railway, from prepared positions in the Tunghua area.[4]

Details pertaining to its subordinate commands were:

> 1. The Forty-fourth Army and the 108th Division will <u>avoid a decisive battle</u> and will exhaust the enemy's fighting strength and delay his advance. Should the enemy infiltrate and advance, these units will try to impair the enemy's fighting capacity by attacking him from the rear.
>
> 2. The Thirtieth Army <u>will destroy the enemy</u>, utilizing prepared positions in the following areas:
> a. The first line of defense (advance positions) will be the principal cities along the Dairen-Hsinking Railway; particularly, Hsinking and Mukden must be secured. b. The second line or intermediate positions will be the line connecting Hailung, Shanchengchen,

---

3. See Monograph No 138, pp 141-3.
4. This referred to the positions in the redoubt area, then only in the planning stages.

MONOGRAPH NO. 155-A
CHART NO. 1

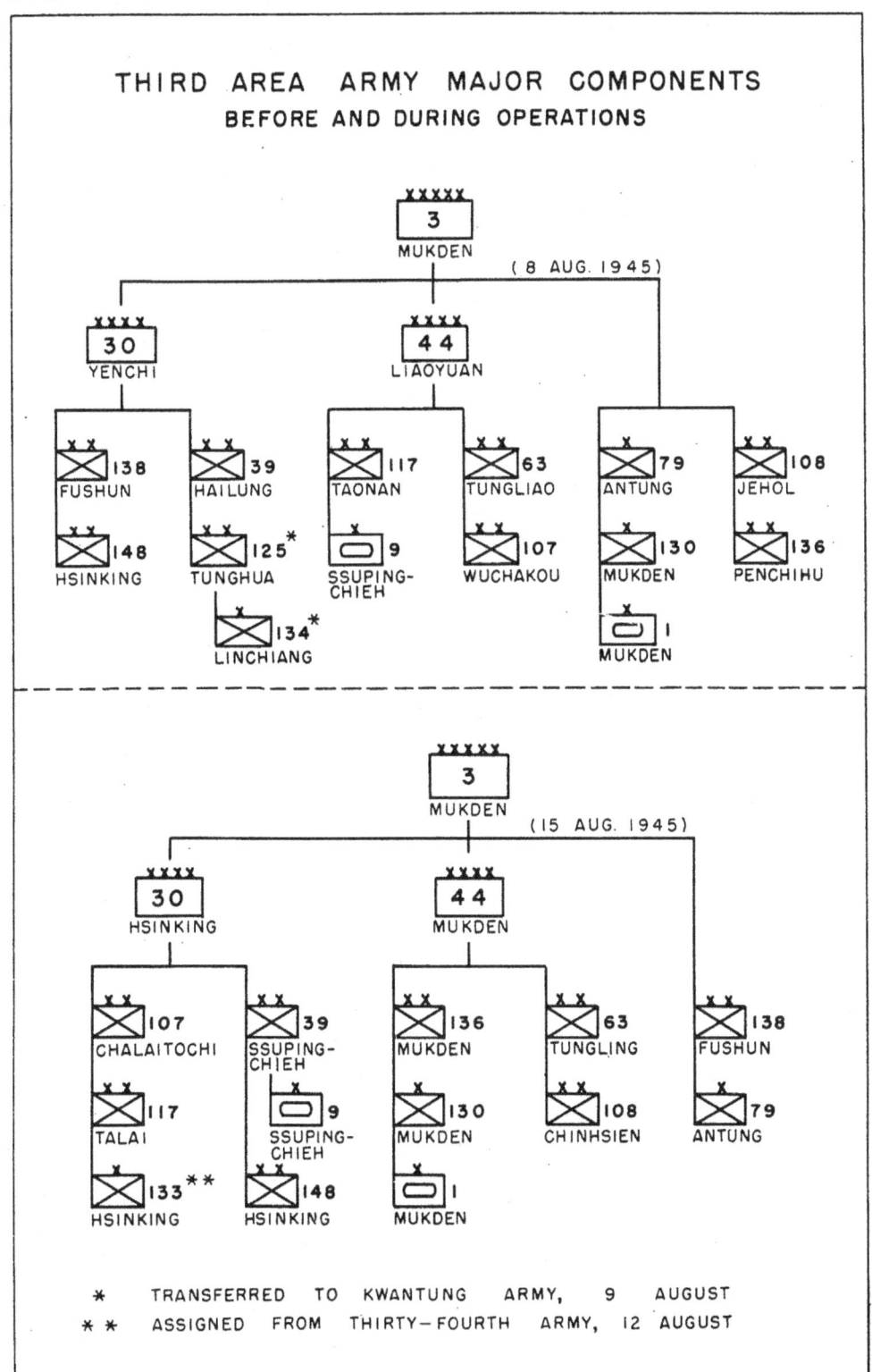

MONOGRAPH NO 155-A
MAP NO. 1

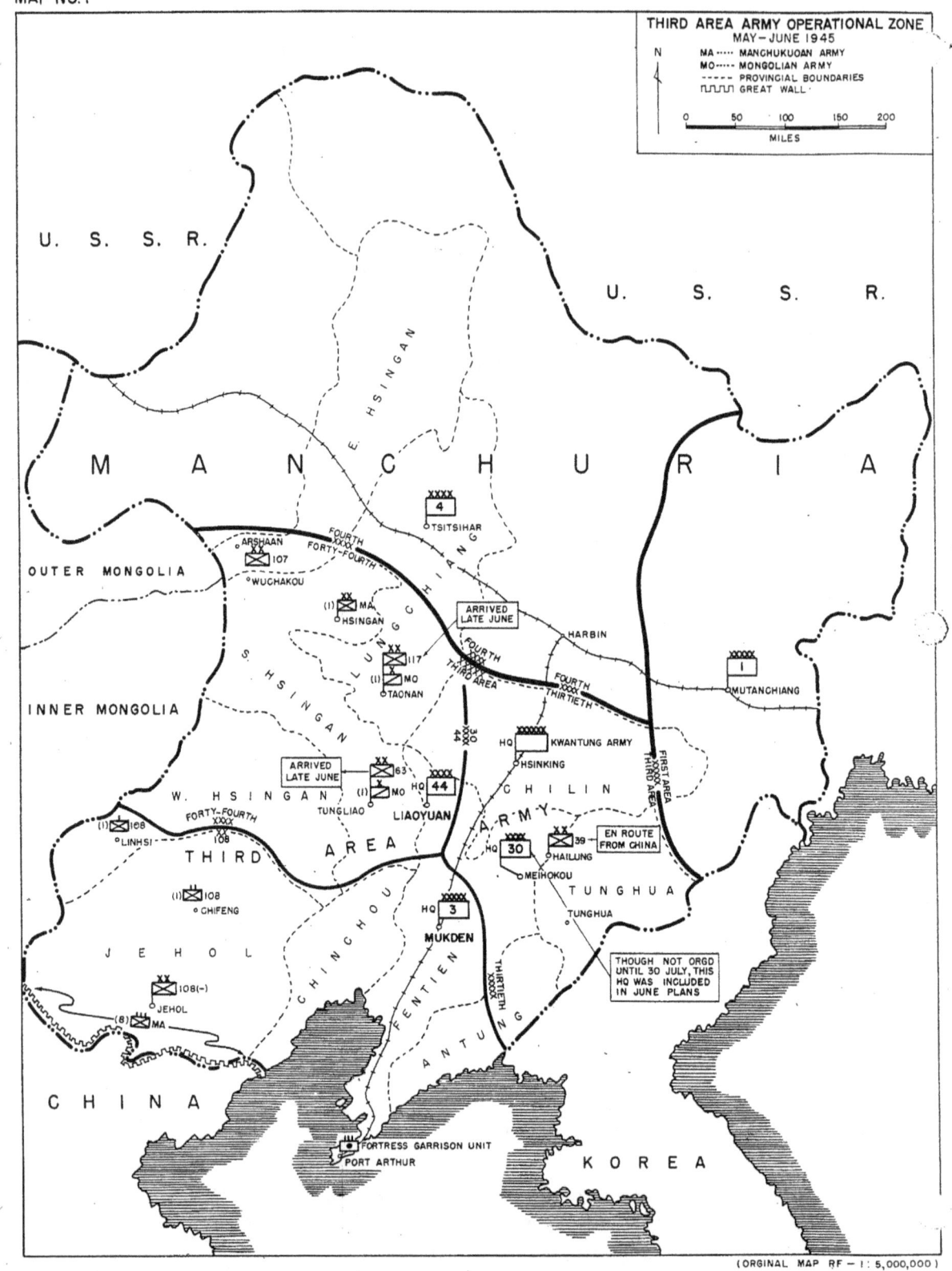

Chingyuan, and the general vicinity of the uplands
west of the Chilin-Mukden Railway, as well as the
area of Penchihu, Fengcheng, Antung, and points on
the Antung-Mukden Railway. c. Third line positions
(main positions) will be the line connecting Chinchuan,
Liuho, Hsinpin, and Huanjen. (See Map No 2.)

3. The operational boundary between the Thirtieth
Army and the Forty-fourth Army will be the Dairen-
Hsinking Railway, the railway itself being included
in the Thirtieth Army's area.

4. The principal Manchurian cities will be utilized
as key defense positions under the guidance of the
Manchukuoan Government; military and civilian organs
will work together to check the Soviet invasion in
depth.

This plan, in effect, gave the important mission of directing the last ditch stand which Kwantung Army planned to make in the Tunghua redoubt area to Thirtieth Army headquarters, which though conceived was as yet unborn. It was to be located at Meihokou.

The commander of the Third Area Army, General Jun Ushiroku, was unalterably opposed to the proposal that his force retreat to the Tunghua area and fight a decisive battle there.[5] His reasons, based entirely on his concern for Japanese residents, can be summarized as follows:

> In the areas under the control of the Third Area Army, there are now about 1,100,000 Japanese residents, most of whom live in the areas bordering the Dairen-Hsinking Railway, particularly in the large cities such as Hsinking (Changchun) and Mukden. The Tunghua area has practically no housing facilities, and it is impossible to prepare billets and to store food there

---

5. For a brief background of General Ushiroku, see Monograph No 154-A, page 11, footnote 10.

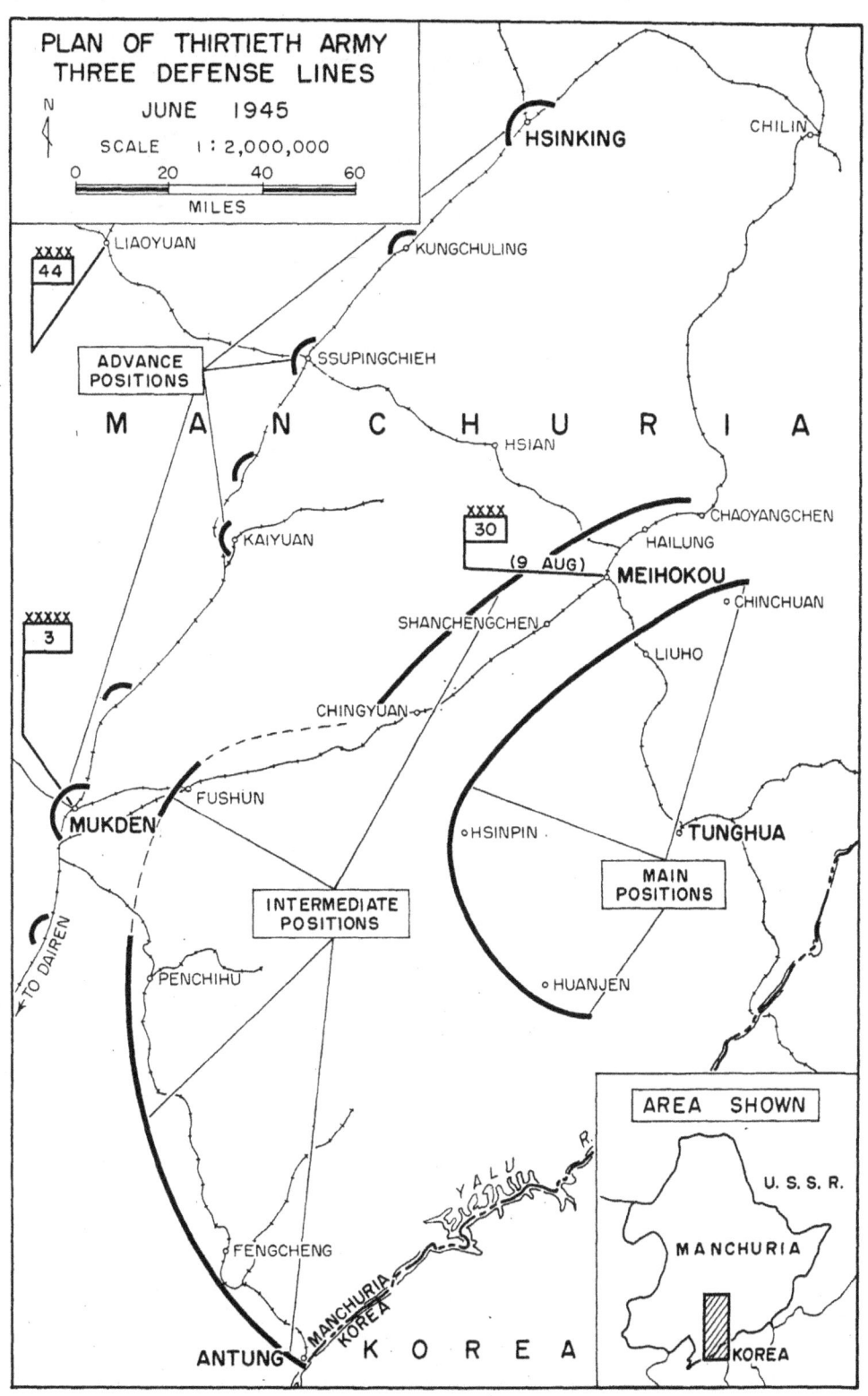

> for residents within the current year since fortifications and storage areas for ammunition and food for military forces alone have yet to be started. Furthermore, the winter cold in the Tunghua area is just as severe as in Tsitsihar, and it is impossible to live there during the winter without housing facilities. In effect, therefore, the Kwantung Army operation plan aims to continue operations by abandoning the 1,100,000 Japanese residents. As commander of the Area Army, I cannot endorse such a policy. Therefore, the Area Army must make its decisive stand in the railway zone contiguous to the Dairen-Hsinking Railway, including the large cities, and share the fate of the residents to the very end.

The seriousness with which General Ushiroku viewed the situation and the firm determination he had to fight the decisive battle in the railway zone were indicated as late as 8 August to Lieutenant General Shojiro Iida, when the latter was departing for Yenchi to assume command of the newly formed Thirtieth Army. General Ushiroku told General Iida: I will defend Mukden to the last, and I want you to defend Hsinking to the last.

Organization and Staff of Thirtieth Army Headquarters

Thirtieth Army Headquarters, the last army headquarters to be formed by the Kwantung Army, was organized at Yenchi in Chientao Province beginning on 31 July 1945. In charge of organizing the new headquarters was Lieutenant General Keisaku Murakami, Commander of the Third Army.[6]

---

6. Further details of the organization of Thirtieth Army Headquarters are given in Monograph No 138, pp 146-8.

Providing personnel for the new army headquarters was a major problem. To command Thirtieth Army, Lieutenant General Shojiro Iida, who had become well known for his occupation of French Indochina in 1941, was called from retirement. Major General Michio Kato was named to be chief of staff. The senior operations staff officer was Colonel Takeshi Yoshikawa; he arrived at Yenchi on 8 August. The junior operations staff officer was Lieutenant Colonel Masahiko Kuwa (author of this chapter), who at the time of his assignment was a hospital patient in Mukden. Major Shinkichi Hirose was assigned as logistics staff officer, but did arrived from Hailar until the war began. The intelligence staff officer was Major Takeshi Yamagishi, formerly on the staff of Kwantung Army; he joined Thirtieth Army on 10 August.

On 30 July Imperial General Headquarters issued the following order of battle for Thirtieth Army:

```
Thirtieth Army Headquarters
39th Division
125th Division
138th Division
148th Division
21st Independent Heavy Field Artillery Battalion
   (150-mm howitzer)
27th Independent Heavy Mortar Battalion
1st Heavy Artillery Regiment (240-mm howitzer)
19th Heavy Artillery Regiment (240-mm howitzer)
7th Independent Heavy Artillery Battalion (300-mm howitzer)
2d Engineer Unit Headquarters
40th Independent Engineer Regiment
Three special guard battalions
Five special guard companies
One special guard engineer company
One motor transport battalion
```

> One transport battalion (horse drawn)
> One road construction unit
> One construction duty company
> One land duty company
> One sea duty company
> One army hospital

Of the four divisions, none had been in the redoubt area prior to June. The 39th was enroute from China, the 125th arrived at Tunghua during June, the 138th was organized in early July and the 148th in late July. Furthermore, as things developed, the Army was to lose during the early stages of operations two of these divisions—the 125th and 138th, although because of the delay in receiving transfer orders, it was to control their operations until about 12 August. Also, as a result of a boundary change on 12 August, the Army was to acquire two additional divisions, the 107th and 117th.

Construction of Positions and Defense of Cities

The operational preparation which Third Area Army undertook in behalf of Thirtieth Army related principally to the construction of fortifications and the defense of cities, and were scheduled to be completed--on the basis of maximum effort--by early November. Actually, because of the many problems involved in getting preparations under way, Third Area Army was able to accomplish little more than the reconnaissance of positions before the war started. The areas reconnoitered were:

> For First Line Positions (in the forward or advance
>   zone): Mukden, Ssupingchieh, and adjacent areas

> For Second Line Positions (in the intermediate zone):
> Fushun, Penchihu, Antung, and adjacent areas
>
> For Third Line Positions (in the rear or main defense zone): Chinchuan, Liuho, and adjacent areas.

Only at Antung, near the Manchuria-Korea border, had the construction of positions been actually begun. In other areas the delivery of fortification materials to the construction sites was delayed; furthermore, the organization of units designated to perform this work had not been completed, and units from China had not yet arrived. In many cases, laborers to assist military units, though ready to work, could not be assigned to duties because the military units themselves had not arrived. Moreover, by the time the military units did become available the Area Army was in the midst of preparations for a training program in the Mukden area. (Scheduled to last one week, this program did not begin until 8 August, and had to be suspended with the outbreak of hostilities on the following day.)

Although Kwantung Army had planned the defense of major cities as early as the beginning of 1945, it had not notified mayors of cities and towns in Fengtien Province of the plan until about 3 August. By that time the attitude of government agencies and private citizens in Manchuria was not cooperative.

Thirtieth Army Headquarters at the Beginning of Hostilities

At the start of the war, Thirtieth Army Headquarters was still in Yenchi completing the final stages of its organization. With the

MONOGRAPH NO. 155-A
MAP NO. 3

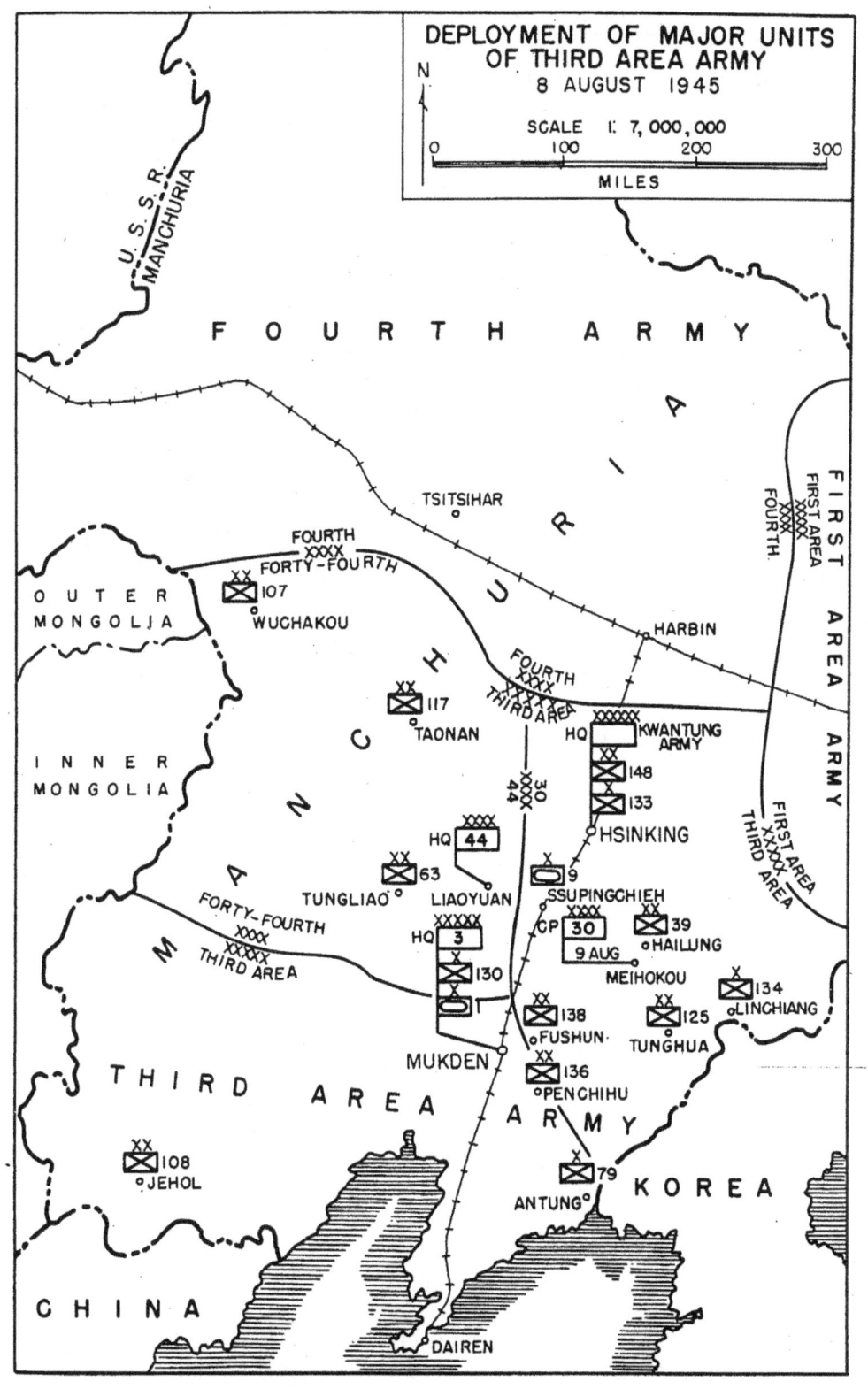

opening of hostilities, General Iida, in company with his chief of staff and his senior staff officer, flew to Meihokou during the morning of 9 August; his senior staff officer continued on to Mukden for consultations with Third Area Army Headquarters. The junior operations staff officer, Lieutenant Colonel Kuwa, was already in Mukden, having only recently been released from the hospital. Meanwhile, the rest of the headquarters started to move to Meihokou by rail, leaving Yenchi on the evening of the 9th.

By the start of the war, the four divisions placed in the order of battle of the Thirtieth Army on 30 July were deployed as follows: the 39th Division Headquarters was at Hailung, with the division's infantry group concentrated in the Hailung, Tungfeng, and Hsian Areas (the division's artillery unit still had not arrived due to transport difficulties); 125th Division Headquarters was at Tunghua, with the division's main body concentrated in the Tunghua and Liuho areas; 138th Division Headquarters was at Fushun, with the main body in the Fushun and Nantsamuhuote areas; 148th Division Headquarters and the main body of the division were concentrated in the vicinity of Hsinking. (See Map No 3, and also Table No 1 for the strength of all divisions in Manchuria).

The following units were in the Tunghua area: 21st Independent Heavy Field Artillery Battalion, 27th Independent Heavy Mortar Battalion, 1st Heavy Artillery Regiment, 19th Heavy Artillery Regiment, and the 7th Independent Heavy Artillery Battalion.

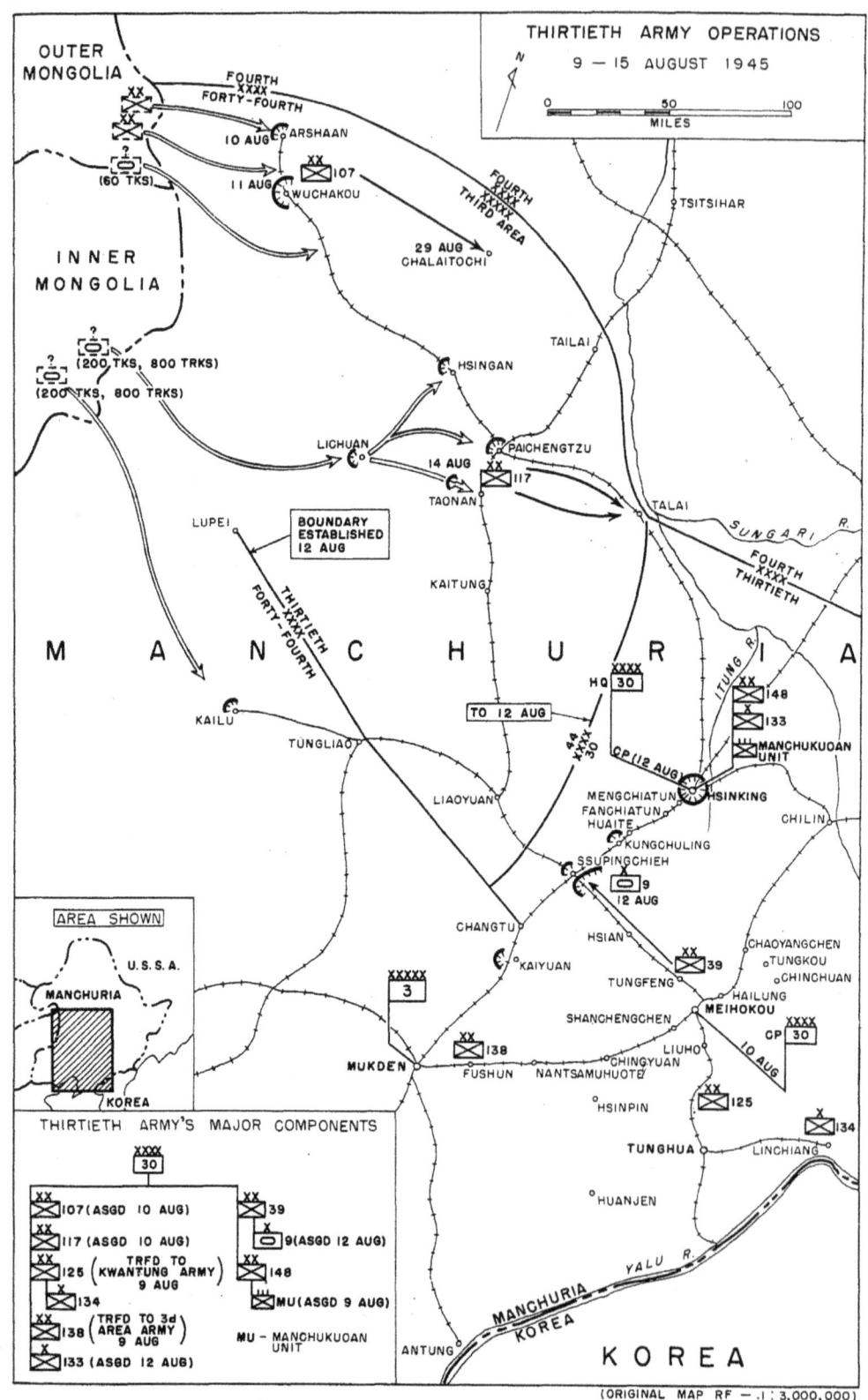

The 2d Engineer Unit Headquarters and the 40th Independent Engineer Regiment were attached directly to the Area Army as soon as they arrived in Mukden from central China in mid-July, and were given the mission of supervising all of the Area Army's fortification work. However, Thirtieth Army Headquarters was unable to assume command of these and other assigned units until the end of the war.

Progress of Operations

Upon arrival at Meihokou on 10 August, Thirtieth Army Headquarters established a command post at the Umenoya Hotel in front of the Meihokou Station. During the afternoon both operations staff officers returned to Meihokou from Third Area Army Headquarters in Mukden, with orders to the following effect:

> The enemy mechanized force in front of Third Area Army has penetrated the border and is advancing eastward in several columns and will reach the areas along the Dairen-Hsinking Railway on about 13 August at the earliest. On the eastern border of Manchuria Kwantung Army positions were breached on 9 August and the enemy reached Suiyang and Hunchun. An element of the enemy mechanized force is pushing toward Mutanchiang. The enemy has penetrated the border at other points but the situation is vague, due to the disruption of communications.
>
> The Third Area Army will start operations according to its prearranged plan. The Thirtieth Army will secure the Hsinking and Ssupingchieh Areas, and will destroy the invading enemy.

In accordance with this Area Army order, Thirtieth Army issued an order to the following effect to the various groups that assembled at Meihokou on the evening of 10 August (See Map No 4.):

> The Army will secure Hsinking and Ssupingchieh, and will destroy the invading enemy.
>
> The 148th Division will secure the special municipality of Hsinking, and destroy the invading enemy.
>
> The 39th Division will advance to Ssupingchieh, securing the upland zone east of the city, and will destroy the invading enemy.
>
> The 125th Division will advance to the sector around Meihokou and prepare for action.

Until the receipt of Third Area Army's order on the evening of 10 August, the Army had not known the enemy situation nor the Area Army's plan, since it had no means of military communication, and the public telephone system had been disrupted. To remedy this, the Army on the morning of 11 August dispatched Major Takeshi Yamagishi, intelligence staff officer, to Kwantung Army Headquarters' rear command post at Tunghua, and Lieutenant Tomiji Onishi, an officer attached to the operations section, to the Area Army Headquarters at Mukden for liaison purposes.

On the night of 11 August, Area Army Headquarters attempted to notify the Army by public telephone of all orders it had issued since the outbreak of hostilities. So many conversations were going over the wires at the time, however, that nothing could be understood except that the 125th Division had been attached directly to the Kwantung Army and that Thirtieth Army Headquarters was under orders to advance speedily to Hsinking.

Erroneously judging from this garbled conversation that the

Area Army plan had been changed to the extent that Ssupingchieh had been deleted from the areas to be defended by Thirtieth Army, the Army ordered the 39th Division at Ssupingchieh to move to Hsinking.

Early on the morning of 12 August, an advance party of the Army (consisting of the Army commander, chief of staff, and the senior operations staff officer) flew from the Tungfeng airfield to Hsinking in a plane provided by the Second Air Army Headquarters for use in evacuation work. At that time the main force of the Army Headquarters still had not arrived at Meihokou from Yenchi due to a train delay caused by bombing in the vicinity of Chilin.

The Thirtieth Army Headquarters at Hsinking

The advance party arrived at Hsinking airfield at noon on 12 August. General Yamada, Commander in Chief of the Kwantung Army, happened to be at the airfield at that time, en route in his withdrawal to Tunghua. He ordered the Thirtieth Army Commander to defend the special municipality of Hsinking, and to assume command of all Kwantung Army units in the Hsinking area.[7] These units were principally:

> 133d Independent Mixed Brigade
> 35th Tank Regiment
> Hsinking Antiaircraft Artillery Unit
> 26th Antiaircraft Artillery Regiment
> Imperial Guard Group (for the Manchukuoan Emperor)
> Cadet Unit of Manchukuo Officers School

---

7. The city of Hsinking (Changchun), unlike other cities, was not under any provincial government. It had independent status under the Manchukuoan Government, (not unlike Washington, D.C.). Hence, it was called the "special municipality of Hsinking." Subsequent textual references will refer to it simply as Hsinking.

At noon on 12 August, Thirtieth Army Headquarters established a command post in the office building of Kwantung Army Headquarters. It immediately contacted Third Area Army Headquarters and was given the following order, which corrected the erroneous assumption made from the telephone conversation of the night of the 11th while at Meihokou:

> The Area Army will destroy the enemy in the Dairen-Hsinking Railway zone.
>
> The Thirtieth Army will secure Hsinking and Ssupingchieh, and destroy the enemy.
>
> The 107th Division at Wuchakou and the 117th Division at Taonan will be placed under the command of the Thirtieth Army.
>
> The boundary of the combat zone with the Forty-fourth Army will be changed from the Dairen-Hsinking Railway line to the Changtu-Tungliao-Lupei line, the line itself being the responsibility of the Forty-fourth Army.

The Army promptly ordered the 39th Division to halt its movement to Hsinking and to reassume its positions in the uplands east of Ssupingchieh, meanwhile retaining the 231st Regiment, which had already arrived in Hsinking, as a reserve.

With the two newly acquired divisions near the Mongolian-Manchurian border, meanwhile, the Army had no means of communication. The 107th Division at Wuchakou, fighting a superior enemy force, was believed to have been encircled. The 117th Division was believed to have withdrawn from the Taonan area and to be retreating toward Hsinking, some elements by rail and some by foot.

On the morning of 13 August, Thirtieth Army issued its first order for the defense of Hsinking. It was substantially as follows:

> The enemy advance is gradually decelerating, and he is not expected to appear in front of Hsinking until about 15 August, at the earliest. The Army will secure Hsinking with its main strength, and will destroy the attacking enemy.
>
> The general disposition of units will be as shown in the attached map. (See Map No 1, Monograph No 155-C.)

Upon receipt of this order on the evening of 13 August, the various Army elements gradually took their positions and began erecting hasty defense works. The next day, the Army received a report from outposts stating that the advance of the enemy mechanized force on the western front was slowing down because of inadequate fuel and rainy weather, and that the enemy could not be expected to reach Hsinking until after 15 August.

The Revolt of the Manchukuoan Army

On the same day a conflict erupted between Japanese and Manchukuoan force within the walls of the old Hsinking city. The Manchukuoan force drew the erroneous impression that the change of disposition toward Itung River ordered for the Imperial Guard Group, in accordance with the Army order of 13 August regarding the defense of Hsinking, was aimed at disarming the Manchukuoan forces. The clash broke out initially between the Imperial Guard Group and elements of the 148th Division, but was extended to the Japanese and Manchukuoan officers on the faculty of the Manchukuoan Officers School. By 15 August, the Japanese and Manchukuoan groups were pitted against each other as distinctly as hostile camps. The conflict continued until about 19 August, but was confined to the city of Hsinking.

End of Hostilities

At about 1400 hours on 14 August, Staff Officer Suehiro of the Area Army Headquarters telephoned Staff Officer Kuwa stating: the Emperor has ordered the cessation of hostilities. Please take charge of Hsinking accordingly.[8] Thirtieth Army immediately issued cease-fire orders to the various units in Hsinking.

General Yamada, upon his return to Hsinking from Tunghua that evening, ordered operations to be resumed because he had not issued a cease-fire order. Thirtieth Army was obliged to reverse it orders to subordinate units. However, until the Imperial Rescript was received it was difficult to restore control over the units.

Transfer to Kungchuling

After the issuance of the Imperial Rescript, there was a discussion as to how the disarmament of the approximately 30,000 men in Hsinking should be conducted. In order to minimize friction with the Soviet forces, it was decided disarm each unit separately at the ordnance depot at Mengchiatun in the southern suburbs of Hsinking, and to move the troops to Kungchuling. On the morning of 18 August, the Thirtieth Army began moving its major elements with the exception

---

8. Earlier, in the morning, Thirtieth Army Headquarters had been informed by Staff Officer Nohara of the Kwantung Army Intelligence Section that the Japanese Government had been broadcasting acceptance of surrender. Colonel Suehiro apparently misunderstood the situation. Although the Japanese Government had been broadcasting acceptance of surrender, the Emperor did not sign the Imperial Rescript until 2300, 14 August 1945.

of the main body of the 148th Division. Thirtieth Army Headquarters reached Kungchuling on the night of 19 August. On the same night, the vanguard of an enemy mechanized force reached Fanchiatun on the Dairen-Hsinking Railway and engaged Japanese units en route to Kungchuling. After a brief clash, the main body of the 231st Infantry Regiment of the 39th Division was disarmed and taken to Huaite.

Disarmament

At noon on 19 August, a Soviet delegation of the Zabaikal Area Army,[9] arrived at the Hsinking airfield in a transport escorted by about fifteen fighter planes. General Matsumura, representing Kwantung Army Headquarters, and Colonel Kuwa, representing the Japanese forces in Hsinking, met the delegates. The Soviets ordered the units still in Hsinking to be assembled for disarmament in the southern suburbs of Hsinking. The units at Kungchuling and Ssupingchieh were disarmed on 20 August. General Suemitsu, assembled units of both the Hsinking Defense District and the 148th Division, at several places, including Chienkuo University, the Tatung School, the Technical College, the Higher Police School, and at the barracks on the southern side of Hsinking. He also turned over the Mengchiatun Ordnance Depot to the Soviets, including one field gun, one 100-mm howitzer, more than ten antiaircraft guns, five tanks and a considerable number of rifles, bayonets, infantry guns, and machineguns.

---

9. Zabaikal means "behind (Lake) Baikal," (as viewed from Moscow).

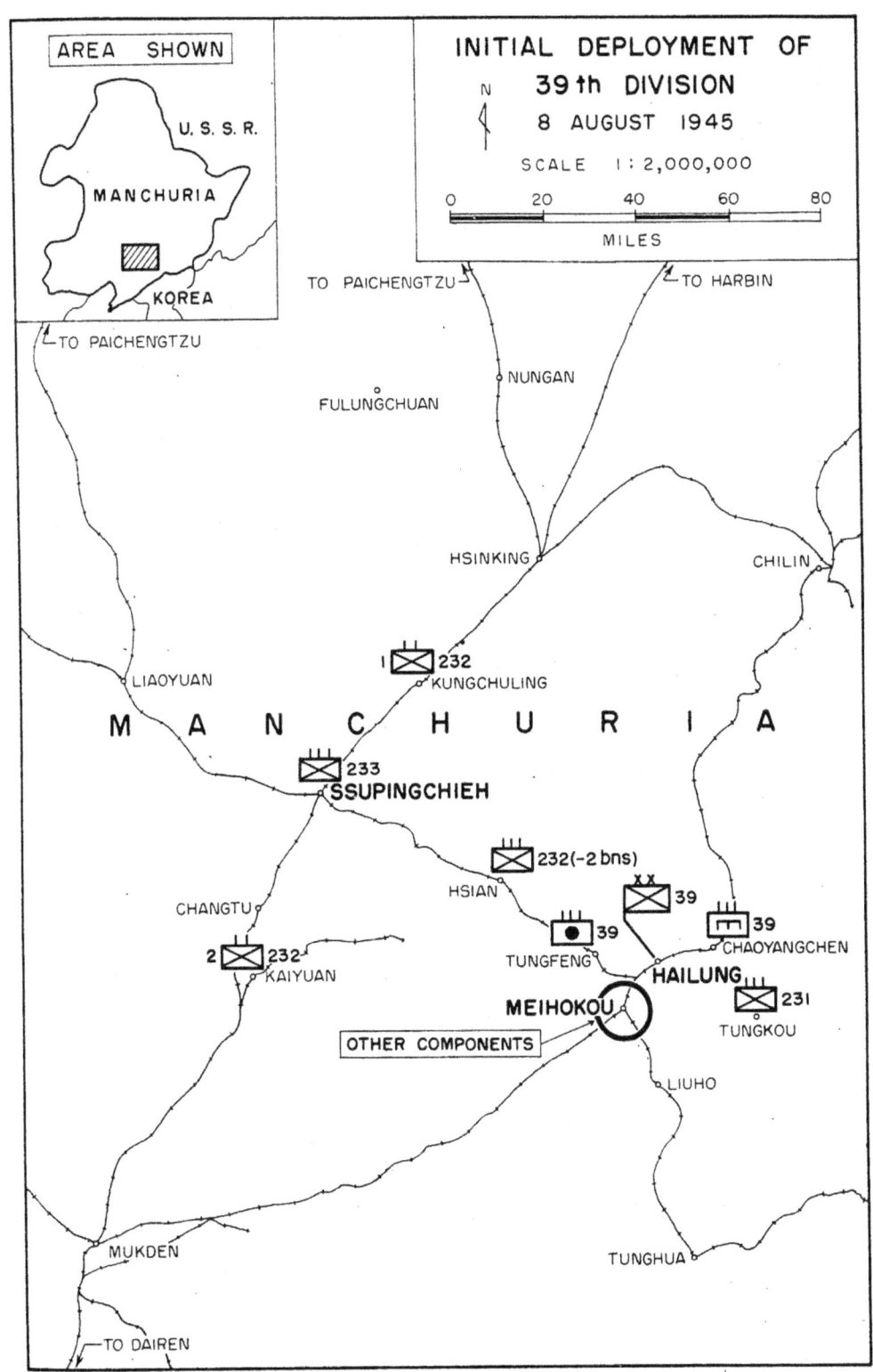

Monograph No 155-B

CHAPTER II

The 39th Division[10]

Transfer from China to Manchuria

Upon receipt of orders that it was to be transferred from its base in China to join the Kwantung Army in Manchuria, the 39th Division early in May 1945 began to assemble in the vicinity of Yingcheng, and marched to Siaokan. On 12 May, it departed Siaokan in five echelons, marching a distance of approximately 280 miles to Kaifeng. Divisional elements began arriving at Kaifeng early in June, and from there were sent by rail to Manchuria. Meanwhile, all artillery guns and about 50 per cent of the division's vehicles were sent by rail from Hankow. Horses were left in Hankow, since they could be replaced from the adequate supply in Manchuria.

On the same day that the journey from China had begun, a staff officer was sent to Mukden by motor vehicle, pursuant to orders from the Third Area Army Commander. The division commander, Lieutenant General Shinnosuke Sasa, also departed, going by air on about 20 May. They immediately conducted a terrain reconnaissance of the proposed positions for the division, extending from Hailung 130 kilometers northwest to Ssupingchieh. As a result of this reconnaissance the division commander suggested to the Area Army that the division's

---

10. Information in this chapter was supplied by Major Shizuo Oguchi, staff officer, 39th Division.

MONOGRAPH NO. 155-B
CHART NO. 1

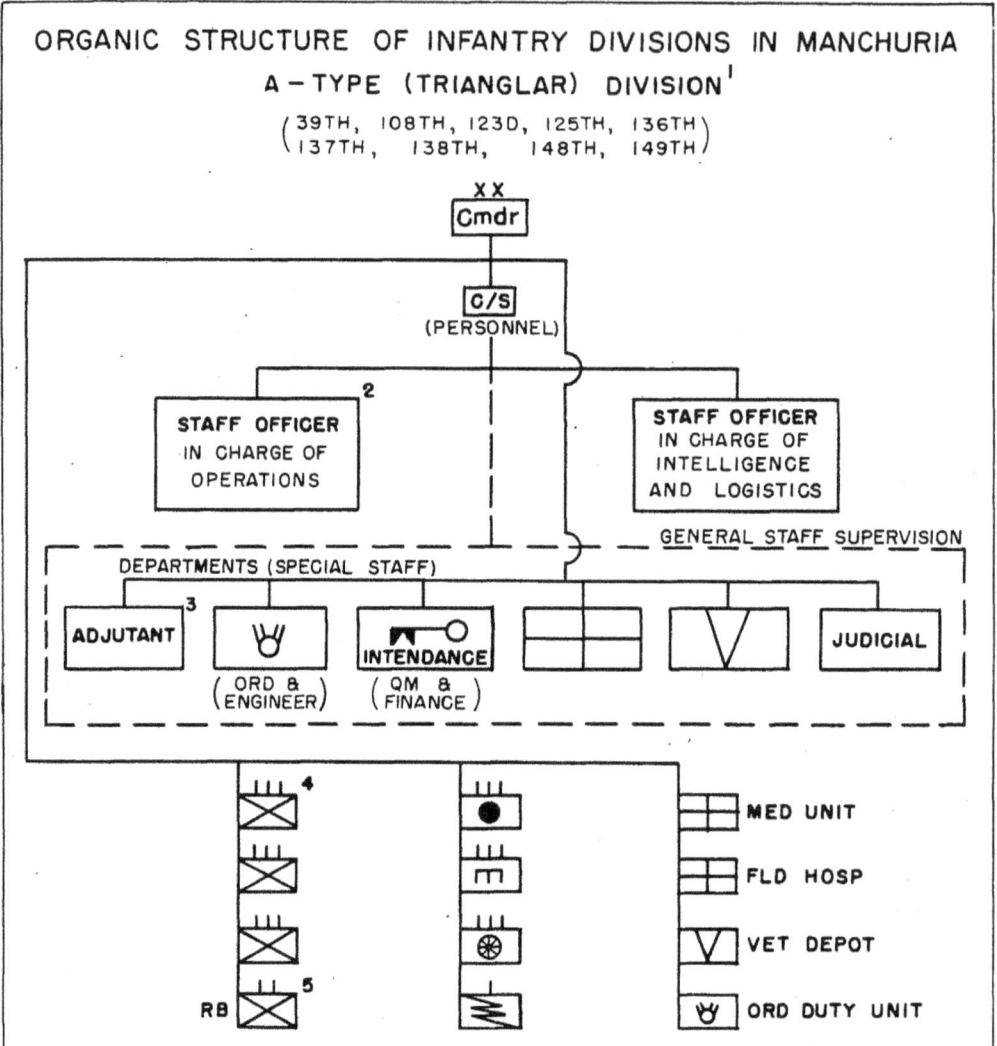

ORGANIC STRUCTURE OF INFANTRY DIVISIONS IN MANCHURIA
A-TYPE (TRIANGLAR) DIVISION[1]
(39TH, 108TH, 123D, 125TH, 136TH,
137TH, 138TH, 148TH, 149TH)

1 — A-TYPE DIVISIONS WERE ORGANIZED FOR TACTICAL OPERATIONS.
2 — NORMALLY, A DIVISION WAS AUTHORIZED THREE "STAFF OFFICERS," ONE FOR OPERATIONS, ONE FOR INTELLIGENCE, AND ONE FOR LOGISTICS. (THE CHIEF OF STAFF WAS RESPONSIBLE FOR PERSONNEL, RECEIVING ADVICE FROM ONE OF THE STAFF OFFICERS). EACH STAFF OFFICER HAD SEVERAL ASSISTANTS, BUT THESE WERE NOT DESIGNATED AS "STAFF OFFICERS."
IN MANCHURIA, TWO RATHER THAN THREE STAFF OFFICERS WAS THE RULE IN SUCH CASES ADJUSTMENTS HAD TO BE MADE. FOR EXAMPLE, THE OPERATIONS STAFF OFFICER MIGHT BE GIVEN RESPONSIBILITY ADDITIONALLY FOR LOGISTICS OR INTELLIGENCE. IF ONLY ONE STAFF OFFICER WAS ASSIGNED TO A DIVISION, HE WAS RESPONSIBLE FOR ALL GENERAL STAFF FUNCTIONS.
3 — NORMALLY, A DIVISION HAD TWO ADJUTANTS. THE SENIOR WAS IN CHARGE OF PERSONNEL AND ADMINISTRATION; THE JUNIOR WAS AN AIDE-DE-CAMP TO THE DIVISION COMMANDER.
4 — NORMALLY, THE THREE INFANTRY REGIMENTS WERE UNDER THE CONTROL OF AN INFANTRY GROUP COMMANDER.
5 — RAIDING BATTALION ASSIGNED TO ALL BUT THE 39TH DIVISION.

main defense position be changed from the Hailung area to the vicinity east of Tungkou because, he felt, it would be difficult to organize positions in the vicinity of Hailung. Third Area Army Headquarters agreed to the establishment of positions for one regiment near Tungkou.

By the middle of June, advance elements of the division reached Manchuria and were deployed in the vicinities of Hailung, Ssupingchieh, Kungchuling, Kaiyuan, Meihokou, Hsian, and Tungkou. Division headquarters was established at Hailung (See Map No 1. See also Chart No 1 showing the organization of a combat division.) The movement of the division was completed early in July. Since Thirtieth Army, to which it was to be assigned, had not as yet been formed the division was assigned on 21 July directly to Third Area Army, which was responsible for operational preparations that were later to be given to Thirtieth Army. On 30 July the division was placed in the order of battle of Thirtieth Army, whose activation at Yenchi was formalized on the next day.

In preparing for operations, the division found that none of its artillery pieces and none of the vehicles shipped separately by train had arrived from China. (50 per cent of the vehicles accompanied troops.) It was not issued any new ammunition and had to get along with what it brought from China. Nor did it receive any fortification materials. These matters tended to lower the division's combat effectiveness, and were aggravated by the fact

MONOGRAPH NO. 155-B
CHART NO. 2

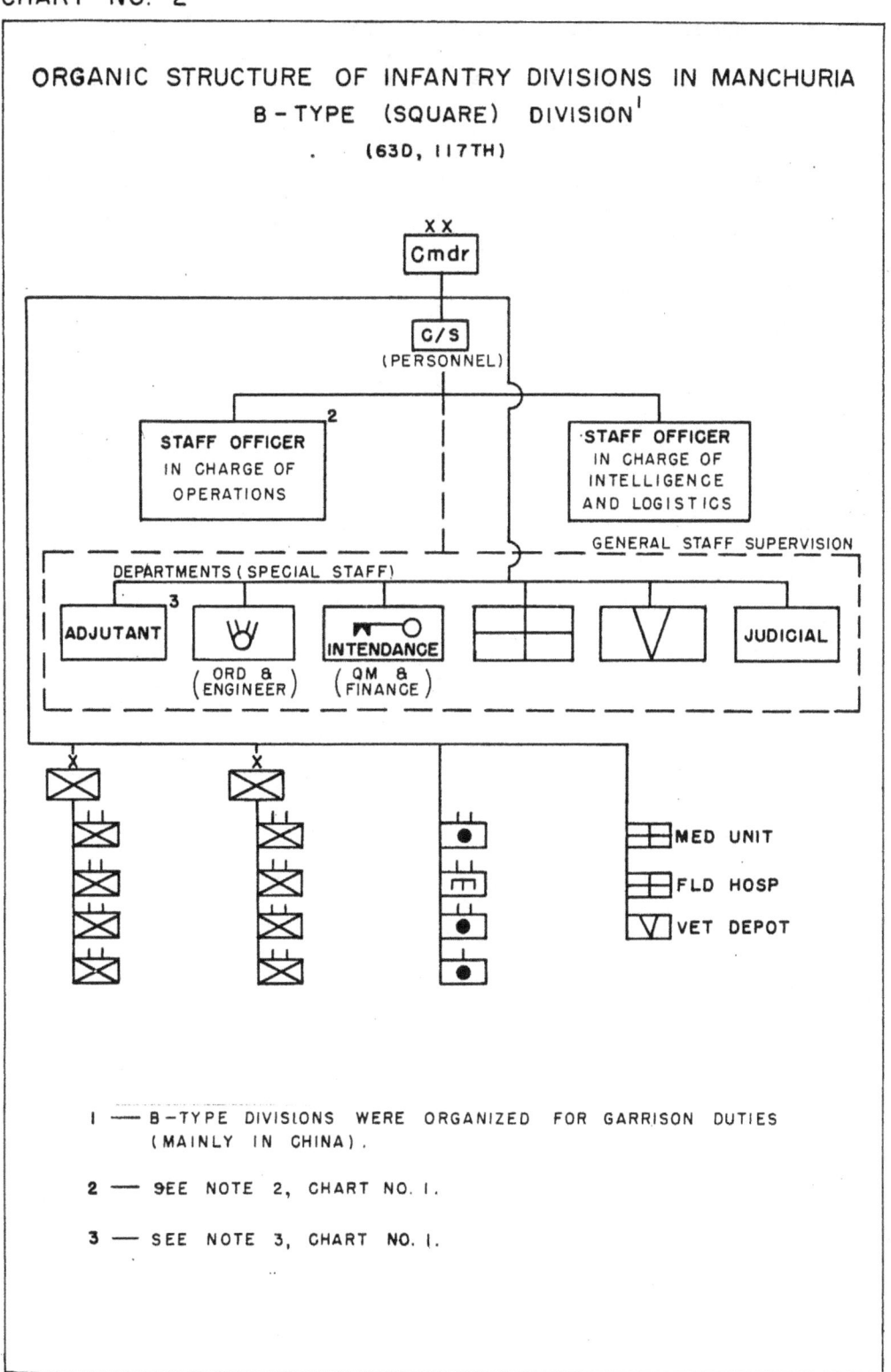

that the division's experience had been limited to the China area, and it was therefore not prepared to fight a well-equipped enemy. These conditions were to be further aggravated during hostilities by frequent changes in assignment and in the orders it was to receive from higher headquarters.

Opening of Hostilities

The division commander learned of Soviet entry into the war by radio on the morning of 9 August, during an inspection of the positions in the vicinity of Tungkou. He immediately set out for division headquarters at Hailung. En route, at Chaoyangchen, he received an order from the Third Area Army to the following effect:

> The Area Army will meet and attack the enemy generally in the area along the Dairen-Hsinking Railway.
>
> The 39th Division will dispatch an element to Hsinking and place it under the command of the Hsinking Garrison Area. The division will meet and attack the enemy at Ssupingchieh with its main body, and at Kungchuling and Kaiyuan with its elements. The division will operate under the control of the Thirtieth Army.

The division immediately ordered the following units to move to Ssupingchieh (the 233d Regiment was already there): from Hsian, 232d Regiment (less two battalions, one in Kungchuling, the other in Kaiyuan); from Tungkou, one battalion of the 231st Regiment (the main body of this regiment was the element to be sent to Hsinking, as ordered by Third Area Army); from Tungfeng, the 39th Artillery Regiment (personnel only, since its 75-mm guns had not arrived from China), and from Chaoyangchen, the 39th Engineer Regiment. Division headquarters and directly attached units also planned to move to Ssupingchieh. Before these moves could be carried out, however, the divisions orders were altered.

At about 0700 hours on 10 August, the division received an Army order to the following effect:

> The 39th Division will cease actions and wait for future orders in its present position.

The division commander transmitted this order to subordinate commander and, perceiving a change in plans, dispatched his staff officer to the Army Headquarters to get clarification of the order. The staff officer returned after learning of the following situation from the Army chief of staff:

> The intention of the Commander in Chief of the Kwantung Army seems to be to assume the defensive in the Changpaishan (Paitaoshan) mountain range. The order to meet and attack the enemy in the areas along the Dairen-Hsinking Railway seems to have been issued arbitrarily by the Area Army commander. Therefore, the Thirtieth Army is suspending actions of its subordinate groups at their present positions and is trying to confirm the intention of the Area Army commander.

The division suspended the actions of its various units accordingly. Then, at about 1200 hours on 10 August, the division received a Thirtieth Army order to the following effect:

> The Army will defend Hsinking with its main body and, at the same time, carry out determined guerrilla operations in the areas along the Dairen-Hsinking Railway.
>
> The 39th Division's main body will advance toward Hsinking; its elements will conduct guerrilla

operations against the enemy in the vicinities of Kungchuling, Ssupingchieh and Kaiyuan.

I (the Thirtieth Army Commander) will be at Hsinking hereafter.

Considering the great deficiencies in rail transportation, the division commander decided that only the 231st Infantry Regiment could be transported by rail to Hsinking, and issued orders to this effect. He directed that the division's main force march to Kungchuling, and then advance to Hsinking. To coordinate the move, he dispatched a staff officer to Hsian and Ssupingchieh.

The difference between the Area Army order and the Army order essentially concerned the deployment of the division's main body: the Area Army on the 9th directed its deployment to Ssupingchieh, while the Army on the 10th, after issuing a halt order at 0700, at noon directed its deployment to Hsinking.

The confusion at division headquarters regarding orders from higher headquarters was compounded at regimental level. When the staff officer arrived at Hsian (the position of the 232d Infantry Regiment, less two battalions) on the evening of 10 August, he learned that the regiment (actually regimental headquarters and one battalion) had already marched a day's distance toward Ssupingchieh but, on the basis of orders received in the morning to halt operations, was now pulling back toward Hsian. To speed the regiment on its way to Hsinking, therefore, the staff officer arranged with the head of the Hsian Railway Station to use a coal train as a troop transport.

The deputy governor of Hsian Prefecture provided 500 carts and placed them under the control of the regimental commander, while the head of the Hsian Railway Station rushed the unloading of coal by his men. The assiduity of the deputy governor of Hsian and the head of the Hsian Railway Station deeply impressed the officers and men of the regiment.

The staff officer sent to Ssupingchieh arrived there at about 1000 hours on 11 August. After noon, he was notified by the railway station commander that the main force of the 39th Division was under orders to be deployed in the Ssupingchieh area. Because it was difficult to contact the Thirtieth Army Headquarters, he confirmed this by contacting the Area Army Headquarters. Therefore, he took the following measures:

> Retained one battalion of the 231st Infantry Regiment at Ssupingchieh and sent the main body of the Regiment to Hsinking. (It left Ssupingchieh in the evening of the 11th.)
>
> Detrained the 232d Infantry Regimental Headquarters and its 3d Battalion at Ssupingchieh (after their arrival by coal train), assigning the 3d Battalion to the mountainous area in the rear of Ssupingchieh to construct positions and prepare for an attack.
>
> Directed the 1st Battalion of the 232d Regiment to remain in the Kungchuling area, and the 2d Battalion to remain in the Kaiyuan area.
>
> Directed the 233d Infantry Regiment to begin constructing positions in the mountainous area to the rear of Ssupingchieh and to prepare for an attack.
>
> Reported his action to the division commander. (Division Headquarters was then en route from

MONOGRAPH NO. 155-B
MAP NO. 2

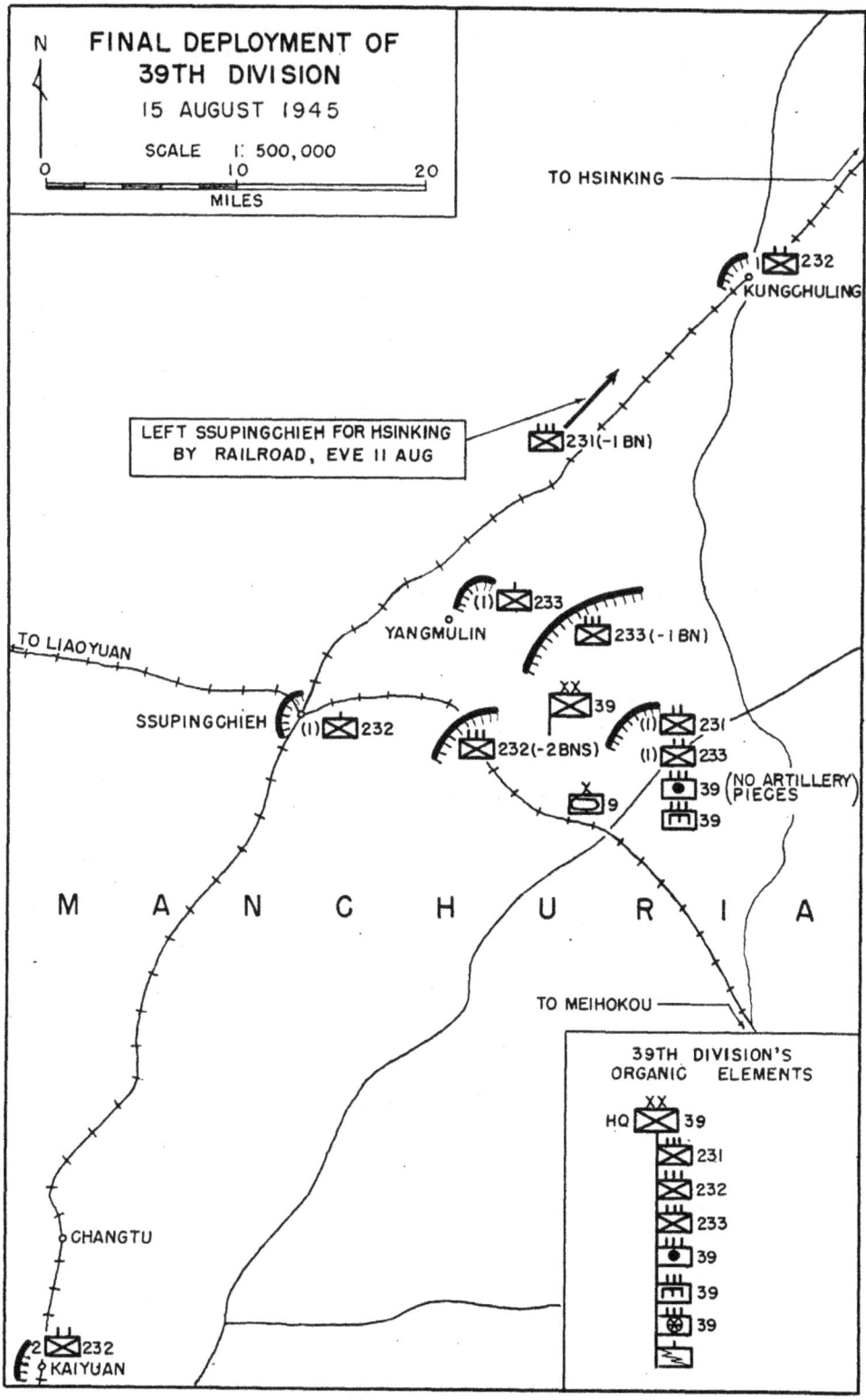

Hailung to Ssupingchieh, and the report did not
reach the division commander until he arrived at
Ssupingchieh the next morning.)

Thus, the actions taken by the staff officers sent to Hsian and Ssupingchieh resulted in the following status in the deployment of division elements on the evening of 11 August: at Ssupingchieh were the 233d Regiment, the 232d Regiment (less two battalions), and one battalion of the 231st Regiment; at Kungchuling, the 1st Battalion of the 232d Regiment, and at Kaiyuan the 2d Battalion; en route to Hsinking was the 231st Regiment (less the battalion left at Ssupingchieh). (See Map No 2.)

During the evening of 11 August, the staff officer met the deputy governor of Ssuping Province at the Provincial Government office and they agreed that the Provincial Government would act entirely in accordance with the directives of the division, and that it would take the following measures.

> Secure and transport provisions.
>
> Organize working parties for constructing positions. (including 5,000 persons under the command of the Chief of the Ssuping Province Civil Engineering Bureau.)
>
> Organize well-drilling parties.
>
> Prepare for the disruption of the traffic net in the area between the Liao River and the Dairen-Hsinking Railway, including the demolition of bridges.
>
> Organize transport parties (15,000 horsecarts).
>
> Instruct the chief of the police department to

collect intelligence, and carry out guerrilla warfare along the line of the Liao River.

Organize intelligence collection.

The provincial deputy governor solemnly swore that he would exert his utmost as a member of the Japanese Army, being no longer a government official of Manchuria, and offered to take all responsibility especially for securing and concentrating provisions and arranging for general transportation. Meanwhile, the staff officer learned from the provincial deputy governor that the Forty-fourth Army Headquarters at Liaoyuan had withdrawn to Mukden.

The division commander upon arriving at Ssupingchieh on the morning of 12 August assembled the commanders of the various groups and ordered them to organize positions in the mountainous area east of Ssupingchieh, to reconnoiter the terrain in the proposed positions, and to make preparation for demolishing bridges over the Liao River at Liaoyuan. Furthermore, by order of the Thirtieth Army, he took command of the various non-divisional units at Ssupingchieh. Except for one tank brigade, these consisted of service units, totaling twenty odd units.

The railway bridge at Liaoyuan was blown up on 13 August by the South Manchurian Railway Company, but since the demolition was not entirely satisfactory, it had to be blasted a second time, by the 39th Engineer Regiment. On 14 August, word was received from the Ssupingchieh Provincial Government that preparations had been completed for the blasts aimed at traffic disruption in the area between the Liao River and the Dairen-Hsinking Railway. (This demolition work was not carried out because of the subsequent cease-fire order.) On 14 August, more than 20 Japanese planes arrived at the Ssupingchieh airfield and proceeded to forward areas where they attacked enemy mechanized forces in the vicinity of Paichengtzu.

End of Hostilities

Upon receipt of the radio broadcast concerning the Imperial Rescript on 15 August, the division issued the following order:

> The division will continue its combat action until an official order is received from the Thirtieth Army.

At the same time, the division commander took the following measures to protect the Japanese residents: he ordered all subordinate units to attach importance to the protection of local residents; he dispatched one infantry company to Hsian and one to Tungfeng to protect Japanese residents there; he ordered the garrison at Ssupingchieh to reinforce sentry standby stations and patrols and, if necessary, to billet groups of several men, mainly officers, at civilian homes.

On 16 August, a staff officer was dispatched to the Thirtieth Army Headquarters. He returned the same day with orders to burn the regimental colors, to surrender weapons, and to assemble units.

(The 231st Infantry Regiment (less one battalion) which on the evening of the 11th had been dispatched to Hsinking, was ordered on the 19th to entrain for Kungchuling. At midnight, while the train was midway between Hsinking and Kungchuling it suddenly came under automatic cannon fire, and the locomotive was destroyed. The regimental commander, Colonel Fukunaga thought at first that the attackers were Manchurian rebel forces, since Manchurian forces had revolted in Hsinking. He therefore ordered the Regiment to engage the attackers. Before dawn, the attackers was identified as members of a Soviet force. Thereupon, the regiment ceased fighting, having first burned the regimental colors. Our casualties during the engagement totaled more than ten. The regimental commander and several officers were immediately taken into custody and were transported by train in the direction of Pamiencheng. The unit itself was taken to Kungchuling under guard. This was reported by a noncommissioned officer who escaped.)

The day before the Soviet occupation (23 August), reports of the Soviet forces advancing eastward from Liaoyuan were frequently received at division headquarters. On the day the Soviets reached the suburbs of Ssupingchieh, the division commander issued instructions to burn the regimental colors. Many Japanese residents and groups of various types assembled at Yangmulin, in the suburbs of Ssupingchieh, for the burning ceremony. Then the colors of the 232d Infantry Regiment and the 233d Infantry Regiment were burned by the regimental commanders in the presence of the division commander.

The Soviet Occupation

On the night of 23 August a Soviet mechanized unit of about 500 men (unaccompanied by its vehicles, which were left behind because the bridge at Liaoyuan had been demolished) reached the suburbs of Ssupingchieh. The 39th Division dispatched a delegate under a flag of truce to the Soviets. The Soviet commander demanded that all the arms and ammunition of Japanese units at Ssupingchieh be surrendered within three hours, and threatened to launch an attack the next morning if this was not done. The Japanese delegate replied that it was impossible to meet the demand. The next morning, the Soviet commander, a lieutenant colonel, came to headquarters. The division told him that at least two days would be required for the surrender of weapons to be completed. He now seemed not too concerned about weapons, and instead demanded that a train be provided for him. A train was made available, and in the evening he went south in the direction of Mukden.

Early in the morning of the 25th, a Soviet unit arrived by train from the direction of Kungchuling and detrained at Ssupingchieh. It had a complement of about 1,000 men, more than ten tanks, more than ten armored cars, and about twenty motor vehicles. It was billeted at Ssupingchieh for the day. Soviet negotiators, a colonel and a major of the Soviet air force, arrived at the Ssupingchieh airfield at about the same time. A conference was held with them at the Ssupingchieh Municipal Office, and the following matters were agreed upon: 1) Japanese forces may remain in the city of Ssupingchieh to maintain peace and order, and may retain a limited number machineguns and smaller arms, the number to be determined by the Soviet forces after an inspection of conditions in Ssupingchieh; 2) Soviet forces will be responsible for the maintenance of discipline among the Soviet occupation troops; 3) arms and ammunition will be collected beginning on the 26th and will be surrendered at the Ssupingchieh airfield on the 28th; 4) a Soviet captain will be appointed garrison unit commander for Ssupingchieh, and the Japanese forces will negotiate with him concerning the maintenance of peace and order; 5) the garrison unit commander will inspect the city by car with a Japanese staff officer tonight with a view toward maintaining peace and order. (When the inspection was actually made, no particular misconduct was noticed and peace generally prevailed.)

At midnight, a Soviet lieutenant general (presumably, commander of a division) and his staff arrived at the Ssupingchieh airfield and, proceeding directly to the quarters of the Japanese division commander, made the following revised demands: 1) all arms and ammunition will be collected and surrendered at the Ssupingchieh airfield on the 26th; 2) the units at Ssupingchieh, Kaiyuan, Tungfeng, and Hsian be assembled, and their movement thereafter strictly prohibited; 3) Soviet forces will be responsible for the protection of Japanese residents; the division headquarters, however, will be permitted to retain a limited number of arms.

This made the previous agreement with the Soviet air colonel absolutely useless.

The collection of arms and ammunition at the Ssupingchieh airfield began promptly on the 26th, but did not progress according to schedule. It was not until the 28th that the surrender of arms and ammunition was completed. On that day, the division commander left Ssupingchieh for Hsinking to join the Kwantung Army general officers being assembled at the direction of the Soviet forces. On the 29th, Soviet forces demolished Japanese tanks and airplanes (training planes and the like), and began transporting captured vehicles and arms by rail in the direction of Hsinking.

On 30 August, another lieutenant general, commander of the Soviet forces in the area, arrived at the Ssupingchieh airfield and directed that all Japanese forces will in the future negotiate with his chief of staff, a Colonel Sokolov. He also demanded that all Japanese forces except division headquarters be assembled at Yangmulin. This was carried out between 31 August and 2 September.

On 4 September, the Soviets demanded that the Japanese form labor groups. Sixteen labor groups were organized in Ssupingchieh, each consisting of between 1,300 and 1,500 men, and each led by a captain or major. The labor groups were transported successively in the direction of Hsinking for the avowed purpose of reconstructing railways. Since the division engaged in no operations, it sustained no casualties. Its strength at the time of surrender was about 16,274.

In mid-October all officers remaining in Ssupingchieh, about 600, were sent to Hsinking. Only hospital personnel and hospital patients remained at Ssupingchieh.

Civil Affairs

The conscientious efforts of the provincial deputy governor and subordinate officers of the Ssuping Provincial Government Office were worthy of special mention as previously stated. The governor of Ssuping Province went into hiding in the city of Ssupingchieh after the termination of war without complying with a request to work for the protection of Japanese residents.

Japanese residents of Ssupingchieh were greatly alarmed when refugees swarmed into the city at the end of the war. Numerous reports were heard indicating that the Manchurians were persecuting Japanese civilians. Although for a while serious social unrest threatened, the city of Ssupingchieh remained generally calm. Koreans were reported to be subjected to considerable persecution by the Manchurians, probably because of long-standing bitterness between them.

In the prevailing confusion, the freight depot (general supplies) was raided by tens of Manchurians, but the raiders were driven off by electrified wire entanglements and by Japanese and Soviet guards. There was also an incident in which Manchurians accompanied by several Soviet soldiers raided a storehouse, and caused several casualties to our people.

Monograph No 155-C

CHAPTER III
The 148th Division[11]

Organization

The organization of the 148th Infantry Division was begun on 25 July at Hsinking and was completed on 5 August 1945. It was one of the last divisions organized in Manchuria.

Officers and noncommissioned officers for division headquarters were obtained mainly from the 101st Guard Unit Headquarters, stationed in Hsinking and responsible for the maintenance of peace and order. In mid-June, prior to the division's formation, the future division commander, Lieutenant General Motohiro Suemitsu, arrived in Hsinking. During early July a large number of officers were transferred from other areas of Manchuria to become troop commanders of the division. Troops for the division were conscripted principally from the Hsinking area, although substantial numbers were obtained from Harbin, Mukden, and other localities. Included were between seventy and eighty Koreans. After its organization was completed, the division had a actual strength of approximately 9,800, compared with an authorized strength of 12,000. (Chart 1 shows the division's command and staff; Chart 2 its equipment.)

---

11. Information in this chapter was supplied by Lt Col Shigeo Maruoka, staff officer of the 148th Division.

Monograph No 155-C
Chart No 1

Command and Staff of the 148th Division* on 5 Aug 1945

Post or Unit	Rank	Name
Division commander	Lt Gen	Motohiro Suemitsu
Chief of staff	Col	Chikashi Sakamoto
Staff officer	Lt Col	Shigeo Maruoka
Staff officer	Major	Yoshitada Iwasa
Senior adjutant	Major	Noboru Takata
Chief of Intendance Department	Lt Col	Kazuo Terauchi
Chief of Ordnance Department	Capt	(Acting) ? Nagasawa
Chief of Medical Department	Col	Naoshi Sazawa
Chief of Veterinary Department	Major	Sadao Imanaka
Duty Company	1st Lt	Torao Yamaguchi
383d Infantry Regiment	Col	Chikamichi Suzumoto
384th Infantry Regiment	Major	Hide Sakata
385th Infantry Regiment	Major	Tsukuru Kagata
Signal Unit	Major	Masataka Ariga
Raiding Battalion	Capt	Makoto Hasuda
148th Artillery Regiment	Lt Col	Kumehiko Takeda
148th Engineer Regiment	Major	Jiro Yokota
148th Transport Regiment	Major	Kichigoro Hayakawa
Ordnance Duty Unit	Capt	Kanichi Kaida
Veterinary Hospital**	1st Lt	? Hosokawa

* Complement of Division: 12,000 men. Complement of Division Headquarters Approx 220 men.

** No field hospital was attached to the Division.

Monograph No 155-C
Chart No 2

Personnel and Equipment of 148th Division

Kind	Percentage of Authorized Number	Remarks
Personnel	81%	Personnel requirement was nearly filled. However, the personnel included Koreans and were generally of poor quality having been drafted in the final mobilization by the Kwantung Army.
Horses	25%	Some of the riding horses assigned were of good quality.
Vehicles	30%	
Rifles	30%	A considerable number of the rifles and machineguns had been requisitioned from the equipment used for military training at universities and middle schools.
Light machineguns	10%	
Heavy machineguns	10%	
Infantry Battalion guns	5%	
Guns	20%	Six field guns type 38; one 105-mm howitzer; one 150-mm howitzer Total: eight guns. Other guns were under request for transport from Harbin when the war ended.
Communications equipment	0.1%	Only a very small proportion of the requirement was obtained from the Manchuria Telegraph and Telephone Company.
Engineer equipment	2%	Only some civil engineering equipment was obtained.
Clothing	30%	A considerable number of draftees continued to wear the clothes they had when they were drafted, such as the Kyowa-Fuku (National Uniform in Manchuria) and the Seinen-Fuku (Young men's Uniform)
Other supplies	10%	

With the formation of the division, the 101st Guard Unit was inactivated and a District Defense Command established for Hsinking under General Suemitsu's command. As garrison commander he was given control of the 4th Antiaircraft Artillery Unit, a regimental size unit of the Manchurian National Army which was responsible for the anti-aircraft defense of Hsinking. One of its battalions, together with two field machine cannon companies of Japanese troops, was responsible for the air defense of the Homan Dam (the Sungari River power plant at the upper reaches of Chilin). In addition, one antiaircraft artillery battery of the Manchurian Army formerly charged with the air defense of the Manchurian Aviation Company at Mukden, was transferred to Kungchuling and assigned to the Hsinking District Defense Command.

The offices and billets of division headquarters and of the District Defense headquarters were established in the building formerly occupied by the 101st Guard Unit Headquarters. Combat elements of the division were billeted, during and after the division's formation, at various schools in Hsinking: Chienkuo University, Technical College, Facheng College, First and Second Hsinkig Middle Schools, and Shiragiku Primary School.

Training

In mid-July, division officers attended a conference of commanders and staff officers of Third Area Army held at the Area Army Headquarters at Mukden. The Area Army Commander, in his instructions to those present, emphasized the training of units, stating that training objectives must be attained by the end of September. He urged particularly that antitank training be stressed, and that close-quarter combat training be thorough.

Carrying out the training programs proved extremely difficult because of the quality of troops, poor equipment, and the pressure of miscellaneous duties day by day. In addition, there was an acute shortage of rifles and bayonets. To compensate for this, five thousand spears were ordered, but were never received.

Headquarters of Third Area Army scheduled a one-week training program for officers and noncommissioned officers in the construction of fortifications. Although this program began on schedule on 7 August, it had to be suspended because of the opening of hostilities.

Mission and Operational Planning

The Kwantung Army operational plan of June 1945 prescribed that the 148th Division would defend Hsinking but that its engagements with the enemy would be limited to light skirmishing, after which the division was to withdraw gradually to the vicinity of Meihokou in Tunghua Province. (However, this mission was changed immediately after hostilities began and the division was ordered to defend Hsinking to the last.)

In view of the Third Area Army Commander's dissatisfaction with Kwantung Army's plan, and his determination to hold the Dairen-Hsinking line, plans were studied jointly with Manchurian civil authorities to establish the main line of resistance in defense sectors surrounding Hsinking. This study proposed that major positions be constructed for defense by the army, and that secondary positions be constructed for defense by the united efforts of the army and the municipal government, the instructions to be given by the army and the work to be carried out under the guidance of municipal authorities. However, construction of positions did not get fully underway until the outbreak of hostilities.

The first reason for the delay was the difference of opinion between the Third Area Army and the 148th Division in regard to the forward extremity of the main positions. The 148th Division Commander stressed the necessity for establishing these positions near the perimeter of the city since the division would have to defend the city alone and also because of the terrain features in the vicinity of Hsinking. The Area Army, on the other hand, was of the opinion that the forward positions should be created in a wide circle considerably outside the city. These two views were never reconciled. Consequently, the division's defense plan was never completed. The second reason was the apparent indifference of city officials and the people in general to the gravity of the war situation. City officials displayed little enthusiasm and wasted much time in desk planning.

Outbreak of Hostilities

At about 0200 hours on 9 August, the division commander was informed of the outbreak of hostilities between Japan and Soviet Russia. He immediately alerted the entire central district. At the time, both he and the chief of staff were at division headquarters in Hsinking; the operations staff officer and a captain of the operations section were at Third Area Army Headquarters handling liaison matters and under-going training in fortifications work; the logistics staff officer had just joined the division headquarters. Soon enemy planes came over and dropped bombs on the completely blacked-out city but inflicted no casualties. The division commander then ordered the units to occupy their respective positions in accordance with prearranged plans. The essential parts of this order were:

0800 hours, 9 August
Division Headquarters

The Soviet Army launched the invasion of Manchuria at 0000 on 9 August, crossing the Soviet Manchurian border on all fronts. A small number of enemy planes raided Hsinking at 0300 hours this morning, but inflicted no damage.

The division with its entire force will firmly occupy the sector surrounding Hsinking, take command of all units of the Manchukuoan Army stationed in Hsinking, and destroy the invading enemy.

The 383d Infantry Regiment is designated the west sector unit. It will occupy positions in the west sector of Hsinking, and will destroy the enemy advancing from that direction.

The 384th Infantry Regiment is designated the north sector unit. It will occupy positions near the forward extremity north of Hsinking, and will destroy the enemy advancing from that direction.

The 385th Infantry Regiment is designated the central sector unit. It will occupy positions in the center of the city, expand the fortified zone near the municipal office, and destroy the enemy infiltrating the first defense line.

The 148th Field Artillery Regiment commander is designated the south sector unit commander. To his command will be assigned his own unit and an element of the engineer unit. He will destroy the enemy advancing from the south. His guns will be disposed mainly for firing any enemy tanks that approach from the north and west.

The Manchukuoan Army force (Military Academy and Guard Unit) is designated the east sector unit. It will occupy positions east of the city and will destroy the enemy advancing from that direction.

Instructions on boundaries between zone of action assigned to these sector units will be issued separately.

The main body of the raiding battalion will advance toward Nungan and an element toward Fulungchuan, to surprise enemy tanks. Another element, of adequate strength, will flood the marshy areas along the Itung River near Hoshunchang (approximately 35 kilometer northwest of Hsinking). The latter element, in carrying out this mission, will coordinate with the vice-governor of Nungan Prefecture and with the town mayor. It will carry provisions for two weeks. The order for departure time will be issued separately.

The engineer unit (less an element) will provide personnel to cooperate with the north, west and central sector units in fortifying key positions and in constructing principal obstacles.

> The division signal unit will rapidly collect and maintain equipment and establish telephone networks between division headquarters and each sector unit.
>
> The 148th Transport Regiment will supply ammunition and provisions first to the north and west sector units and then to the central and south sector units.
>
> Lt Gen Motohiro Suemitsu
Division Commander

Staff officer Maruoka who had been on an official trip to the Third Area Army Headquarters since 7 August, started his return trip immediately after the suspension of the conference and fortifications training for officers and noncommissioned officers. While the train was stopped at Ssupingchieh at about 1500 hours on 9 August, he received an order by telegram directing him to proceed to Thirtieth Army Headquarters in Meihokou for orders. At 0700 hours on 10 August he arrived at Meihokou. The Thirtieth Army Headquarters, at that time was quartered in the Umenoya Hotel in front of Meihokou Station. On the evening of 10 August, he was given a Thirtieth Army order which stated, in effect:

> The enemy mechanized force that crossed the western border is pushing eastward in several columns in front of the Third Area Army, and will reach the sectors along the Dairen-Hsinking Railway about 13 August at the earliest. On the eastern border, the enemy penetrated our frontier positions on 9 August and advanced to Suiyang and Hunchun. Enemy mechanized elements are speeding toward Mutanchiang. The enemy has crossed the border at all points, but the situation is vague due to the disruption of communications.
>
> The Army will secure Hsinking and Ssupingchieh and destroy the invading enemy.

> The 148th Division will secure Hsinking and destroy the invading enemy.
>
> The 39th Division will secure the hill east of Ssupingchieh and destroy the invading enemy.
>
> The 125th Division will advance to the sector surrounding Meihokou and prepare for subsequent actions.

In the early morning hours of 11 August, staff officer Maruoka left Meihokou for Hsinking with Colonel Yoshikawa, an Army staff officer. Since the Manchurian Railway line was choked with refugees from the Hsinking area, and the Hsinking Station precincts were congested with trains, the two officers were unable to reach Hsinking, but were forced to detrain at Mengchiatun. They arrived at the division headquarters at midnight, 11 August.

On 11 August the Kwantung Army Surveying Unit, composed of 300 men, including civilian employees, and commanded by Colonel Yamaguchi was assigned to the division. On 12 August the division was newly reinforced by approximately 3,000 men mustered from Hsinking and its vicinity. It had difficulty controling them, not only because of the lack of military discipline among the reservists but also because of the shortage of arms and clothing.

On the morning of the same day, Lieutenant General Iida, Thirtieth Army Commander, together with his chief of staff and other officers, reached Hsinking and established a command post in the building of the Kwantung Army General Headquarters. The Thirtieth Army had originally planned to concentrate its entire strength in

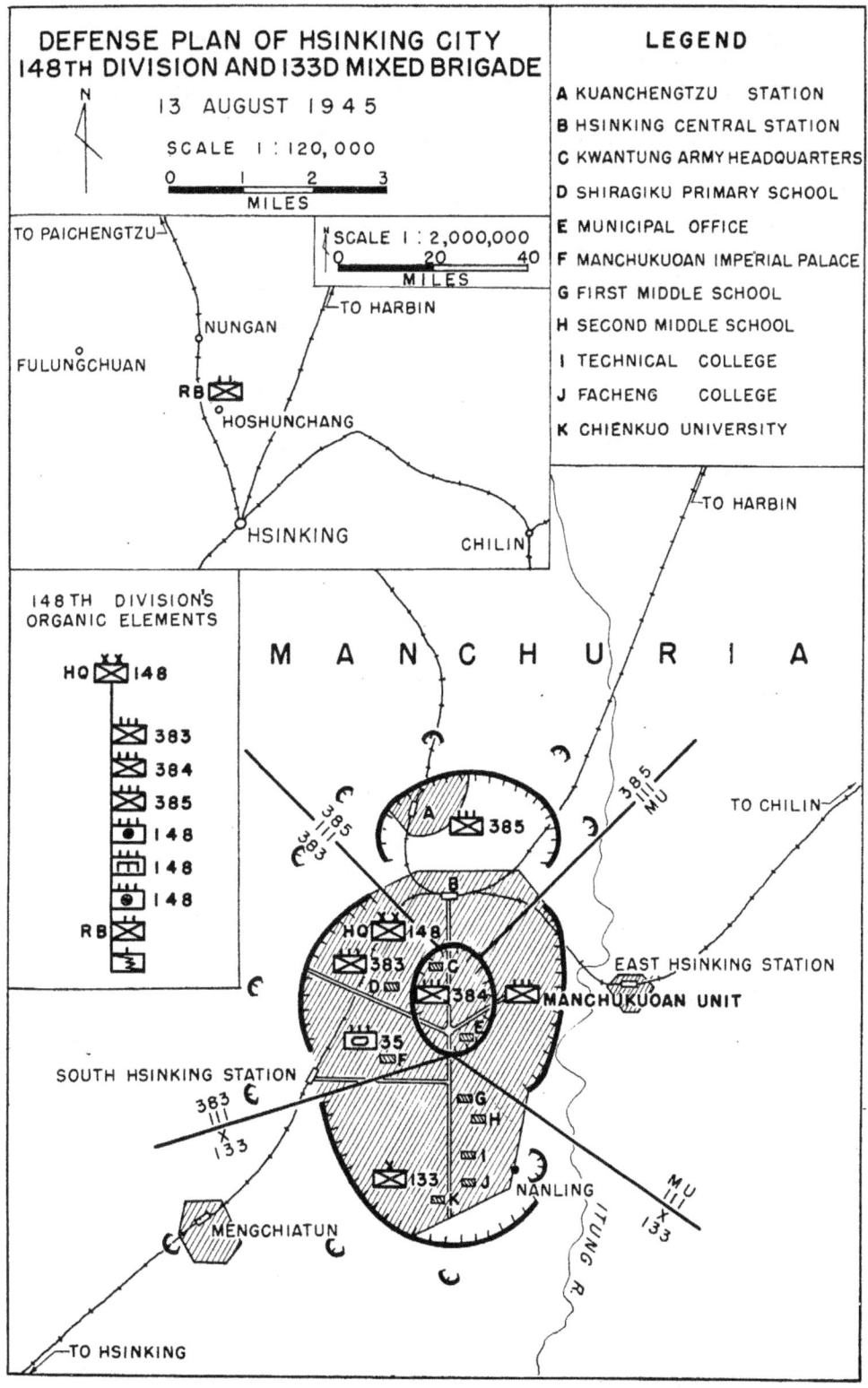

Hsinking for the decisive battle, but later decided to secure both Hsinking and Ssupingchieh. Based on this change, the division on the morning of 13 August issued orders to the following effect:[12] (See Map No 1.)

> The enemy, gradually decelerating his advance, is expected to appear in front of Hsinking about 15 August at the earliest. The Army intends to destroy the invading enemy by securing Hsinking with its main strength.
>
> With the reinforcement of the Hsinking sector, the division will attempt to destroy the invading enemy. The following units will be newly attached to the division:
>
> > 35th Tank Regiment
> > Hsinking Antiaircraft Artillery Unit
> > 26th Antiaircraft Artillery Regiment
> > Various supply depots in Hsinking
> > Remaining personnel of the Military Hospital
> > Guard Unit of the Manchukuoan Army and
> >   Military Academy Cadet Unit
>
> The 133d Independent Mixed Brigade is expected to occupy positions in the south sector of Hsinking.
>
> The Raiding Battalion will complete its previously assigned mission. The time of departure will be this evening. The west sector unit (383d Regiment) will continue its assigned mission. The central sector unit (385th Regiment) will move to the sector north of Hsinking and will hereafter be known as the north sector unit.
>
> The unit formerly called the north sector unit (384th Regiment) will occupy the center of Hsinking and will be redesignated the central sector unit.
>
> The east sector unit (Manchukuoan troops) will effect

---

12. Cf Chapter I, p 14.

necessary reorganization of positions according to the change of positions of the north (now central) sector unit.

The order on boundaries between zones of action for each unit will be issued separately.

The 148th Field Artillery Regiment will occupy positions at the northwest sector in the city. Its main body will cooperate in the battles of the west sector unit and an element with the north sector unit. As occasion demands it will engage in antitank combat.

The 35th Tank Regiment will wait in readiness near the Manchukuoan Imperial Palace and prepare for antitank operations. One element will reconnoiter closely the movements of the enemy mechanized units in Huaite and Nungan areas.

On the afternoon of 12 August another unit, the Liaoyang NCO Candidate Unit, was assigned to the division. This battalion-size unit of the 107th Division, unable to rejoin its command near Wuchakou, had detrained at Hsinking. Meanwhile, the 148th Division was preoccupied mainly with strengthening its defense positions and acquiring additional arms and clothing. Toward the latter end it diverted one of its elements from construction work, sending it to supply depots and civilian outlets.

On the night of 12 August, a telephone call from the Paichengtzu Garrison Unit revealed that the 107th Division was fighting a superior enemy near Wuchakou, and that its routes of retreat gradually were being cut at several points. The call also revealed that the 117th Division was withdrawing from the Paichengtzu and Taonan areas, and that the Paichengtzu Garrison Unit was steadfastly engaging the enemy to cover that division's withdrawal.

According to information received from the Manchukuoan Government on the evening of 13 August, cease fire negotiations were under way in the homeland. Nevertheless the division continued to perform its mission.

One company of the 40th Independent Engineer Regiment (transferred from the Central China area) arrived at Hsinking on 13 August and was assigned to the division which reassigned it to the 148th Engineer Regiment. (This company was ordered to join the main body of the regiment but was sent to Hsinking by mistake.)

On the morning of 14 August the Thirtieth Army issued a cease-fire order but it was promptly countermanded, and orders to continue operational actions followed. However, the general situation pointed to low morale among troops and lack of enthusiasm in building fortifications. The rebellious atmosphere in the Manchukuoan Army sector became increasingly serious on the afternoon of the 14th, and this area was kept under surveillance. It was reported that Japanese officers assigned to the Manchukuoan Army were shot to death by Manchurian officers in the Itung River area.[13]

On 15 August, squad-size elements of the 384th and the 385th Infantry Regiments were dispatched to suppress the mutinous troops

---

13. The Manchukuoan Government and the Manchukuoan Army consisted of both Japanese and Manchurian nationals. The Japanese officers with the Manchukuoan Army were not part of the Japanese Army, even though they were Japanese nationals. There were relatively few of these, and they were assigned to key posts.

of the Manchukuoan Army. They succeeded in disarming part of them after a skirmish, at a cost of twelve dead and about fifteen wounded on our side. Major Irie, staff officer of the Kwantung Army, and Major Yamagishi, staff officer of the Thirtieth Army, while riding on the outside of a tank and moving among the positions of the Manchukuoan Army to survey the situation, were shot and killed by snipers. Street fighting abated somewhat but did not stop. On 16 August Chief of Staff (Colonel) Sakamoto negotiated with the Manchukuoan Army and arranged for the assembly of the Manchukuoan forces in the areas east of the Itung River; afterwards, the firing stopped completely.

Post-war Situation

Beginning on 15 August events moved rapidly. On that day about 3,000 reservists who had been called to active duty from Hsinking were released from service.

The following day about 5,000 men of the 117th Division withdrawing from forward areas reached Hsinking by train and were attached to the division. Thirtieth Army Headquarters, the 133d Independent Mixed Brigade, and the 35th Tank Regiment started to move to Kungchuling on the morning of 18 August.

The units stationed in Hsinking, pressed with the necessity of immediately completing the tasks created by the termination of war (e.g. burning of top-secret documents) before the arrival of the Soviet occupation forces, were busily engaged in such tasks on 18

August. To our great regret, the temporarily assigned logistical units (various supply depots and others in Hsinking) arbitrarily and rashly destroyed fuel, arms and clothing.

On the night of 19 August, the advance unit of an enemy mechanized force reached the Dairen-Hsinking Railway and attacked our units moving to Kungchuling at Fanchiatun. The main body of one infantry regiment of the 39th Division was captured and taken to Huaite area. Meanwhile small units of the 117th Division from the Paichengtzu area continued to arrive in Hsinking to join the division. Trains transporting Japanese refugees from the northern areas reached Hsinking in increasing numbers and the city fell into confusion. Moreover, since the end of the war on 15 August, there had been frequent occurrences of unlawful entry by Koreans and Manchurians into the homes of Japanese residents, and peace and order were gradually disrupted.

About noon of 19 August, the Soviet military representatives reached Hsinking by air and went immediately to division headquarters. Initially, they ordered that all units in Hsinking be completely disarmed, but as a result of negotiations they agreed to permit about 1,000 men, armed only with rifles, to remain in the city in order to protect Japanese residents and to maintain public peace. They also agreed to permit the division headquarters to remain in the city for negotiations and liaison work and for preserving public peace.

About 22 August, the Soviet Army ordered this peace and order force to move to a provisional internment camp in the vicinity of Hsinking and Nanling where the main body of the division already was assembled. After the withdrawal of this force, the Soviets stationed Japanese and Manchurian military police at key points in the city and placed them in charge of maintaining public peace and order, the Japanese covering the new city and the Manchurians covering the old city. One of the problems confronted by the military police was the quelling of riotous acts by the communist elements of the Manchukuoan Imperial Palace Guard Unit and within the Manchukuoan Military Police Unit itself.

Relations between the Japanese and Manchurian cadets at the Military Academy Cadet Unit were generally good. This Unit was disbanded peacefully after the termination of the war. The Japanese land development groups (about 14) in the area surrounding Hsinking were looted by Manchurians between 16 August and 18 August and suffered many casualties. They requested help from the Japanese Army, which promptly dispatched an element of the division to their aid.

In late August by order of the Soviet Army the division headquarters and the military police in charge of maintaining public peace also evacuated Hsinking and joined the main body of the division. The division commander and his staff moved to the Manchurian Motion Picture Company, near the southern extremity of Hsinking. General Suemitsu, commander of both the 148th Division and the Hsinking

Garrison was ordered to assume control of the approximately 20,000 men from units formerly in Hsinking that were assembling in the vicinity of Nanling.

Beginning in early September, the units near Hsinking were gradually organized into labor battalions. The first and second labor battalions (1,000 men each) were organized on 1 September. One battalion departed early on 2 September. It returned the same day after repairing nearby roads. Its return lessened fears about being sent to the USSR. Although the subsequent organization of labor battalions was generally accomplished without anxiety, after the organization of the third labor battalion, restlessness spread among the officers and men, who feared deportation to Soviet Russia, and the number of deserters gradually increased.

In all, fifteen labor battalions, 1,000 to 1,500 men each, were organized in the Hsinking area (including two battalions composed of residents). In addition to these, two battalions of officers were organized.

The transportation of labor battalions from Hsinking to Soviet Russia was completed on 12 November and the departure of the officers' battalions began. Two companies of convalescents, and one unit of Japanese senior officials of the Manchukuoan Government were detained in the provisional internment camp in Hsinking.

Monograph No 155-D

CHAPTER IV

The 138th Division[14]

Organization

According to plans, the organization of the 138th Infantry Division was to begin in early July and to be completed by the end of the month. It was to be organized in key towns and villages along the Chilin-Chaoyangchen section of the Chilin-Mukden railway. Division headquarters was to be at Panshih, one infantry regiment in Chaoyanchen and others in nearby towns, with supporting units chiefly in Chilin. The authorized strength of the division was to be 16,000. Besides headquarters and the three regiments, the division was to consist of a dismounted raiding unit, an artillery unit, engineer unit, a signal unit, ordnance duty unit, and a transport unit. The organization of the division was to be carried out by the 1st Mobile Brigade (commanded by Colonel Kinoshita), and under the general supervision of the Third Area Army.

In carrying out the actual organization of the division, the 1st Mobile Brigade deviated somewhat from the general method employed in organizing divisions. After initially forming the headquarters

---

14. This information in this section was furnished by Colonel Sadaji Sato, chief of staff of the 138th Division from 26 July 1945 until the end of the war.

Monograph No 155-D

CHAPTER IV

The 138th Division[14]

Organization

According to plans, the organization of the 138th Infantry Division was to begin in early July and to be completed by the end of the month. It was to be organized in key towns and villages along the Chilin-Chaoyangchen section of the Chilin-Mukden railway. Division headquarters was to be at Panshih, one infantry regiment in Chaoyanchen and others in nearby towns, with supporting units chiefly in Chilin. The authorized strength of the division was to be 16,000. Besides headquarters and the three regiments, the division was to consist of a dismounted raiding unit, an artillery unit, engineer unit, a signal unit, ordnance duty unit, and a transport unit. The organization of the division was to be carried out by the 1st Mobile Brigade (commanded by Colonel Kinoshita), and under the general supervision of the Third Area Army.

In carrying out the actual organization of the division, the 1st Mobile Brigade deviated somewhat from the general method employed in organizing divisions. After initially forming the headquarters

---

14. This information in this section was furnished by Colonel Sadaji Sato, chief of staff of the 138th Division from 26 July 1945 until the end of the war.

except in one or two matters. The division commander, Lieutenant General Tsutomu Yamamoto, had not arrived; bombings in the homeland had delayed the delivery of his orders. Moreover, some mistakes were made in the assignment of officers. In several instances, new officers were given assignments intended for experienced officers. These errors were later corrected.

Equipment

Personnel transferred from other units brought with them a limited quantity of small arms and ammunition. Other than this the division had no small arms or ammunition and no artillery pieces, until the end of July. There appears to have been a plan to give the division the artillery pieces of the Manchukuoan Army unit in the Harbin area. Men dispatched to get them never returned because of the outbreak of hostilities. Another plan was to turn over the pieces of the Manchurian unit in the vicinity of Chilin, but hostilities ended before this could be done. The only weapons actually received by the division were rifles, and these not until about the time the cease-fire order was issued.

In the matter of clothing, the same situation prevailed. Officers and men transferred from other units wore regulation clothing; draftees wore what they had, some military uniforms and some national uniforms for civilians. No new supply of clothing was issued to the division. Although the division's supply of equipment and clothing was wholly inadequate, actually nothing could be

MONOGRAPH NO. 155-D
MAP NO. 1

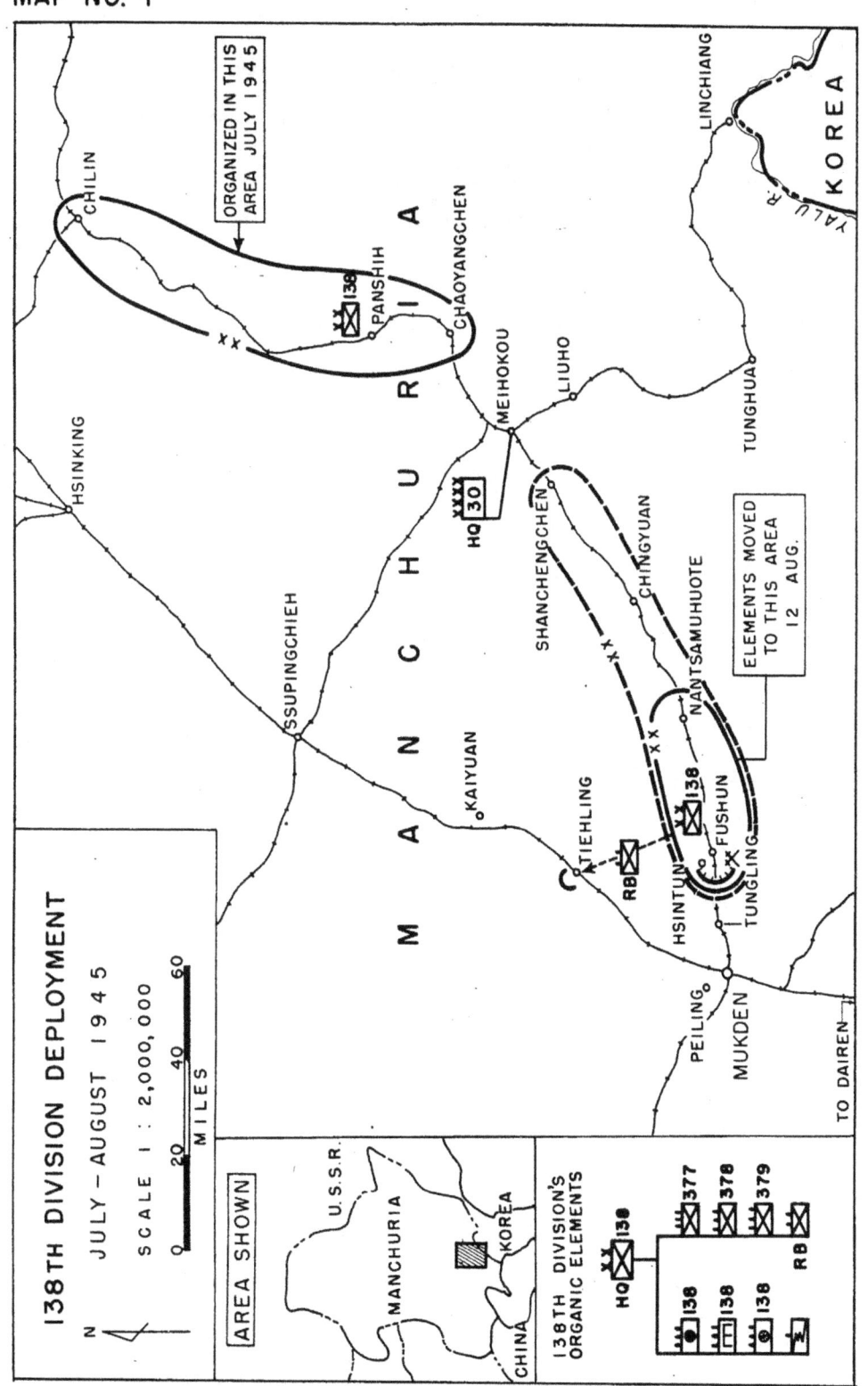

done about it. But it meant that the organization of the division could not be completed in the true sense of the word. Despite this, ground work for the unity of division elements was established.

Deployment and Fighting Effectiveness

While being organized, division elements were deployed at various places along the Chilin-Chaoyanchen section of the Chilin-Mukden railway. Immediately prior to the Soviet entry into the war, the disposition of units was the same as at the time of their formation. However, the division was preparing to move to the district between Shanchengchen and Fushun, and to establish division headquarters at Chingyuan. (See Map No 1.)

On 6 August Third Area Army called its subordinate commanders to a conference at Mukden and issued operational instructions. Since General Yamamoto had still not joined the division, the chief of staff attended, and received instructions concerning the division to the following effect:

> The 138th Division will promptly construct positions for the defense of cities in its new area, and will complete them by the end of August. During operations, when the Kwantung Army assembles in the Tunghua area, the division will prepare to occupy the highlands south of Liuho.

Since the division was able to learn these intentions of superior authorities only three days before the Soviets entered the war, it could make little or no significant operational preparations.

Opening of Hostilities

Shortly before daybreak on 9 August, Soviet aircraft bombed major towns where the division was stationed, including Chilin, but inflicted no serious damage. Examination of bomb fragments revealed that the bombs were made of cast iron and were very ineffective. This fact suggested a weakness in Soviet air power. Furthermore, judging from the bombing tactics used by the Soviets, especially in the avoidance of important targets, it appeared that the bombings were carried out as threats or to achieve political aims.

Among the things handicapping the division at the outbreak of hostilities, aside from the shortage of arms and equipment, was the total absence of communication with Third Area Army Headquarters. Within the division itself, wireless telegraph communication was available, but personnel operating it had not shown any degree of efficiency. Another handicap was the fact that the division commander had not yet arrived.

In the darkness, as the first enemy planes appeared over the division's area, ground fire signals communicating with enemy aircraft were seen at various places. By this fact, we realized that Soviet underground forces, mixing with civilians, had infiltrated into the remotest corners of South Manchuria. Japanese and Manchurian civilians appeared to be undisturbed by the opening of hostilities. Japanese civilians in particular apparently did not realize the significance of the war, and regarded it with total indifference.

On 9 August, while the division in accordance with prearranged plans was preparing to move to its new location between Shangchengchen and Fushun, it received preparatory orders from Third Area Army. (Although the division had been under Thirtieth Army, it was assigned directly to Third Area Army at the outbreak of war). On the following day it received confirmatory orders stating:

> The 138th Division will use its raiding unit to check the enemy advance in the vicinity of Tiehling. The division's main body will proceed to Fushun to delay the enemy advance and then to defend that city.

Accordingly, the main body of the division was immediately dispatched to Fushun. However, the raiding battalion could not be sent promptly because it was still unequipped.

The orders from Third Area Army were delivered by train. Since only one train arrived daily, orders were naturally delayed. Moreover, the orders received on the 9th assigned a combat mission to the unarmed troops of the Raiding Battalion. In view of these mounting difficulties, division headquarters dispatched staff and liaison officers to Third Area Army Headquarters, to explain the division's difficulties. On 10 August, Lieutenant General Yokichi Nakajima, the chief of the Ordnance Department of the Kwantung Army, was appointed division commander, and immediately took his post. (General Yamamoto never joined the division.)

On 12 August division headquarters moved to Fushun and, assuming direct command of one infantry regiment which had arrived there earlier, directed the preparation of positions to defend Fushun, a coal mining area. It also supervised the construction of positions undertaken by civilian authorities to defend the city. Other elements of the division as well as new draftees continued to arrive in the Fushun area. The division gradually built up its main strength in Fushun city, and deployed one element along the railway approaching the city from the northeast.

Termination of Hostilities

While directing the preparation of positions by its own elements and supervising the work of civilian authorities, the division learned by commercial radio that the war had ended. Since it had no adequate communication with Third Area Army Headquarters, the division, on its own, took action to maintain order, discipline, and morale, assembled the division at Fushun city, and took steps for the protection of Japanese residents. Fortunately, the division was able to control its units, and no untoward incidents occurred.

Also on its own initiative, the division decided to demobilize all locally drafted personnel, including commissioned officers, and return them to their homes. While this demobilization was under way, an order was received from Third Area Army directing each unit to cease fighting, and to obey the enemy's directives without committing any hostile acts.

Meanwhile, rumors circulated that some units in various parts of Manchuria had gone into the mountains to continue resistance, and that other units had disbanded, their members fleeing in all directions. It was horrible to contemplate what the Russian Army would do to Japanese and Manchurian people under these circumstances. It was expected that officers and men of the division would be interned by either the Soviets or the Chinese, and be used for reconstruction work for an indefinite time. Such being the case, and since no demobilization instructions had yet been received, it was decided to return as many officers and men as possible to their homes promptly. Accordingly, the following measures were planned: 1) draftees arriving by train at Fushun from the north were to be demobilized immediately, paid traveling expenses, and returned to their homes; 2) personnel of division headquarters and of units assigned to the division were to be demobilized in three phases, locally drafted enlisted personnel first, all drafted commissioned officers (except important staff members of the headquarters) second, and all others, third. After completion of the third phase, the division was to have only officers and men transferred from other units, and these were to be reorganized into a single unit.

To prevent unrest among officers and men, and to insure the smooth execution of the first phase, knowledge of the second and third phases was withheld from everyone except division staff officers. While the first phase was being carried out, orders were received from the Area Army directing the demobilization of local draftees. The division completed the first phase, returning almost all noncommissioned officers and men to their homes, but was strictly prohibited from carrying out phases two and three by Third Area Army Headquarters.

Disarmament

On 19 August Soviet occupation forces began to arrive in the Mukden area. It was not until the 23d, however, that a representative sent from the commander of the Soviet forces in Mukden arrived in Fushun. On the 28th, a Soviet unit occupied Fushun and directed immediate disarmament.

The division immediately disarmed itself and surrendered all weapons and materiel. At the direction of the Soviets, the division also disarmed various army and naval units at Fushun, including the Fushun Guard Unit, the Naval Fuel Depot Unit, and a Manchurian anti-aircraft artillery unit. Considerable difficulty was encountered in disarming these units because the Soviet order gave no time for preparation and demanded execution and completion within an impossibly short time. Nevertheless, disarmament was completed without incident.

During disarmament, divisional units were temporarily billeted at primary schools and elsewhere. The units stationed in Fushun remained in their own barracks. After being disarmed, all units were assembled at Hsintun, about 8 kilometers from Fushun; division elements were billeted in tents, while other units utilized buildings. While at Hsintun, the division commander was taken away, and the chief of staff assumed control of all Japanese units in the area.

Attitude of Soviet Army toward the Japanese Army

One unit of the Soviet Army--alleged by the Soviets to be a regiment--occupied Fushun, and detached one of its elements, commanded by a captain, to Hsintun. It was apparent that the Soviets in Fushun were extremely fearful of disturbances, particularly of resistance by the Japanese Army. They endeavored to avoid incidents by a generous policy until they had completely disarmed the Japanese Army and rendered it impotent and unimportant. This attitude stemmed, it appeared, from the fear that the small and inferior Soviet force which first arrived could not control the Japanese Army units.

The attitude of Soviet officers toward the Japanese was outwardly cordial. For example, when a Soviet Army commander who identified himself as General Kurautsuenko arrived on 24 August, he shook hands with the division commander and his staff, and said: "I think you are tired after this long war and need a rest. In about three months you will all be free." The Soviet occupation force did not impose any severe restraints upon the daily life and conduct of the Japanese Army at Fushun and Hsintun, and entrusted the prevention of escapes to the Japanese Army staff. Furthermore, the Soviet senior staff officers exerted every effort to prevent malfeasance by subordinates.

Junior staff officers, however, always used lies in dealing with or directing the Japanese Army. All ranks of the Soviet force seemed particularly anxious to propagate the idea that "the Japanese Army will be repatriated soon." They undermined the Army organization, destroyed the unity of command, and removed all general officers.

Japanese units governed their daily life according to their own former practices, under the supervision of the Soviet regimental commander at Fushun, and no particular difficulties were encountered. There were a few deserters in each unit, but no one was convicted by the Russian Army. Efforts were made to save provisions in view of shortages and in anticipation of a long stay.

Transfer from Hsintun to the Mukden Internment Camp

On 15 September the Soviet Army ordered all personnel of the army and naval units at Hsintun, about 5,000 men, to march to Mukden. The march began promptly and was under the control of the chief of staff of the 138th Division. Upon reaching Mukden, all personnel were interned at the Peiling Internment Camp. This was the first time they had been in a camp surrounded by wire entanglements.

Thereafter, Japanese units were ordered to organize 1,500-man labor battalions, consisting of officers of the grade of captain and below, noncommissioned officers, and men. One by one, these labor battalions were transported north by rail. Within a few days the personnel of the 138th Division and units formerly stationed at Fushun had departed Mukden. Meanwhile at Mukden the Soviets launched a large scale investigation of field grade officers, especially those who had been in intelligence.

Shortly after the departure of the labor battalions, officers interned at Peiling were formed into battalions. There officers were mainly from Kwantung Army Headquarters, units that had been stationed in the vicinities of Hsinking and Mukden, and various supply depots. The officer battalions left Mukden by rail on 20 October, passed through Harbin, Suihua, and Heiho, arriving in November at Blagoveshchensk. Then they were sent west, and were interned at Morshansk in European Russia on 23 December. Some officers sent to the same destination were routed through Manchouli. During all transportation movements the Soviets continued to assure the Japanese troops that they were being repatriated to the Japanese homeland.

Civil Affairs

As soon as Soviet forces entered Mukden on 19 August, they halted traffic around Mukden at a radius of 20 kilometers. All Japanese refugees arriving from Chilin and other interior areas were sent to Fushun. The number of refugees assembled there increased daily. The chief of the Fushun Coal Mine Company, in cooperation with Fushun city authorities, provided shelter and protection for these refugees, utilizing his well-organized management system and his abundant commodities.

From the time the Soviets entered Mukden until they arrived at Fushun, all Japanese agencies in Fushun cooperated in taking steps regarding the reception and treatment of the Soviet Army, the prevention of uprisings, and even in gathering information on Soviet and Manchurian rebels in Mukden. By virtue of the joint efforts of these officials of the division, the city, and the mine company, the mumber of violations and disturbances in the Fushun area were kept at a minimum. To a large extent this orderliness was attributable to the power and influence of the mine company. Nearly all Manchurians in the area depended upon the company for their livelihood directly or indirectly; none of them revolted. The company also took such measures as issuing ample rations to the Soviet troops and keeping licensed brothels to prevent violent acts.

In the sector lying between Fushun and Mukden, numerous acts of plunder by rebels were reported. Many members of the division who had been released from active service and were returning home fell victim to these rebels and were robbed of money and personal belongings supplied by the division.

The Manchurian Army and Police

Immediately following the cease-fire order, Japanese officers assigned to the Manchurian Antiaircraft Artillery Unit in Fushun were relieved of their duties. Order was maintained thereafter by the Manchurian officers. However, these too were disarmed (at the same time as the Japanese Army), and were later sent home. Until the Soviet forces entered the city, Manchurian police helped to maintain order. When the Soviets arrived, they made a special investigation of underground activities of the police, and detained all senior police officers, Japanese and Manchurians.

Manchurian People

The Manchurians in the Fushun area, unlike those in the Mukden area many of whom rebelled and resorted to plunderous acts, remained calm and showed no change in their attitude towards Japan. The general observation was that the Manchurians were favorably disposed toward Manchukuo and the Japanese because the development of Manchukuo over the years had steadily improved the peoples' welfare. This attitude was understandably altered during the closing phase of the war when the Japanese commandeered human and material resources, and forced other hardships on these people. However, after the war, the general public still maintained such goodwill that no anti-Japanese feeling was in evidence. There were, of course, some uprisings, subversive activities, and revolts by politically or socially rebellious Manchurians or by personally disgruntled people. These were more than compensated by the countless instances wherein Manchurians who were grateful for past kindnesses protected the Japanese in a self-sacrificing manner at the end of the war.

The feelings of the Manchurians toward the Soviets were anything but good. A few incidents can illustrate this feeling. While Japanese army and navy units were being marched under guard from Fushun to Mukden, Manchurians in Tungling were asked to give lodging to soldiers. There were some who were willing to accomodate Japanese soldiers but all persistently refused to harbor the Soviet troops guarding the Japanese. That same night a Soviet officer assaulted a Manchurian woman on the roadside.

Monograph No 155-E

CHAPTER V

The 125th Division[16]

Organization

The origin of the 125th Infantry Division is traceable to Kwantung Army's decision to organize the 122d to 128th Division in order to replace the many units that had been transferred to the Pacific fighting front.

Late in January 1945, Kwantung Army notified Lieutenant General Tatsuo Imari that he had been appointed to command the 125th Division. (General Imari was then in Tungan as commander of the 8th Artillery Command.) At about the same time Kwantung Army also notified Colonel Sanehiko Fujita of his appointment as chief of staff, and Major Bunichi Hirata of his appointment as staff officer. (These officers had been, respectively, regimental commander of the 1st Tank Division, and staff officer of the 4th Border Garrison Unit.)

Kwantung Army directed the division commander and other staff officers to report to Fourth Army Headquarters in Sunwu by the middle of February to receive orders. At Sunwu, General Imari learned from the Army commander that his division was to be organized mainly in Shenwutun, Heiho Province, and that the task was to be the responsi-

---

16. The information in this chapter was furnished by Lieutenant General Tatsuo Imari, commander of the 125th Division.

bility of the 6th Border Garrison Unit commander. He immediately sent Colonel Fujita and Major Hirata, the prospective staff officers, to Shenwutun to coordinate matters with the 6th Border Garrison Unit.

The division was organized principally from demobilized elements of the 13th Border Garrison Unit at Fapiehla, and the remnant of 57th Division scheduled for transfer to the homeland. (Other border garrison units in the area--the 5th near Shengwutun, the 6th at Aihun, and the 7th at Hsiheiho--were reorganized into the 135th and 136th Independent Mixed Brigades during July-August 1945.)

By mid-March a major part of the organization of the division had been completed. The elements organized, the degree of organization, the location, and the commanders are shown in the following chart:

Element	Commander	Degree of Completion	Place
Division Headquarters	Lt Gen Tatsuo Imari	Less 1 staff officer and the chiefs of the intendance, ordnance, medical, and veterinary sections	Shenwutun
274th Infantry Regiment	Col Miyagishi	Headquarters, signal section, 3 battalions, machinegun unit, infantry gun unit, mounted plat.	Hsiheiho
275th Infantry Regiment	Col Masao Segawa		Fapeihla
Division Artillery	Maj (unknown)	Hq, cmd Co, 3 Btries, ammo train, (type 38 guns and type 4 150-mm How)	Shenwutun
Signal Unit	Capt Toyonobu Kondo	No wireless equipment	Shenwutun

MONOGRAPH NO. 155-E
MAP NO. 1

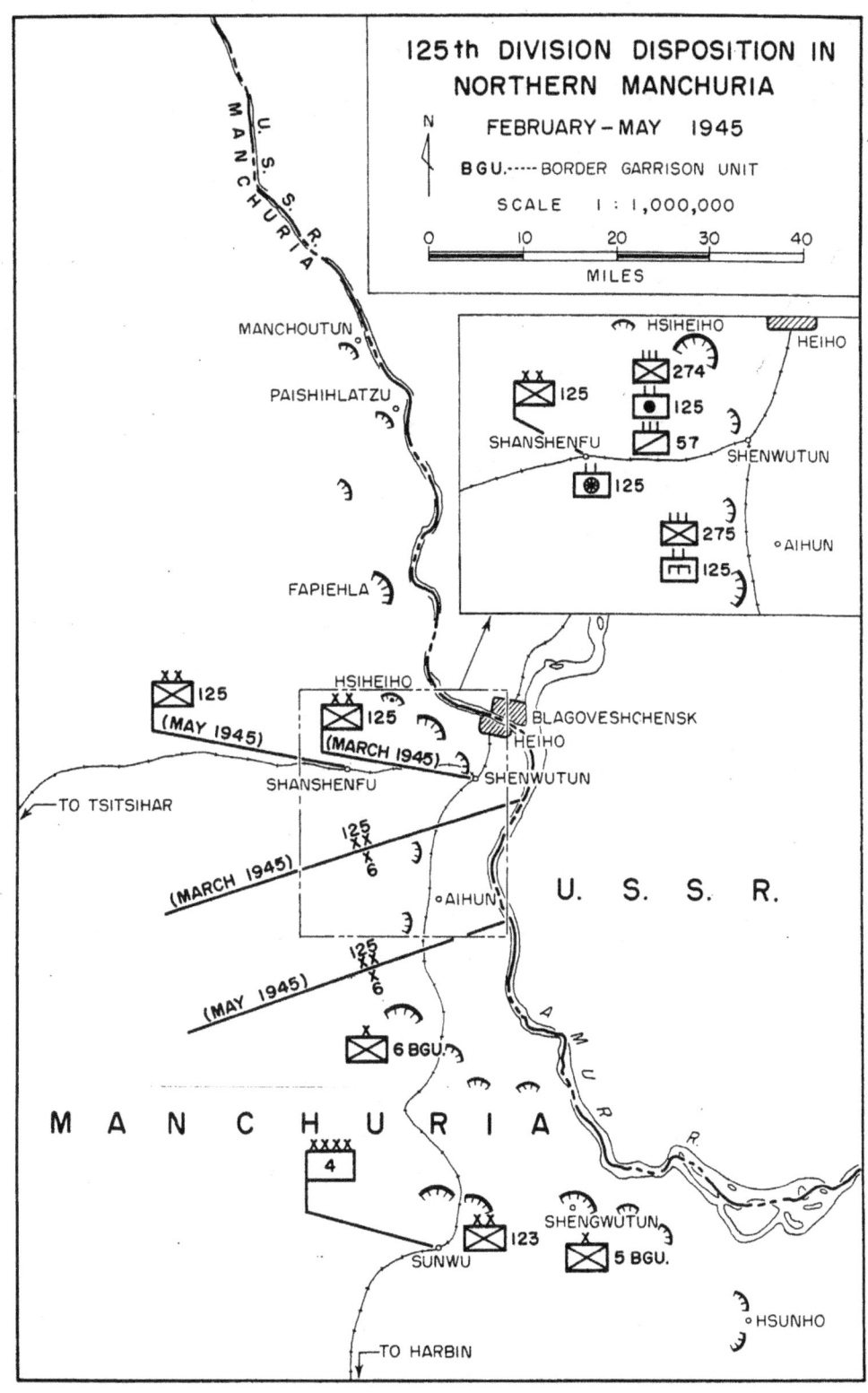

Engineer Unit	Maj Toru Mitano	Hq, 2 Companies	Shenwutun
Transport Unit	Maj (unknown)	Hq, 2 Companies	Shenwutun

The delay in organizing other elements was due mainly to the lack of adequate personnel. On paper, but not organized was the 276th Infantry Regiment.

The mission assigned to the division was to carry out reconnaissance along the border formed by the Amur River (from the lookout post about 10 kilometers southeast of Heiho through Heiho City, and northwestward through Hsiheiho, Fapiehla, Paishihlatzu, to Manchoutun), and also to defend the area lying south of this line as far as the garrison sectors of the 123d Division (at Sunwu), and the 6th Border Garrison Unit. (See Map No 1).

Late in March, division headquarters conducted an inspection of armaments and also, in view of the scattered disposition of elements, took steps to establish unity in the division. Late in April, the commanders of the 274th and 275th Regiments went to Tokyo and received their regimental colors.

Early in May, a major re-disposition of divisional elements took place after the 57th Division, whose main force had been in Shanshenfu, was transferred to the homeland. At the same time, the 125th Division acquired the 57th Reconnaissance Regiment (one light armored car company and one cavalry company) from the transferred division. After the re-disposition was completed, all divisional elements were in the Shanshenfu area, except the 275th Regiment and the Engineer Unit, which were at Aihun. (See Inset of Map No 1.)

In mid-May, the division commander summoned each unit commander to his headquarters for conferences, and late in the month himself visited each unit at its station, inspecting combat readiness and strengthening the unity of the division.

Transfer of Division to Tunghua

When it became apparent that war with the Soviet Union was inevitable, Kwantung Army decided to mobilize eight divisions and seven independent mixed brigades by calling for a mass-mobilization of men living in Manchuria. Although this was not begun until July, Kwantung Army in June ordered the 125th Division to detach certain of its elements and leave them at their stations under Fourth Army, and to move the remaining elements including division headquarters, to Tunghua, where the division would be reorganized under the direct command of the Third Area Army. The units to be left behind were the 274th Regiment, the 57th Reconnaissance Regiment, the Artillery Unit, the Transport Unit, the Ordnance Duty Unit, and the Intendance Duty Unit.

At about the same time that these orders were received from Kwantung Army, other orders were received from Third Area Army directing the division commander to report to its headquarters in Mukden. Upon reporting, he was instructed to conduct a one-week reconnaissance of positions in the Changpaishan Range in Tunghua Province,

MONOGRAPH NO. 155-E
MAP NO. 2

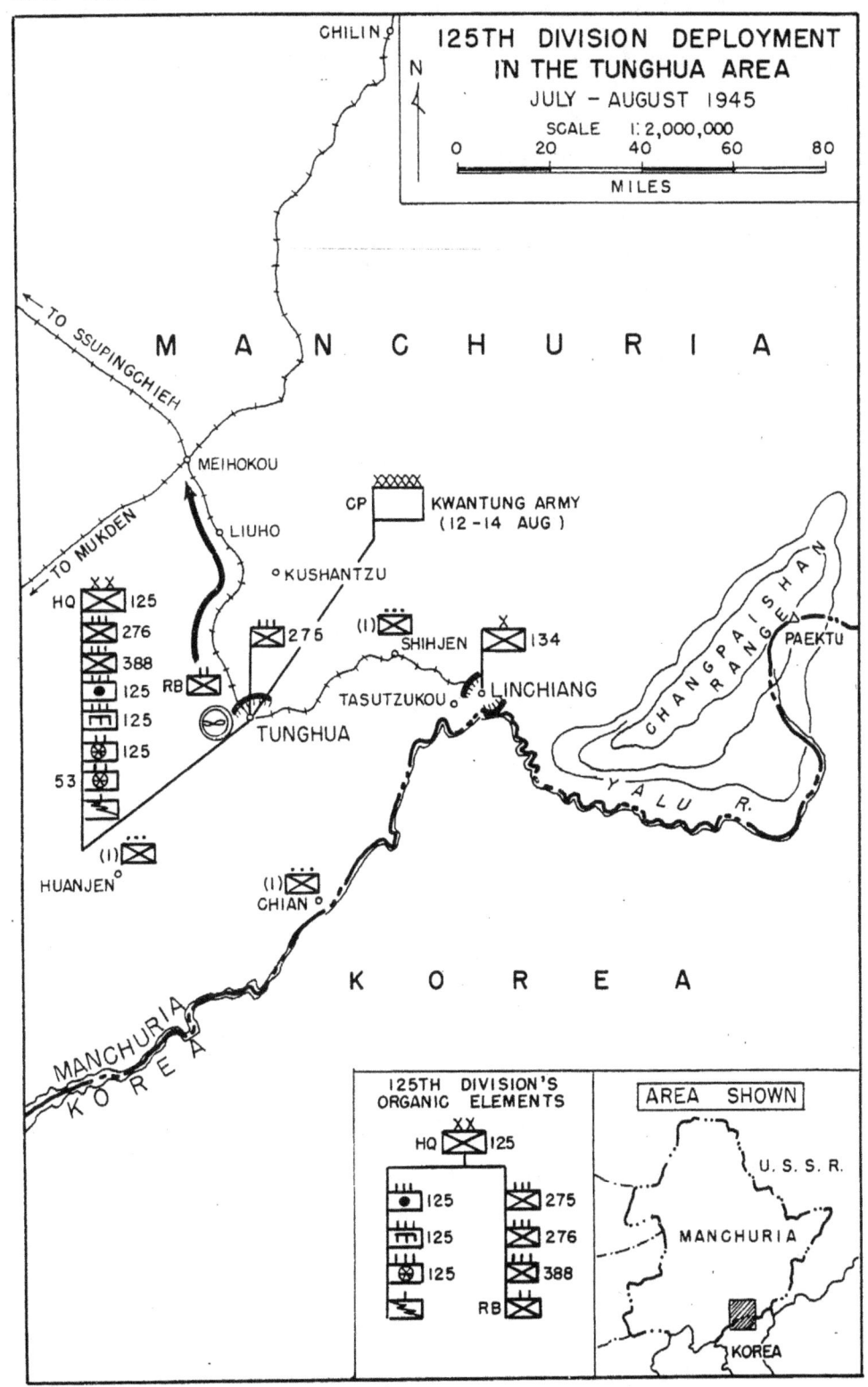

which was to form the last defense line of Kwantung Army to prevent a Soviet invasion of Korea. General Imari immediately left Mukden by train, accompanied by his chief of staff.

After surveying the mountain range, General Imari and Colonel Fujita went to the city of Tunghua and during the few days there made a thorough map study of the range. General Imari then reported to the Area Army Commander that: "The occupation of positions is possible if adequate time is allowed, and personnel, materiel, and funds are adequate."

The division's move to Tunghua began early in June, division headquarters going first. At two-day intervals the other elements involved in the transfer moved in the following order: Signal Unit, 275th Regiment, Engineer Unit. The trip was made by rail and took about one week. Upon arrival at Tunghua, division headquarters was stationed in the First Primary School, the Signal Unit in the area formerly used by the Manchukuoan Army Ordnance Depot, the 275th Regiment in the barracks outside Tunghua City formerly used by the Manchukuoan Army, and the Engineer Unit occupied hastily built barracks in the compound of the Tunghua Iron Foundry. Aside from this disposition, the division sent one guard unit of platoon strength to Linchiang (where Kwantung Army General Headquarters planned to direct the last-ditch stand), one to Chian (where the railroad bridge crosses the Yalu River leading to Pyongyang), and one at Huanjen, a rice producing district where a Japanese land development group was located. (See Map No 2.)

Reorganization

The division reorganization began early in July and consisted principally of bringing existing units up to strength and forming new units with personnel obtained during the July mass-mobilization. Of the existing units, the 275th Regiment was ordered to furnish an element for the organization of a raiding unit, and was itself replenished with recruits. The Engineer Regiment formed a headquarters and three companies from personnel of the original organization plus conscriptees.

The first of the new units formed was the raiding battalion. It consisted of a headquarters and three companies, and was stationed in the Normal School in Tunghua City. Next to be formed was the 276th Infantry Regiment. It was to consist of 2,500 men, but was able to obtain only 660. The regiment was bivouacked in the plaza in Tunghua City. The 388th Infantry Regiment was also to consist of 2,500 men, but it obtained only 460 men; it was bivouacked on the grounds of the Tunghua Iron Foundry. The plan for mobilizing the 125th Artillery Regiment (horse drawn) required the formation of a headquarters, a command company, three battalions, and an ammunition train. The Regiment actually got only 500 men and 200 horses for all these units. It was billeted in the Second Primary School, although some units had to be bivouacked in the grounds nearby. The Transport Regiment (horse drawn) required an organization of a headquarters and three companies, but actually got only 300 men and 100 horses. It was bivouacked in the city plaza. The Ordnance Duty Unit required 200 men but got only 110, and was stationed in the Manchukuoan Army Ordnance Depot. The Veterinary Hospital required 100 men but got only 36; it occupied buildings attached to the airfield on the outskirts of the city. All of these units were only partially equipped.

On 25 July, when the division's reorganization was far from complete and its equipment far from adequate, Kwantung Army instructed it to bring reorganization procedures to an end. From that date till the end of the month, the division commander, with a view to raising morale, conducted an inspection of the equipment of each unit. The leading commanders of the division at that time were:

    Division Commander   - Lt Gen Tatsuo Imari
    (Chief of Staff)   - Col Sanehiko Fujita
    275th Regiment   - Col Masao Segawa
    276th Regiment   - Col Kaoru Okano
    388th Regiment   - Col Shigeru Imada
    Artillery Regiment   - Maj Akizo Yokoyama
    Signal Unit   - Capt Toyonobu Kondo
    Engineer Regiment   - Maj Toru Mitano
    Transport Regiment   - Lt Col Sen Nagai
    Ordnance Duty Unit   - 1st Lt Ichiro Yamamoto
    Veterinary Hospital   - 1st Lt Toshio Ogawa

Assigned directly to Third Area Army, the division was given the mission of constructing strong positions capable of checking an enemy tank advance in the mountain region extending from the west foot of the Changpaishan Range to Tunghua along the railroad and the paralleling road, and of conducting training in these positions.

Anticipating the difficulty of conducting mass training once the construction of defense positions was started, the division in early August assembled regimental and battalion commanders and officers in charge of training. Under the personal supervision of the chief of staff division headquarters gave instructions on antitank operations in the defense of positions.

Also early in August, the division's strength was reinforced by the assignment of the following units: 134th Independent Mixed Brigade, the 53d Independent Transport Battalion, the 88th Land Duty Company, the 604th Special Guard Battalion, the 36th Field Hospital of the Kwantung Army, a Special Service Agency (intelligence) unit, and a military police detachment. The brigade was to be assigned to Linchiang for its defense, and at the same time the Linchiang Guard platoon was to move to Shihjen. Other units were stationed at Tunghua and its vicinity.

On orders from Third Area Army, all units moved to their assigned sectors and began constructing positions and stockpiling provisions along the railroad south of Liuho. In preparing its antitank positions, the division stressed the use of explosives against tanks. Since it had received no supply of explosives from Kwantung Army, it undertook in early August the manufacture of a quantity for its own use, commandeering yellow powder and other substances from Tunghua Province.

Opening of Hostilities

On 6 August the division commander went to the area south of Liuho for what was to be a five day detailed study of the Liuho positions. When the war started he was inspecting positions at

Kushantzu.

At about 1600, 9 August, he received a report that the Soviets had begun a full scale war, crossing the north, east, and west borders of Manchuria. He immediately started back to Tunghua. Arriving at division headquarters at midnight, he was informed by the chief of staff of the receipt at noon of orders assigning the division to Thirtieth Army.

On the following morning, the division commander received a Thirtieth Army order directing him to concentrate the division in the vicinity of Meihokou. On the morning of the 11th, he received a contradictory order from Kwantung Army instructing him that the division was being attached directly to Kwantung Army and was to defend Tunghua and its vicinity. Thus within three days the division had three different assignments.

On receipt of the Thirtieth Army order, General Imari ordered division headquarters, the Signal Unit, the Raiding Battalion, the 275th Regiment, and the Engineer Regiment to proceed immediately to Meihokou and its vicinity, and ordered other units to remain at their stations, completing preparations for operations. While preparing to initiate these movements, the division received the Kwantung Army order. General Imari immediately countermanded his previous orders. He ordered the Raiding Unit to concentrate its main body in the sector south of Meihokou, and to deploy elements in the city of Tunghua. He ordered the 275th Regiment to occupy positions from the end of the defile 10 kilometers north of Tunghua to the hill immediately north of Tunghua, with the mission of preventing the penetration of enemy tanks. He ordered other units to continue their previously assigned missions.

General Imari reported these measures personally to the Kwantung Army Commander-in-Chief when the latter arrived at the office of the vice-governor of Tunghua Province on the evening of 12 August. The arrival of General Yamada in Tunghua signalled the withdrawal of Kwantung Army Headquarters to the redoubt to direct the last ditch stand in Manchuria. He was accompanied by Major General Matsumura, his assistant chief of staff, Lieutenant Colonel Sejima, Operations Officer, and Major General Komatsu, chief of the Special Intelligence Department. Also arriving in Tunghua the same day were other members of the General staff and of the Adjutant's Department, as well as the Kwantung Army's Ordnance Depot, and an element of its Signal Unit.

On the afternoon of 14 August, General Yamada hurriedly left Tunghua to return to Hsinking, taking with him General Matsumura, Colonel Sejima, and an aide. During the morning, an element of the Air Officers School had arrived at the Tunghua airfield in about fifteen planes and was quartered at Tunghua. (This unit flew to the homeland on the 16th.)

Termination of Hostilities

On 15 August division headquarters heard a radio broadcast of the Imperial Rescript on the Termination of the War. The broadcast was not clearly received because of noise, so the Telegraph News Service was contacted and in the evening a printed copy of the Rescript was received. All were awed and alarmed.

Orders and directives concerning the cease-fire were not received from Kwantung Army until 17 August, and may be summarized as follows:

> In compliance with Imperial Command, Kwantung Army will cease fighting.
>
> Each unit will remain in its present area and will be disarmed on orders of the Soviet Army.
>
> Officers will be permitted to wear decorations and swords, but warrant officers and enlisted men will not be permitted to carry swords or bayonets.
>
> Demobilization of the Kwantung Army will be effected after negotiation with the Soviet Army.
>
> Officers and men of the Kwantung Army, although under the control of the Soviet Army, will not be regarded by Japan as prisoners of war (in the sense of being subject to court-martial).
>
> Officers and men must not take rash actions detrimental to the future welfare of Japan.

Based on these Kwantung Army orders and directives, the division issued its own orders to subordinate units. Some officers expressed reluctance to comply with the orders, but the division commander, after much persuasion, finally succeeded in obtaining their understanding. The division chief of staff, Colonel Fujita, accompanied by his family, secretly took flight on 17 August.

Meanwhile, after learning of the Imperial Rescript on 15 August, the division began burning secret documents. On the 20th the colors of the 275th Infantry Regiment were burned in the presence of the regimental commander. The division commander on the 21st toured all areas in Tunghua under his jurisdiction, exhorting officers and men to avoid rash acts and to submit to the Soviet Army authorities in an orderly manner.

On the 23d the division commander appointed Colonel Segawa, 275th Regimental Commander, to be chairman of a group of officers charged with collecting all weapons of Japanese and Manchurian Army units in the Tunghua area. This task was completed at about 0100 on 24 August. After returning to his quarters, Colonel Segawa was offering prayers to the gods when he met a violent death from rifle bullets fired by Japanese soldiers.

At about 1100 hours on 24 August, a Soviet delegation (consisting of two lieutenant colonels, a major, and an interpreter) accompanied by one escort tank company arrived at Tunghua Station. Informed of their arrival, Colonel Kadota, who had succeeded Colonel Fujita as chief of staff, went to the station to meet them, and led them to division headquarters. There the following agreement was concluded:

> Disarmament will begin on the evening of 24 August. Arms and equipment will be delivered to the Soviet Army. The platoons in Huanjen, Chian, and Shihjenkou will be disarmed last. Disarmament will be completed by the evening of 26 August.

Disarmament of Japanese units at Linchiang will be conducted by Soviet forces there.

The Japanese Army will be authorized the use of 1,000 rifles with bayonets, for the maintenance of peace and order in Tunghua City. Responsibility for public peace and order will be transferred to the Soviet Army at noon of 30 August.

The division and units under its command will be transferred to Chilin. Three trains will be provided on 26 August, two on the 27th, four on the 28th, and one on the 31st.

Families of military personnel will be detained in Tunghua. The safety of their lives and property will be guaranteed by the Soviet Army.

Pursuant to these terms, approximately 12,000 Japanese personnel were placed under the control of the Soviet Army. The breakdown of this figure is:

Officers	600
Noncommissioned Officers	1,400
Division guards	180
Men of the Segawa Unit (275th Regt)	2,100
Men of the Okano Unit (276th Regt)	660
Men of the Imada Unit (388th Regt)	460
Men of the Yokoyama Unit (Arty)	500
Men of the Mitano Unit (Engr)	600
Men of the Nagai Unit (Trans)	300
Men of the Sugihara Unit (Raiding Bn)	800
Men of the Kondo Unit (Signal)	160
Men of the Yamamoto (Ichiro) Unit (Ord)	110
Men of the Ogawa Unit (Vet)	36
Men of the Takenaka Unit (53d Ind Trans Bn)	900
Men of the Goto Unit (134th Ind Mix Brig)	700
Men of the Yamamoto (Kazuo) Unit (88th Land Duty Co)	460
Men of other units	2,034

Weapons, ammunition, and equipment delivered to the Soviet Army were as follows (ammunition given in parenthesis):

Rifles	5,000	(1,100,000)
Heavy machineguns	15)-	(45,000)
Light machineguns	57	
Heavy grenade dischargers	50	(3,500)
Revolvers	50	(9,000)
Infantry guns	3	(1,200)
Antitank guns	2	(900)
Mountain guns	2	(2,500)
Powder (yellow)	30 tons	
Vehicles (trucks)	100	

The move of the division and units under its control to Chilin was carried out on schedule and as planned. The first group to depart consisted of the Goto, Segawa, and Mitano Units; the second group consisted of the Takenaka, Ogawa, Nagai, Yokoyama, and both Yamamoto Units; the third group consisted of the Imada Unit and various units under the division's control; the last group consisted of division headquarters and the Sugihara Unit. On 30 August, approximately 1,200 horses were taken overland to Chilin.

Since division headquarters left Tunghua in the last echelon, it did not learn until later that as troops detrained at Chilin they were formed into battalions of approximately 1,000 men each, with no regard to their original organizations. Supplies taken by the units to Chilin (clothing, tools, provisions) were collected by the Soviet forces. It was unavoidable that large quantities of these supplies were looted.

The division commander arrived at Chilin on 1 September. He was met by a Soviet Army major who directed him, his senior adjutant, interpreter, and orderly, as well as Major General Niimi, Chief of the Military Service Department of the Kwantung Army and other general staff officers who arrived at Chilin at the same time, to the Chilin Provincial Government Office. All these people were detained until 5 September and, meanwhile, were briefly questioned regarding their personal history. On the afternoon of 5 September all were flown to Voroshilov.

Civil Affairs

Japanese residents in the area under the division's jurisdiction numbered about 10,000. The bulk of these were personnel connected with the branch office of the iron-foundry. The minority groups were a land development group and the families of military personnel. The land development group was settled in Huanjen, a rich rice-producing district in Antung Province, near the southwestern border of Tunghua Province, and accessible by both trucks and boat. After the termination of the war, as the pressure of Manchurians upon this group increased, the community was withdrawn to Tunghua escorted by an element of the division.

As for the families of military personnel, of whom there were about forty, although the terms of the agreement provided for their protection by the Soviet Army, they actually joined the other Japanese residents. Their care was entrusted to the chief of the Japanese residents group.

Public peace in Tunghua, well maintained during the Soviet occupation, deteriorated after the Chinese communist troops replaced the Soviet force late in 1945. Sharp increases in extortion of money or articles of value was noted, but cases of violence or murder were not in evidence. However, the Japanese-sponsored Governor Yang, as well as Vice-Governor Sugawara, and Mr Kawase, chief of the Police Affairs Agency, were arrested and apparently shot to death while proceeding to Antung under escort. Also, two advisers to the Manchurian Government, former lieutenant-general Inoue, and Mr Takahashi, formerly president of an insurance company, were arrested and sent to Pyongyang, and finally to Siberia. In February 1946, Colonel Fujita, former division chief of staff, secretly entered Tunghua from his hiding place and led an abortive rebellion. He was later arrested and executed. As a result of this attempted rebellion, Japanese residents were subjected to extremely cruel treatment, and many innocent men were shot.

The Emperor of Manchuria and his family had fled to Tasutzukou, west of Lichiang, on about 12 August. After the end of the war he left Tunghua Province by place on about 16 August. He was arrested at Mukden, while en route to Japan, and sent to Siberia.

Manchurian Army troops in Tunghua province had been transferred to Chinhsien in the middle of June. Hence there was no problem with them. Nor was any oppressive action taken against the Japanese by Manchurian police in Tunghua. Also, between the Manchurians and Koreans residing in Tunghua there were no riotous acts.

Monograph No 155-F

CHAPTER VI

The Forty-fourth Army[17]

Origin of Forty-fourth Army Headquarters

Southern Manchuria, with its heavy industrial concentration and its critical rail network, was the base of the line of communications of the Kwantung Army. In mid 1944 American planes flying from China bases bombed key industrial and rail targets in the Anshan, Dairen, Penchihu, and Suichung areas, and the necessity for strengthening the defenses of these vital areas assumed major importance. To accomplish this Kwantung Army Headquarters on 1 September 1944 transferred Kwantung Defense Army Headquarters from Hsinking to Mukden, and directed it to improve the air defenses of southern Manchuria. At the same time it emphasized the importance of maintaining public peace in key cities, and of suppressing the China Eighth Route Army in Jehol Province.

The Kwantung Defense Army was a "peace and order" army. Not a tactical command, it was untrained for use in offensive operations. At the time its headquarters was transferred to Mukden, the only forces in southern and southwestern Manchuria were the 107th Division,

---

17. The information in this chapter was prepared by Major Takeo Kato, staff officer, Forty-fourth Army Headquarters.

stationed in the vicinity of Arshaan, the 108th Division in Jehol Province (engaged in suppressing communist bandits), elements of the Manchukuoan Army (about one division in the vicinity of Hsingan, and eight regiments along the Great Wall), and about two brigades of the Mongolian Army--one near Taonan and one near Tungliao. Southern and southwestern Manchuria were considered a vacuum zone, and the weakest part of Kwantung Army's defense system.

With the sudden change in the war situation in early 1945 (the surrender of Germany and the annihilation of the Japanese on Okinawa), the threat of a Soviet invasion increased. The matter of improving the defense of southern Manchuria became urgent.

At the time the only units that could be said to be deployed anywhere near the border facing Inner Mongolia[18] were, in the 108th Division's area, one company at Linhsi and one battalion at Chihfeng, and in the 107th Division's area, small elements near Arshaan and Wuchakou. This limited deployment emphasized the weaknesses of defenses in this area and posed a direct threat to the Dairen-Hsinking Railway, the main artery in Manchuria. The commander of the Kwantung Defense Army felt the urgency of strengthening this front, and submitted appropriate proposals to the Commander in Chief of the Kwantung Army.

---

18. Actually, Inner Mongolia was under Japanese control. The Soviet Army would have to come from Outer to Inner Mongolia to reach the Forty-fourth Army's border (except for a short distance in the north). Most of this area is desert land.

On 10 May Kwantung Army sent General Matsumura, its assistant chief of staff, and Lieutenant Colonel Miyata[19] (Prince Tsunenori Takeda), operations staff officer to Mukden to notify Kwantung Defense Army Headquarters of plans underway to strengthen Manchuria defenses in general, and southern Manchuria defenses in particular. They stated that a plan for the improvement of defenses on the western front in general had been submitted to Imperial General Headquarters.

The plan provided for 1) the deployment of one tactical army consisting of three divisions in the south and southwest, 2) the reorganization of Kwantung Defense Army Headquarters into a tactical headquarters for this purpose, and 3) moving Third Area Army Headquarters from Tsitsihar to Mukden to assume the peace and order responsibilities of the Kwantung Defense Army. The divisions for the new army were to be one division (the 107th) already in the Wuchakou-Hsingan area, and two divisions (the 63d and 117th) to be transferred from China.

On 20 May, Kwantung Defense Army Headquarters was informed that this plan had been approved, and on the following day staff officers of Third Area Army Headquarters arrived in Mukden to survey the office space and officers quarters which their headquarters personnel were to take over from the Kwantung Defense Army Headquarters.

At about the same time, the Defense Army Headquarters, on instructions from the assistant chief of staff of Kwantung Army, sent

---

19. This was a pseudonym adopted as a security measure.

its chief of staff and other officers to inspect the prospective sites for the new army headquarters and its subordinate commands. As a result of this survey, it was decided that army headquarters would be established at Liaoyuan, 63d Division Headquarters at Tungliao (with division elements deployed along the Liaoyuan-Tungliao Railway), 117th Division Headquarters at Taonan (with division elements along the Ssupingchieh-Taonan Railway). This recommendation was submitted to the Commander in Chief of the Kwantung Army.

On 27 May the Kwantung Defense Army Headquarters sent an advance party to Liaoyuan. On the 29th the Third Area Army Commander and his headquarters arrived in Mukden and immediately assumed the duties of the Kwantung Defense Army Headquarters. Defense units, air defense units, and garrison units in the area maintained their status quo, but were placed under the command of the Third Area Army commander.

The main body of the Defense Army Headquarters left Mukden on 30 May and completed its move to Liaoyuan on 1 June, when it immediately began defense planning. On 5 June, the Kwantung Defense Army Headquarters was redesignated the Forty-fourth Army Headquarters. It was placed under the command of the Third Area Army commander, and was issued the following order of battle:

> Forty-fourth Army Commander - Lt Gen Yoshio Hongo
> Headquarters
> 63d Division (Joined on 19 June)
> 107th Division
> 117th Division (Joined on 25 June)
> 9th Independent Tank Brigade (Joined on 30 July)
> 29th Independent Antitank Battalion
> 2d Raiding Unit (Joined on 30 July)

17th Heavy Field Artillery Regiment (150mm howitzer)
30th Heavy Field Artillery Regiment (100mm gun) (Joined on
      30 July)
6th Independent Heavy Artillery Battery (300mm howitzer)
    (Joined on 30 July)
14th Independent Field Artillery Battalion
31st Signal Regiment
605th Special Guard Company
607th Special Guard Company
619th Special Guard Company (Joined on 30 July)
643d Special Guard Company (Joined on 30 July)
644th Special Guard Company (Joined on 30 July)
648th Special Guard Company (Joined on 30 July)

Zone of Communications Units
  127th Special Field Duty Company
  75th Line of Communications Duty Company
  112th Independent Motor Transport Battalion (Joined on
      30 July)
  277th Independent Motor Transport Company (Reattached to
    the Inspectorate of Supply on 30 July)
  73d Independent Transport Company
  47th Field Road Construction Unit
  55th Casualty Clearing Platoon
  40th Construction Duty Company
  82d Construction Duty Company (Reattached to the Thirtieth
    Army on 30 July)
  41st Sea Duty Company (Reattached to the Thirtieth Army
    on 30 July)
  Arhshaan Army Hospital
  Paichengtzu Army Hospital
  2d Hailar Army Hospital
  19th Field Ordnance Depot (Less one mobile repair section)
  19th Field Motor Transport Depot
  19th Field Freight Depot (Less one mobile repair section)

<u>Disposition of Units Assigned to the Army</u>

    The 107th Division disposed its main force in the Arshaan area and an element in the vicinity of Wuchakou and Tepossu, leaving its reconnaissance and transport units at Tsitsihar. The Army, however, considered it more advantageous to withdraw the division's main force to prepared positions in the vicinity of Wuchakou for delaying operations, and suggested this to the Kwantung Army General Headquarters. After obtaining approval, the Army transferred the main body of the division to Wuchakou in the middle of June and supervised the organization of established positions to make them suitable for one division. The reconnaissance and transport units left at Tsitsihar were also transferred to the vicinity of Wuchakou. In late June, the Army commander conducted his first inspection of 107th Division positions.

The 63d Division moved in echelons from North China beginning in early June. It consisted of two infantry brigades (each with four battalions) an artillery unit, an engineer unit, and a transport unit.

Upon arrival in Manchuria, the division's headquarters and its main force were deployed in the vicinity of Tungliao, with elements at Kailu, Liaoyuan, and along the Liaoyuan-Tungliao Railway. The transfer was completed in about a week. The division's assignment to the Forty-fourth Army became effective as of 19 June. At the beginning of July, by order of the Area Army, one infantry battalion of the division was placed under the command of the 108th Division then engaged in operations against China's Eighth Route Army in Jehol.

The 117th Division received orders transferring it to Manchuria while it was engaged in the Laohokou Operation in North China. After overcoming the enemy resistance in that operation, the division assembled in the vicinity of Hsinhsiang, its former garrison, and started moving to Manchurian in the middle of June. Its composition was similar to that of the 63d Division.

The division's headquarters and its main force upon arriving in Manchuria, were deployed in the vicinity of Taonan, with elements at Paichengtzu and along the Ssupinchieh-Taonan Railway. The movement was completed at the end of June, and the change of assignment made effective as of 25 June. However, two infantry battalions remained in North China, engaged in the operations there.

Units under the Direct Command of the Army

The Forty-fourth Army's tank brigade and most of its directly assigned artillery units were organized or joined during July. Because of their lack of equipment and training, very little could be expected of their fighting capacities. Logistical groups also arrived during July from Hailar and Tsitsihar, and had just begun their tasks when the war with Russia started.

The 31st Signal Regiment was transferred from Central China to Pamiencheng in the middle of June. The 17th Heavy Field Artillery Regiment, assigned from Third Army, was deployed at Kaiyuan at the beginning of July. The 29th Independent Antitank Battalion arrived in Taonan in early July. The 2d Raiding Unit remained in Hsingan.

The Kwantung Defense Army had had no supply depots, only one field road construction unit, some transport units, and one hospital. The Forty-fourth Army order of battle included a considerable number of logistical units.

The 19th Field Supply Depot was obtained from Fourth Army and moved from its former stations in the Hailar and Tsitsihar sectors. The main dumps of the Field Ordnance Depot and the Field Motor Transport Depot were moved to the vicinity of Ssupingchieh. As for the Field Freight Depot, its main dump was moved to Liaoyuan, with its branches in the vicinities of Wuchakou, Taonan and Tungliao. Upon the assignment of these depots in the middle of July, they immediately began supply operations.

The 47th Field Road Construction Unit had been stationed in Tungliao since March and was engaged in the maintenance of the Tungliao-Kailu road. The 73d Independent Transport Company moved to the vicinity of Liaoyuan early in July. Medical Units were moved from their stations in Hailar by the middle of July and assigned to the station of each major divisional element, where they established casualty convalescent stations. The line of communications duty unit moved to Liaoyuan in the middle of July.

Operational Preparations

Although the organization of the Forty-fourth Army Headquarters was completed on 5 June, higher headquarters did not immediately reveal operational plans to it. (The Army's deployment of the 63d and 117th Divisions was tentative). It was not until 14 June, when the Army commanders were assembled at the Kwantung Army Headquarters, that the draft of operational plans was disclosed. Not waiting for Third Area Army to issue its plan (see below), the Army drew up its own

MONOGRAPH NO. 155-F
MAP NO. 1

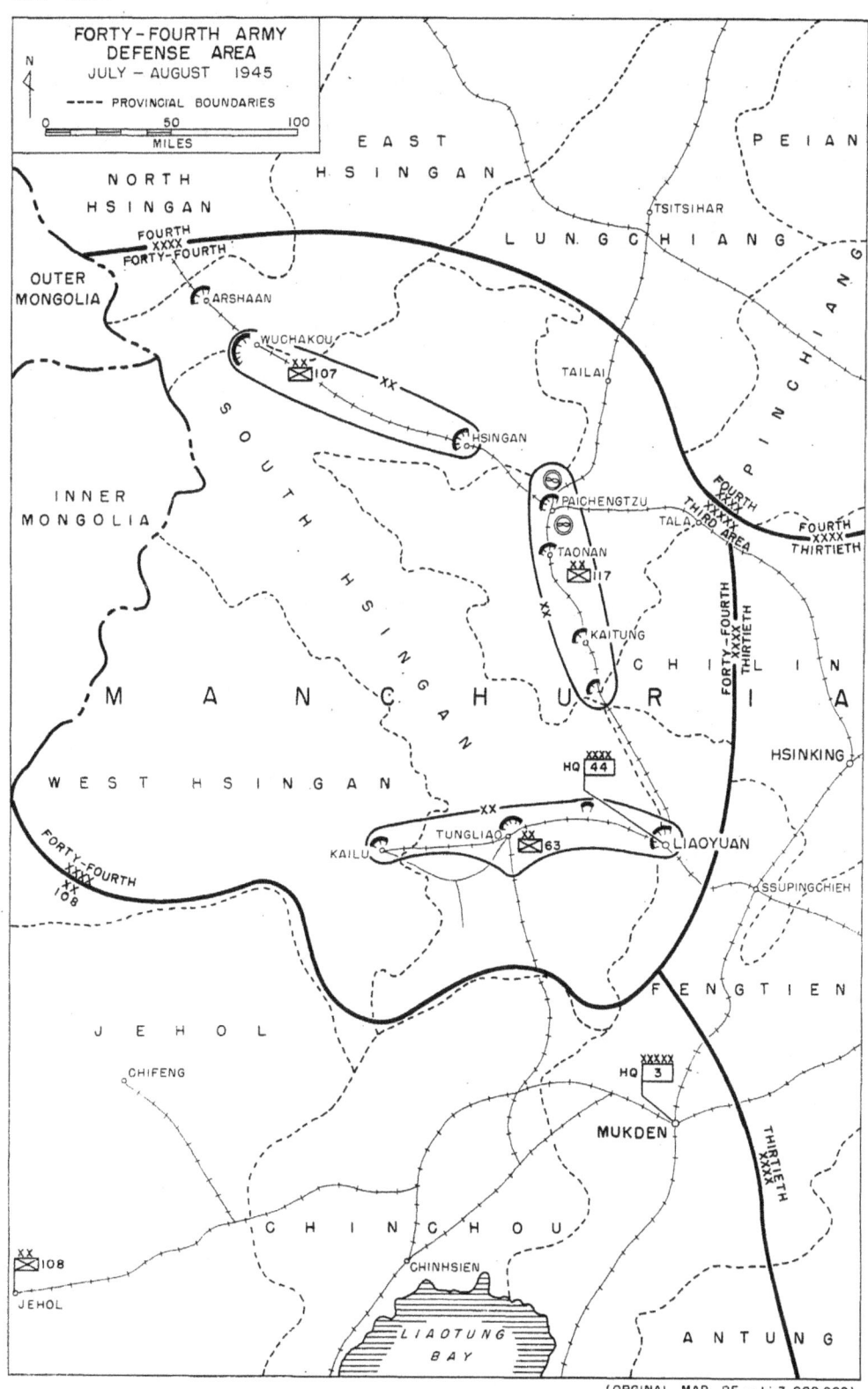

operational plan and explained it at the meeting of unit commanders held at the Army Headquarters in Liaoyuan early in July. The gist of the Army's operations plan, presented informally, was as follows: (See Map No 1.)

> The 107th Division will secure the prepared positions in the vicinities of Wuchakou and Hsingan and the rest of the commands will secure the key traffic points along the Ssupingchieh-Taonan Railroad and the Liaoyuan-Tungliao Railroad and check the enemy advance at these positions.
>
> Positions will be organized at key traffic points; guerrilla warfare will be carried out with these positions as the bases of areas of approximately 20 kilometers radius. If the enemy detours around these positions, he will be attacked in the rear.
>
> The artillery units presently under the direct command of the Army will be attached to the 63d and 117th Divisions to become the nuclei of the positions respectively in the Liaoyuan and Tungliao area and the Paichengtzu and Taonan area, as well as other areas.
>
> The Tank Brigade, supported by an infantry element, will assume a defensive role in the vicinity of the Paichengtzu airfield. To counteract the action of enemy paratroop forces, it will employ its tanks as mobile pillboxes.
>
> Defense positions at Wuchakou will be reformed so as to be adjustable to changes in strength.
>
> Positions will be prepared in the Hsingan area to thwart an enemy detour.

"Defense" Mission (Public Peace and Order)

Aside from its mission of preparing for operations against the Soviets, the Forty-fourth Army, after its headquarters was transferred to Liaoyuan, was given the mission of maintaining public peace and order, and was accordingly designated additionally as the Western District Defense Command.[20] In this capacity it replaced the 107th Division. The defense districts in its jurisdiction covered the same areas as its operational districts. These were the provinces of West Hsingan and South Hsingan, and the Tailai prefecture of Lungchiang Province as well as the Liaoyuan prefecture of Ssuping Province. Divisions under the Army's operational control were given defense responsibility for their respective districts. Thus the Army's operational and defense areas were integrated.

Although the Army had issued defense instructions to its subordinate commands as soon as they joined, it was not until late July or early August that it prepared a formal defense plan based on an outline furnished by Third Area Army in mid July. On 4 August the Army held a conference with the chiefs of staff of subordinate commands, during which the defense plan was discussed.

Since the maintenance of peace and order among the civilian populace was essential to the execution of military operations, the defense mission was closely related to the operations mission. For the defense of the Western Defense District, the Army plan provided for the establishment of strong positions for carrying out guerrilla

---

20. Similar defense (peace and order) commands existed in all parts of Manchuria. The Central District Defense Command was the 148th Division in Hsinking. The Southwestern District was the 108th Division at Jehol. The Pinchiang Province Defense Command was the 131st Independent Mixed Brigade in Harbin.

warfare, and the collecting of timely intelligence. Subordinate commands were instructed to make special efforts to win the confidence of the people, with the object of getting every town and village to help the military in resisting enemy attacks by such measures as constructing moats and other obstacles at important points in and around towns and villages.

In actual practice this did not work out, and no noteworthy construction was carried out by the people. Even the people's confidence was lost, principally as a result of the unfavorable turn of the war situation, but also because of the Army's severity in commandeering commodities and requisitioning personnel. The construction by civilians of positions for guerrilla warfare, therefore, was mere desk theory.

South Manchuria had always been the focal point in defense plans of Manchuria, and the western sector merely played a supporting role in the defense of South Manchuria and the Hsinking area against air attacks from China. Although the air defense setup had been kept in readiness, the maintenance of the communications network had deteriorated. By re-arranging the positions of lookout sentries, the Army planned to strengthen the communications network for air defense. However, because of shortages of equipment and materials, such plans could not be carried out satisfactorily. Furthermore, to forestall enemy sabotage after the outbreak of the war, the Army instructed military police units, railroad garrison units, and Manchukuoan Army units to protect principal traffic lines, power sources, and buildings.

The seat of the administrative organs of Hsingan General Province (North, East, South, and West Hsingan), which represented a major part of the Army's defense sector, was Hsingan City. Since for liaison purposes the city was inconveniently located with respect to Liaoyuan the provincial government sent a councillor to Liaoyuan in mid-June to act as liaison officer.

As for security measures in its area, which had been infiltrated by armed spies from Mongolia since May, the Army requested each subordinate command to take thorough counter-espionage measures, and instructed border observation units and border police units to be especially vigilant in apprehending spies.

Fortifications

Prior to its designation as Forty-fourth Army the Kwantung Defense Army had taken steps to strengthen border positions in the Linhsi sector of Jehol Province, to construct permanent antiaircraft artillery positions in central and south Manchuria, to construct a bombproof command post, and to construct positions in the Antung and Port Arthur-Dairen areas for defense against a possible invasion by United States forces. However, with the transfer to Liaoyuan, Third Area Army took over these tasks, and Forty-fourth Army started to construct fortifications in its new operational sector only. Large scale maps of this sector were not available, however, and each unit was compelled to do its own surveying of positions.

The prepared positions in the vicinity of Wuchakou, 80 kilometers in circumference, were too scattered. Readjustment of these defenses was undertaken by the 107th Division to adapt them to the strength of the division. Progress was so difficult, due to the total lack of fortification materials--particularly explosives and rock drills--that at the time of the outbreak of war, they amounted to nothing more than field positions. The division's front was a vast and barren plain with almost no trees. Late in July the Army dispatched the main body of the 47th Field Road Construction Unit to obtain timber from the forest along the Paichengtzu-Arshaan Railroad, particularly in the vicinity of Pailang. In August the Army assumed direct command of the 1st Transport Company of the 117th Division, and sent this company also to Pailang to transport the timber. However, while this transport unit was in the vicinity of Hsingan, en route, Soviet Russia entered the war, and it returned to its original command. The Field Road Construction Unit also returned to its original station.

Great difficulty was encountered and much time was wasted in the establishment of the Army's lines of supply, mainly due to inadequate transport facilities. At the time of the transfer of the 19th Field Supply Depot to the Army, much time and effort were spent in negotiations with the Fourth Army and the Kwantung Army in regard to the personnel, supplies, and equipment in former positions. Although the deployment of the various sub-depots for continuous supply

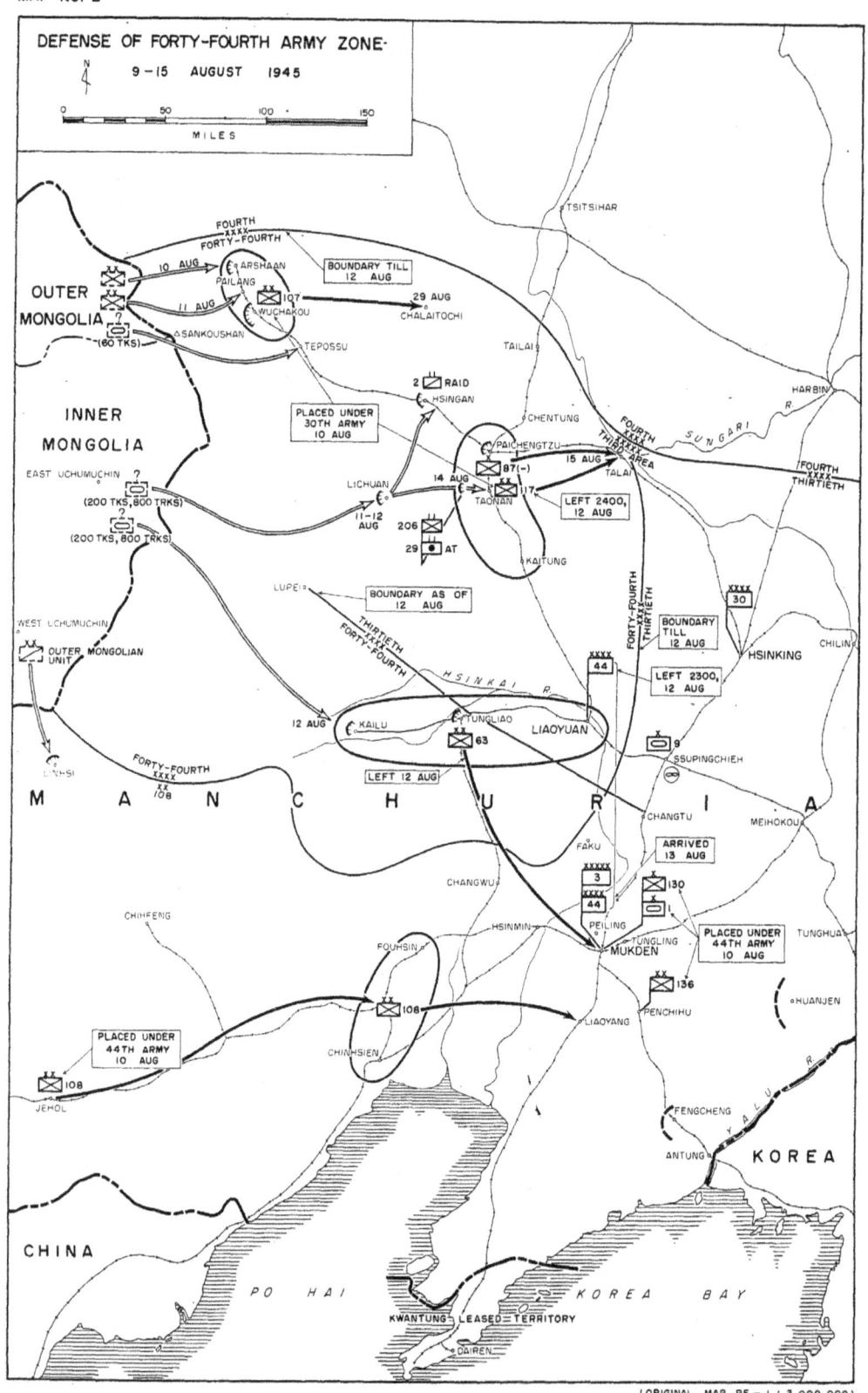

generally proceeded satisfactorily, the war began before the stockpiling of materials, in accordance with the operations plan, could be started.

As for accommodations for the recently acquired commands, the Army was confronted with providing shelters for winter as well as for summer, and for peace as well as for war. However, the capacity of existing accommodations was less than one-third of requirements, and the Army had to accommodate the majority of its personnel in small huts and tents. The Army was also preparing to build Manchurian type houses and had accumulated considerable quantities of materials for this purpose from civilian administrative agencies. The war broke out while it was making arrangements for the construction of these houses by the Labor Service Corps.

Transportation

The railroads in the operational zone were the north-south Ssupingchieh-Tsitsihar line, the east-west Arshaan-Talai line, and in the south the Liaoyuan-Tungliao stem. (See Map No 2.)

Management of the railroads was under the general control of the Continental Railway Force, which was directly under Kwantung Army. Railroads in the Army's northern sector were under the direct jurisdiction of the manager of the Tsitsihar Branch, and those in the southern sector under the jurisdiction of the manager of the Chinhsien (Chinchou) Branch. Since both these managerial areas were outside the Army's operational and defense district, the Army was at a dis-

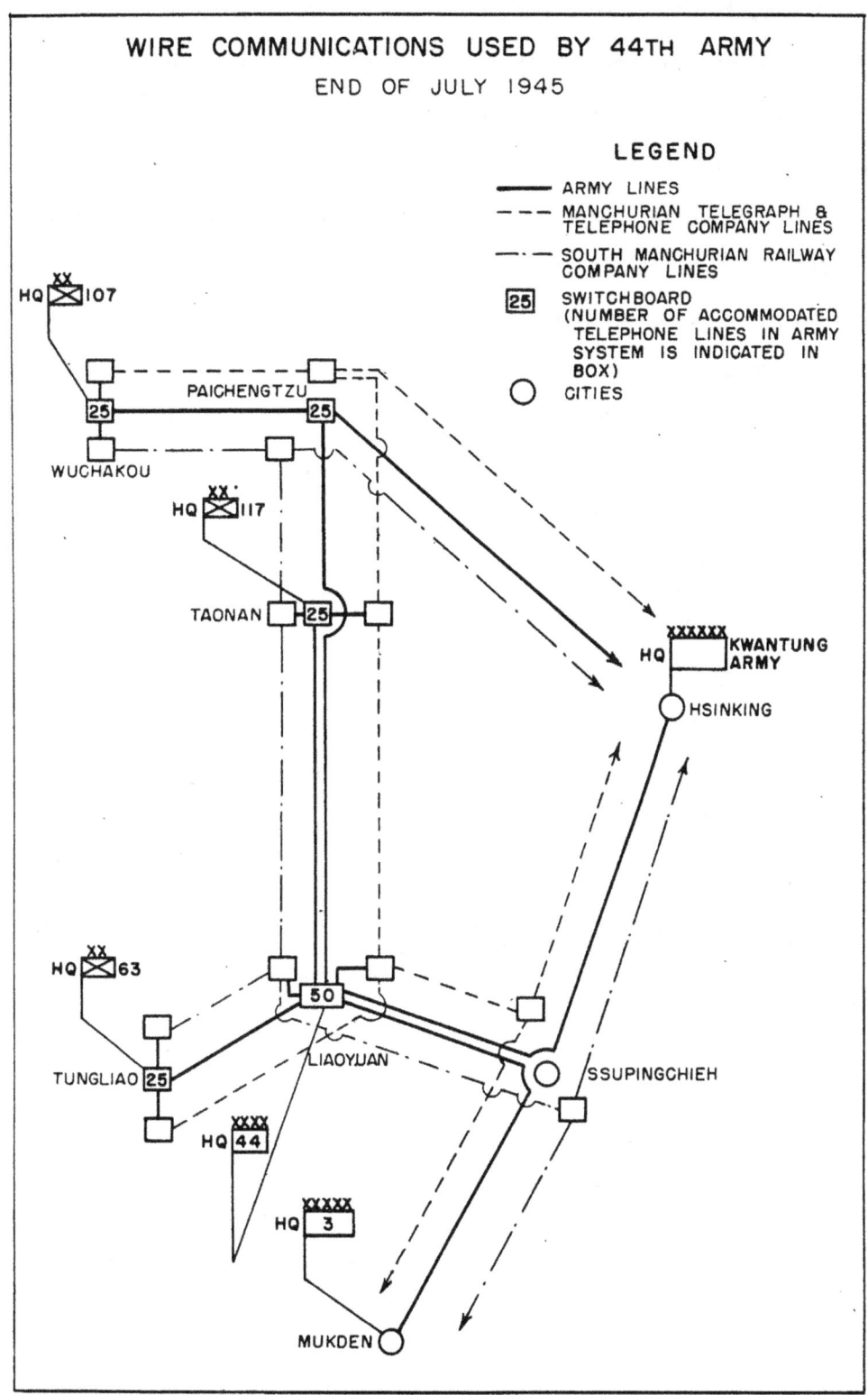

advantage, and requested Kwantung Army to provide a managerial branch within the Army's area. This was not approved, and the existing system proved to be a serious obstacle to the movement of units after the outbreak of war.

Unimproved roads were generally of little value as operational roads, although the Tungliao-Kailu road (86 kilometers), after improvements were undertaken in March, was used by the Army, government and the public. The Army sent representatives to higher headquarters requesting improvement of principal roads in order to have some suitable supply routes. This resulted in getting the Ministry of Communications of Manchuria to draw up plans for improving, first, the Ssupingchieh-Liaoyuan-Tungliao road, and then the Liaoyuan-Paichengtzu road. However, this plan was finally abandoned.

Communications (See Sketch No 1.)

Prior to the establishment of the Forty-fourth Army, the only communications unit in the border areas was an element of the Kwantung Army Signal Unit, stationed near the 107th Division. After the Army was organized in Liaoyuan, and given the defense mission, its signal equipment and personnel were increased. In the middle of June, the 31st Signal Regiment was assigned to the Army, giving it a signal force of full strength. However, this regiment did not install any new long-lines of communication.

Between major headquarters--Kwantung Army, Third Area Army, Forty-fourth Army, and subordinate commands--direct military lines were used, except that between Army Headquarters and 107th Division Headquarters communication went through the Army's switchbord at Paichengtzu. For auxiliary communications, the telephone exchanges of the South Manchurian Railway Company and the Manchurian Telegraph and Telephone Company were used.

Both military and commercial lines, however, had deteriorated, and were subject to frequent breakdowns. The Army notified Kwantung Army of this situation. At the same time the Army drew up a plan for improving the military lines, and requested the Manchurian Telegraph and Telephone Company to make improvements, first, on the Ssupingchieh-Liaoyuan-Tungliao-Kailu line, and then the Liaoyuan-Taonan-Paichengtzu line. Reconditioning of the first of these was completed as far as Tungliao by the time war broke out. The Army also requested that the Manchurian Telegraph and Telephone Company reorganize its own commercial lines in order to adapt them to defensive operations in the Army's zone. This was done to some extent. Furthermore, the Army requisitioned additional wireless telegraph equipment which it considered absolutely necessary for guerrilla warfare in its vast operational zone, but due to the shortage of such equipment the request was not approved.

Training

In the middle of June the Army prepared training instructions and announced them at the meeting of the chiefs of staff of subordinate commands. The instructions emphasized guerrilla warfare training, and antitank close-quarter fighting. It was not considered practicable to conduct a regular training program over an extended period. Therefore, training was accelerated so as to be accomplished in the minimum time to achieve the stated objectives.

Because of the excellence of guerrilla warfare training in the 107th Division, one of its infantry battalions had been selected to supervise this phase of training at the Liaoyang Training Unit, a center operated by the Kwantung Army for the benefit of all divisions. Some personnel of the 63d and 117th Division were sent there to take the guerrilla warfare training. These divisions had already gained some experience in guerrilla tactics during operations in North China, and so both officers and men developed great confidence in it. They had not, however, been thoroughly trained in antitank combat. Despite difficulties caused by the shortage of materials for training, each group carried out programs. Even at the time of the inspection by the Army Commander and the Area Army Commander, training in close-quarter attacks on tanks was being pushed. The training given to the units organized in early July, additionally emphasized the strengthening their unity; because of the shortage of weapons and materials and the lowering of the caliber of officers and noncommissioned officers of these new units, however, the training did not produce noticeable results.

For practical training in guerrilla warfare, maneuvers were carried out in Chilin during mid-July by the mobile brigade, pursuant to orders of the Kwantung Army. The maneuvers were observed by the Army Commander and the chiefs of staff of all units.

Intelligence

Early in July, the Army was notified by the Third Area Army of a plan for collecting intelligence. After forming its own intelligence collection plan in accordance with the operations plan, the Army announced it at the 4 August meeting of the chiefs of staff. The principal object of this plan was, first, to determine the time of commencement of hostilities by the Soviet Union and, second, to collect information necessary for exploiting guerrilla warfare. For this purpose, the 107th Division was charged mainly with collecting information regarding Outer Mongolia by its border lookout sentries. Other commands were charged mainly with the collection of information for guerrilla warfare in their respective sectors.

The collection of intelligence on the Soviet Army then was conducted almost exclusively by the Kwantung Army itself, and the Area Army and lower levels of command relied solely upon the border lookout sentries. This limited the intelligence operations in which the Army could engage. The Army, however, was in critical need of information on the situation in Outer Mongolia, especially as regards the enemy's troop concentration, the change of railway gauge, the extension of the Tamsag Railroad, and extent of motor transport facilities in Outer Mongolia. But as the collection of this type of intelligence by the Army itself was stricly prohibited to avoid provoking Soviet Russia, the Army directed the Hsingan Special Service Agency, assigned to the Army in the middle of June, to obtain the desired intelligence. A telephone interception section dispatched from the Harbin Special Service Agency was stationed on the border of the Arshaan sector. Thereafter, Army Headquarters received intelligence reports directly from the section. The Hsingan Special Service Agency had its own secret battle plan called "Midori Kosaku" (Green underground activity) and operated from bases within the military district of the Army.

In July, with the situation becoming tense, a revision in the intelligence plan was proposed whereby information collected by the border lookout sentries would be sent directly to the Kwantung Army from the border observation parties.

Investigation of Military Topography and Geography

After the Army was transferred to Liaoyuan, it became aware of the fact that information concerning the military topography and geography in its operational zone was altogether incomplete, and felt the necessity for speedily completing new studies. Late in June the Army held a meeting at its headquarters of officers from various units, from the special service agency, and from the Manchurian Army. The Army assigned the districts to be investigated, and directed that the investigation be made principally from the standpoint of guerrilla warfare operations. This meant that emphasis would be placed on the condition of principal traffic networks, rugged terrain, and inhabited areas, including the sentiment of inhabitants.

The results of the first investigation were submitted in the middle of July. The Army planned to dispatch a second investigation party, but was prevented from doing so by the outbreak of war. Meanwhile, as the situation grew worse late in July, the Army planned to demolish the principal roads which might facilitate a Soviet invasion of Manchuria from Outer Mongolia and Inner Mongolia across the Hsinganling Mountains. It could not fix the date for the demolishment, however, because of the extremely serious effect it would have on Manchurian public sentiment and because secrecy was impossible. It, therefore, decided to postpone it until such time as Soviet Russia's intention to start the war became apparent. The Army finally ignored the opportunity to execute the plan.

Organization of New Units

Under the total mobilization of July 1945 draftees were recruited to the fullest extent from the members of the Manchurian Government staff, the police force, and the employees of commercial companies. The mobilization was conducted in accordance with a Kwantung Army directive to draft all except those who were unquestionably unfit for military service due to poor health. Under these circumstances, the poor quality of the draftees can readily be guessed. The units whose mobilization was administered by the Army were as follows:

Unit	Date Organized	Place
9th Independent Tank Brigade	1 July 45	Ssupingchieh
6th Independent Heavy Artillery Battery (300-mm howitzer)	10 July 45	Kaiyuan
30th Heavy Field Artillery Regiment (100-mm gun)	10 July 45	Kaiyuan
Raiding Battalion of 107th Division	10 July 45	Wuchakou

To form the new units, about one-tenth of the men and somewhat less than 30 percent of the officers and noncommissioned officers were transferred from existing units, and the resultant vacancies were filled by draftees. However, due principally to the drop in the quality and quantity of officers and noncommissioned officers, the fighting effectiveness of the existing units declined to about two-thirds of what it had been.

The supply of weapons and clothing for the newly mobilized units was extremely inadequate. The tank brigade was short of tank machine-guns. The heavy field artillery regiment and the heavy battery had no guns up to the time the war started. According to the instructions from Kwantung Army, the distribution of equipment to the newly organized units was scheduled for the end of December.

During this period much equipment in Manchuria was being withdrawn for use in the homeland. About half of the antitank guns of the 107th Division were withdrawn in the middle of June. The equipment authorized the Division Artillery Regiment was reduced, and as a result large quantities of its ammunition and motor fuel were diverted to the homeland. The 31st Signal Regiment though fully armed and fully equipped, lost some communications equipment to the Kwantung Army, particularly wireless telegraph sets, because of the latter's shortage.

The greatest concern of the Army from the point of view of imminent operations was ammunition, especially antitank explosives. At first the Army had none. Just prior to the outbreak of war it obtained about two tons. This fulfilled immediate requirements.

At about this time the Thirtieth Army was being organized, and the 82d Construction Duty Company and the 41st Sea Duty Company were transferred to its command. (These units had been stationed in Hsinking under the command of the Kwantung Army.)

Estimate of Soviet Strength

Until the outbreak of war, no large concentration of Soviet forces was reported in Outer Mongolia. Ever since mid-June, however, when intelligence reports relative to Outer Mongolia forces began to be made available to the Army, there had been signs indicating the possibility of such concentrations. (The Soviet Zabaikal Area Army that invaded our area at the outbreak of hostilities had been stationed in the sector west of Manchouli-Karymskaya, and must have advanced to our Army front immediately before the oubreak of war.)

Even prior to this, however, some evidence of Soviet activities had been laid bare. In the middle of May, for example, in front of positions at Arshaan, three members of a five-man border patrol of the 107th Division were killed and two captured by armed spies. These spies were later seized by one of our border police units. After late May, and especially following the deployment of the Army in June, the entry of armed spies into Manchuria from Outer Mongolia was frequently reported. Spies were usually clad in Japanese Army uniforms and carried radio sets. Some of them were known to have penetrated as much as 100 kilometers into Manchuria.

In general, however, enemy activities on the western front of Manchuria were not as conspicuous as those on the eastern front. Against the eastern front the Soviet were expected to hurl approximately eight infantry divisions, two tank divisions, and 1,000 planes. No such concentration was detected on the western front. In fact, in the immediate vicinity of the Forty-fourth Army border, there were absolutely no indications of a large concentration of troops even immediately prior to Soviet Russia's entry into the War.

After the middle of July, an increasing number of reports of enemy activities along the western front--a vast desert area--were received, particularly as regards the movement of motor vehicles. Also reported were frequent border crossings by motor vehicles from Outer Mongolia into Inner Mongolia. Although Inner Mongolia was under Japanese influence, its barrenness rendered it a no-man's land, and such crossings into Inner Mongolia had not been previously observed.

It was estimated from these various reports that Soviet Russia must have had some kind of reconnaissance plan, and it was evident that it had made considerable preparations for operations. This belief was later supported by the fact that early in the morning of 8 August the enemy at the border of the 107th Division at Arshaan, issued an order stating in plain text: "Launch the offensive when attack preparations have been completed." Furthermore, during operations the enemy seemed prepared for the crossing of the Tungliao area, which had been flooded by our forces, since the crossing was spearheaded by amphibious tanks, as was also the crossing of Liao River in the vicinity of Hsinmin.

Opening of Hostilities   (See Map No 2.)

Army Headquarters learned of the Soviet invasion from a Third Area Army Headquarters message, received at 0200 hours on 9 August, stating that the Soviets had penetrated the Heiho, Tungning, Hutou and Manchouli fronts, and had bombed Mutanchiang, Manchouli, Hailar, Hsinking, and other places. This information was immediately relayed to all assigned units, and a state of emergency was declared. Then, at 0300 hours, when the alert was flashed throughout Manchuria, the army put into effect a prearranged wartime defense plan, placed the Manchurian army, civilian police, and military police under its command for defense matters, and fully entered a war status.

At 0500 hours, the chief of staff of the 107th Division reported by telephone: "The enemy strength in the Arshaan front is approximately one sniper division with tanks, and is gradually increasing. Scores of enemy tanks are crossing the border in the sector south of

Sankuoshan and are making a detour around the rear of the division. The enemy radio, located in front of our positions, transmitted an order to attack and advance as soon as preparations are completed. The division considers this to be an earnest attack by the Soviet Army and will smash the enemy in front of its position."

Other information received on 9 August concerning the enemy situation in front of the Army was as follows:

> Approximately 1,000 tanks and vehicles are advancing east on the East Uchumuchin-Lichuan road.
>
> A mechanized unit (approximately 1,000 tanks and vehicles) covered by three fighter planes is advancing southeastwardly on the East Uchumuchin-Kailu road.
>
> About one division of the Outer Mongolian cavalry is advancing south on the West Uchumuchin-Linhsi road.

Information obtained by the Army on enemy movements elsewhere on the western front indicated that the strength of the enemy advancing south on the Chilalin-Hailar road appeared to be one mechanized division, and that of the enemy advancing eastward on the Manchouli-Hailar road, approximately two divisions.

The Army requested the Area Army to continue air reconnaissance of the enemy situation in front of the Army, and, at the same time, based on the above reports, attached the 29th Independent Antitank Battalion in Taonan to the 117th Division, directing the division to make preparations for destroying the enemy tank units in the Lichuan area as well as to collect information. At the same time, the Army ordered the 63d Division to demolish bridges and flood the Kailu area at opportune moments according to prearranged plans.

Two reconnaissance planes were attached to the Army from the Third Area Army for liaison purposes and were assigned to Ssupingchieh airfield. The Army endeavored to maintain contact with the 107th Division by telegraph, but failing to receive a response due to the division's defective sending set, the Army had no alternative but to continue sending messages. (We were later informed that the 107th Division's telegraph receiver was functioning normally and could receive the Army's transmissions but that its transmitter was out of order.)

There was no great change on 10 August in the enemy situation on the western front. The enemy forces in front of the 107th Division appeared to be about two divisions, but they did not press the attack. On other fronts, the enemy in eastern Manchuria made a rapid advance and was nearing the Muleng sector. The Hailar front was under attack by the enemy. The Aihun and Hutou fronts reported that Japanese forces were resisting the enemy and carrying out vigorous raiding attacks at border positions.

At about 0900 hours on 10 August the Army received the following order from the Third Area Army:

> The 107th Division, 117th Division, and 9th Independent Tank Brigade will move to Hsinking and be commanded by the Thirtieth Army Commander; the Army Headquarters, the forces directly attached to your command, and the 63d Division will move to the vicinity of Mukden. The 108th Division, 136th Division, 130th Independent Mixed Brigade, and 1st Tank Brigade will be placed under your command.

At 1000 hours, the Army issued separate orders. It then began making arrangements with the Tsitsihar and Chinhsien branches of the Continental Railway Force concerning the railway transportation of units mentioned in the order. The gist of the Forty-fourth Army order was as follows:

> The 107th Division will check the enemy advance at its present position, then destroy the Paichengtzu-Arshaan Line, Hsinganling Tunnel, and other technical objects to obstruct his advance, and will then redeploy to the vicinity of Hsinking as soon as possible where it will be placed under the command of the Thirtieth Army commander.
>
> The 117th Division will dispatch an element to the vicinity of Paichengtzu to cover the withdrawal of the various units in the Paichengtzu-Arshaan Line area. The division's main body will quickly move to the vicinity of Hsinking, where it will be placed under the command of the Thirtieth Army commander.
>
> The 63d Division will move rapidly to the vicinity of Mukden. One engineer company will be attached to the Army at Liaoyuan.

At 1100 hours, the senior staff officer of the Army transmitted this order directly to the chief of staff of the 107th Division by both telephone and telegram and transmitted the order to each of the other groups by telephone. Telephone communication to the 107th Division was interrupted immediately after the order was given. As a precaution the Army contemplated sending a written order by messenger but abandoned this idea because of three unfavorable developments: the severance of the Paichengtzu-Arshaan Line in the vicinity of Pailang by enemy tanks, the burning of Hsingan by enemy bombing, and the rebellion of the Mongolian Army. The Army had previously requested the Kwantung Army, in view of communication difficulties, to communicate directly with the 107th Division in an emergency, and now requested Kwantung Army to effect direct liaison with the division since its own communication with the division had been disrupted.

The 117th Division reported on the afternoon of 10 August that approximately 1,000 enemy tanks were advancing toward Lichuan and that the division had dispatched one infantry battalion and the Independent Antitank Battalion to the vicinity, about 30 kilometers west of Taonan, to check the enemy advance. At the same time, the report added, the division was attempting to concentrate its strength in the vicinity of Taonan.

Also on 10 August the Area Army commander summoned the Army commander to Mukden. In his place, however, the Army commander sent his chief of staff, who left the Army Headquarters in the afternoon, stayed overnight at Ssupingchieh, and then flew to Mukden.

Reports were received on 11 August that enemy tanks had attacked Lichuan [Tuchuan?], some 95 kilometers west of Taonan, and that the prefectural government office and other buildings had been set afire. Later, a patrol reported that this tank force had stopped at Lichuan and that it showed no indications of making further advances. The Army was not able to determine whether the enemy tank unit would advance northward to the vicinity of Hsingan and cut the 107th Division's retreat or attempt an attack on Taonan after replenishment and servicing.

In either event, the Army feared that the tank force would seriously hinder the planned withdrawal, and requested the Third Area Army Headquarters to deliver an air strike.

The Area Army's answer was to direct the Forty-fourth Army to use the 117th Division to attack the enemy mechanized unit and later withdraw. Since an orderly retreat of the division would be impossible if it launched an attack, Forty-fourth Army instead directed the 117th Division to put out a rear guard while effecting the withdrawal of the main body promptly. It also instructed the 117th Division to destroy military installations, including the airfield and fuel dumps, in the vicinity of Taonan during its withdrawal.

The enemy situation in front of the 107th Division near the border was totally obscure. In front of the 63d Division positions at Tungliao to the south, the slow-moving enemy was still a considerable distance from the division, which had previously destroyed the bridges on the Hsinkai River and inundated the area.

During the day a minor problem arose regarding the withdrawal of Military Police Unit at Hsingan. The chief of that unit phoned Army headquarters stating: "The Paichengtzu-Arshaan Railway has been cut in the vicinity of Pailang and enemy units are steadily closing in on Hsingan. Therefore, it is desirable that a withdrawal order be issued to us immediately." The Army, which had control of MP units only in matters of peace and order, replied that the withdrawal of the MP Unit at this time would be premature in view of the revolt of the Hsingan Mongolian Officers School, and the bombings which were disturbing the public peace, adding that in any event withdrawal orders for the MP Unit should properly come from the MP commandant in Hsinking rather than from the Army.

A call to Hsinking MP General Headquarters evoked the response that all MP units had been assigned to the Army. The Army, however, had never received such orders. In the end, the matter of withdrawal was left entirely to the discretion of the local military police unit commander.

On 12 August, while the enemy mechanized unit was still in Lichuan, the Army was continuing to make urgent requests to the Tsitsihar Branch of the Continental Railway Force to allot trains to transport the units ordered to Hsinking and Mukden. Although no trains were made available for the 117th Division, late in the day trains were sent from the Chinhsien Branch to transport only the 63d Division to Mukden.

The Army ordered the 63d Division to leave three patrol squads behind (each led by an officer and composed of about ten persons, with horses and radio sets) for the purpose of tracking the enemy advancing along the Kailu-Changwu-Hsinmin-Mukden roads. It also ordered the division's engineer company, previously placed under its direct control, to make preparations to demolish bridges, railway stations, and military installations near Liaoyuan.

The 63d Division's main body left Tungliao by rail on the afternoon of 12 August. Eighty miles to the west, meanwhile, an enemy tank unit was entering Kailu, but the garrison unit there had already withdrawn.

The Army chief of staff, who had gone to Mukden on the 10th to prepare for the withdrawal to and the defense of that city, returned to Liaoyuan on the 12th and reported to the Army commander. The latter promptly emplaned for Mukden accompanied by his senior staff officer. Forty-fourth Army Headquarters started entraining at 2300. Meanwhile, there were no prospects whatever of obtaining train transportation for the 117th Division, so its main body started the move to Hsinking on foot.

The curt answer given by the Area Army on the preceding day to the request for an air strike on Lichuan was partly explained at about 2000 hours, when a liaison officer from the Hsinking Air Brigade arrived at Liaoyuan airfield. He stated that although his brigade had flown sorties to Lichuan during the morning, the planes had been unable to locate targets. He added that another bombing mission with about twenty-five planes was scheduled for dawn on the 13th. His request for information about targets was answered in considerably detail.

At about 2100 hours, the chief of the Hsingan Special Service Agency arrived in Liaoyuan and reported that the 2d Raiding Unit, which operated under its control, was in action near Hsingan, adding that the Special Service Agency[21] was itself preparing to carry out guerrilla warfare.

Forty-fourth Army Headquarters arrived at Mukden on the afternoon of 13 August and immediately established a temporary headquarters in the Clothing Hall in the northwestern sector of Mukden. The senior staff officer of the Army, who had arrived earlier with the Army commander, during the morning had reported to the Third Area Army Headquarters for operational instructions. Construction of defense positions in the vicinity of Mukden were begun by the 63d and 136th Division, the 130th Independent Mixed Brigade and the 1st Tank Brigade. Meanwhile, the 108th Division was placed under the command of the Army for use in the vicinity of Liaoyang.

In the afternoon the Army learned that the Area Army was planning to move to the Fengcheng and Huanjen areas, and that it had already dispatched its signal staff officer to the Huanjen area to make a preparatory survey. The Area Army placed nearly all the units in the Mukden area under Forty-fourth Army, but the number of these units was so great (more than seventy) that the control was extremedly difficult. In fact, the Army Headquarters did not know of the location of some of these units.

---

21. A Special Service Agency carried out espionage and counter-intelligence activities, and employed polygot personnel: Manchurians, Mongolians, Koreans, and White Russians, besides Japanese officers and noncommissioned officers. There were eleven such agencies in Manchuria. Besides the one at Hsingan, these were located at Hailar, Sanho, Heiho, Chiamussu, Tungan, Mutanchiang, Yenchi, Mukden, Dairen, and Apaka (Inner Mongolia).

At about 1200 hours on 14 August, while in the midst of preparing for operations pursuant to Area Army instructions, the Army was given a general cease-fire order. The senior staff officer of the Third Area Army who brought this order also transmitted verbal orders to suspend operational action by 2200 hours of the same day.

The Army immediately sent its senior staff officer to the Area Army Headquarters to obtain further details and to transmit the cease-fire order to all subordinate units, using the communications network of the Area Army Headquarters. He returned at about 1800 hours, bringing new orders from the Area Army rescinding the previous cease-fire order and calling for continued operations. At the same time, the Army was informed that an important message would be broadcast at noon on 15 August.

An inquiry was made of the Area Army's reasons for its imprudent action on such serious matters as the ordering of a cease-fire and its rescission. The answer was that the Kwantung Army would continue its operations because the previous cease-fire order had been received from an Imperial General Headquarters staff officer dispatched to Tunghua and was not an official command. The Army's staff, that night, kept awake and remained generally unconvinced.

Disposition at Termination of War

Nearly all Forty-fourth Army units, except those enroute to new stations, were in the vicinity of Mukden when the war ended. The main body of the 63d Division was holding its positions near

Tungling east of Mukden. The main body of the 136th Division was in the western sector of Mukden, and that of the 130th Independent Mixed Brigade near Peiling north of Mukden. The 108th Division was near Liaoyang. The 1st Independent Tank Brigade was near Tungling, and the Raiding Unit was at Hsinmin. The main body of the antiaircraft artillery unit was in the city of Mukden preparing for antitank action. The main body of the 31st Signal Regiment was at Peiling north of Mukden.

The 14th Independent Field Artillery Battalion and the 17th Heavy Field Artillery Regiment were at Changtu. The 30th Heavy Field Artillery Regiment and the 6th Independent Heavy Artillery Battery were at Kaiyuan. The 112th Independent Motor Transport Battalion was at Tiehling. The 73d Independent Transport Company, the 47th Field Road Construction Unit, the 40th Construction Duty Company, the 127th Specially Established Field Duty Company, and the Paichengtzu Military Hospital and Hailar 2d Military Hospital were at Mukden.

Casualties

Considerable damage presumably had been inflicted on the enemy at the Arshaan front but details were unknown. More than ten enemy tanks of the enemy mechanized unit at Lichuan were presumed to have been destroyed during the bombing carried out on the 13th.

Casualties suffered by units of Forty-fourth Army were difficult to determine. The heaviest losses were sustained by the 107th Division. According to an investigation conducted at the time it halted operations at Chalaitochi, the division determined that more than 1,000 of its officers and men had been killed. The 63d Division sustained only a small number of casualties, perhaps ten, and the forest cutting unit near Pailang was presumed to have suffered some losses but this was not confirmed.

Situation at the Termination of War

Most of the units assigned to or under the command of the Army, were newly organized units. Some were still in the process of being organized and, of course, were not yet equipped. Therefore, the units were at less than half of their fighting capacities.

Confirming the termination of war through the broadcast at noon on the 15 August, the Army tried to communicate the cease-fire order to patrols remaining in the vicinities of Tungliao, Hsinmin, and Liaoyuan, the Hsingan Special Service Agency, and the 2d Raiding Unit. It reached all but the Hsingan Special Service Agency and the 2d Raiding Unit. Reports from patrols revealed that some elements of the Soviet Army had reached Liaoyuan and some were in Tungliao.

Although the cease fire had been broadcast, continued construction of antitank ditches in Mukden City was ordered. Kwantung Army was determined to carry on its operations since no order had been received from the Imperial Headquarters. This created an embarrassing situation but, in the spirit of the broadcast, the Army did not change its policy of halting combat operations.

The Army Headquarters moved to the Asahi Girls School in Mukden city on 16 August according to prearranged plans. The commander and the chief of staff conferred with General Ushiroku, the Area Army Commander, General Wang, commander of the 1st Army District of Manchuria, as well as with the vice-governor of Mukden Province (Mr Matsuzo Genda), on the maintenance of public order and other matters. The Forty-fourth Army Headquarters was designated defense headquarters for Mukden Province, and all combat units and zone of communication units in the province were placed under its command.

Meanwhile the 108th Division, which at the time was moving to the Liaoyang area, reported that public order at Chinhsien was bad, and that there was a great danger that a Manchukuoan Army force, about 10,000 strong, which was assembled in the vicinity after having fought in various parts of North China,[22] might revolt. Since there was only one infantry company in Chinhsien, the Army rushed one battalion of the 63d Division to protect the residents there and also requested the commander of the 1st Army District to suppress the Manchurian Army force. On 17 August, the danger of a revolt appeared to subside somewhat.

The Area Army on the 17th ordered the demobilization of personnel who had been conscripted from the South Manchuria Railway Company, the Manchurian Telegraph and Telephone Company, the Manchuria Electric Industry Company and other commercial agencies. It also ordered the demobilization of servicemen with families in Manchuria and the release of civilian employees. The Army complied with these orders

---

22. See pp 123-4, Monograph 138.

on the same day, releasing all personnel in the above categories from assigned units. However, it proclaimed that military law was still in force, and that any person who violated military discipline would be punished.

Public order in Chihsien improved slightly on 18 August. In Mukden city, however, looting and rioting were rampant and the Army had to call out troops and tanks.

Various intelligence reports indicated that the Soviet mechanized unit advancing toward Mukden from the direction of Tungliao could reach Mukden on the evening of 19 August. Army Headquarters therefore began burning its documents. With a view to preventing confusion likely from the Soviet Army's occupation of the city, the Army sought to have the Soviet force halt its troops on the western outskirts of Mukden, and at the same time began preparing billets for the Russians in the Tiehhsi sector of Mukden. Three patrol squads dispatched by the 63d Division to contact the Soviets returned with five men lost. Survivors revealed the position of the Soviet force, and also reported that the Hsingan Special Service Agency, after learning of the cease fire, had assembled in the vicinity of Faku.

On 17 August Imperial General Headquarters modified its attitude towards "prisoners of war." It announced that Japanese servicemen whose surrender to the enemy was the result of the cease-fire order would not be regarded in the same light as those who surrendered or were captured during operations. This step was necessary because existing orders relating to surrender did not contemplate the ultimate defeat of Japan and therefore contained no provision defining the status of servicemen after Japan's defeat. In the absence of such a provision, the exising law would prevail, and all Japanese servicemen would naturally consider themselves as being within the purview of the existing law.

Existing law--that is, Army and Navy regulations--strictly prohibited the surrender of servicemen. Morally, the offense was considered shameful and dishonorable; the military code required fighting "to the end" rather than surrender. Legally, the offense was liable to court martial, with the penalty of death most likely.

Taking cognizance, however, of the fact that the Government's cease-fire order, not the individual will of the serviceman, delivered Japanese forces into the enemy's hands, Imperial General Headquarters published War Ministry Secret Order No. 14415, announcing that the Japanese Government, and the nation as a whole, would not regard servicemen delivered to the enemy as a result of the cease-fire order as having surrendered under the meaning of the old law, and hence would absolve them from the stigma attached to surrendering and remove them from liability to reprisals.

This action had a tremendous psychological effect on all Japanese men in uniform, rescuing all from dishonor and many from the obligation to commit suicide. On 19 August Kwantung Army General Headquarters transmitted this government decision to its subordinate commands.

At the same time that Forty-fourth Army received this announcement, it received details of the cease-fire agreement concluded between the Kwantung Army and the Soviet Army.

Also on the 19th cease-fire negotiations with the Soviet Army were held by Forty-fourth Army as well as by Third Area Army. At about 1100 hours, Major General Blittora, military envoy of the Soviet Army, arrived at the north airfield of Mukden, accompanied by a woman captain acting as interpreter and two lieutenant colonels. They were met at the airfield by Major Shii of the Third Area Army who, after a brief interlude (see below), escorted them to the Area Army Headquarters. Ceasefire negotiations were then begun with the commander of the Third Area Army and the commander of the Forty-fourth Army. In the course of the day's negotiations, General Blittora demanded 1) disarmament, 2) a ban on troop movements, 3) suspension of railway operations, and 4) control of communications by the Soviet Army. At the request of the Japanese Army, the Soviets agreed to permit units in the vicinity of Mukden to retain one-third of their arms for self-defense and to maintain peace and order. The rest of the arms were to be turned over to the Soviets at each unit's area. (When the Soviet party arrived at the airfield, the Emperor of Manchukuo and his retinue were resting on the second floor of the Manchuria Air Company building, awaiting a flight to Japan. Their presence was discovered when Lieutenant General Yasunao Yoshioka, the Manchukuo Imperial Palace Commissioner, went downstairs to the lavatory. The Emperor and his staff were immediately sent to Soviet territory by air.)

Meanwhile the mechanized unit of the Soviet Army reached the western suburbs of Mukden at about 1800 hours. Its officers and men were quartered in billets which had been prepared for them.

At about 0900 hours on 20 August, negotiations at Third Area Army Headquarters were resumed. The Soviets demanded that all units of the Japanese Army in the Mukden vicinity be completely disarmed and then be withdrawn from the city and assembled within three hours about sixteen kilometers north of Mukden. Excepted were the headquarters of both the Area Army and Army, and the 1st Special Garrison Unit in charge of maintaining peace and order. The Army commander insisted that the time limit set by the Soviets was unreasonable. He asked that the garrison unit be specifically permitted to retain all its arms in order to maintain public order and that other units be allowed to leave sufficient personnel behind to guard the collected weapons. The Soviets agreed to this and also the the withdrawal of the units within six, instead of three, hours.

The Soviet forces assumed control of railroads and communications facilities and requisitioned additional buildings for their quarters. Moreover, it frequently happened that Japanese army vehicles operating in the city, whether passenger cars or trucks, were halted and requisitioned on the spot by Soviet soldiers. Horses were also seized and generally were sold to Manchurians. The weapons turned over to the Soviets were removed on trucks; Soviet soldiers gave some of the rifles and ammunitions to Manchurians.

Consequently, upon withdrawal of the Japanese troops, public peace was suddenly disrupted and the situation became uncontrollable, with mob looting and outrages occurring in various places.

Prior to this, the Soviet force had demanded that Japanese officers of general rank in Mukden assemble at Third Area Army Headquarters. At about 1100 hours, after the Third Area Army commander introduced every general to the Soviet representative, the latter requested all the generals to go to the Mukden north airfield to meet the Soviet Far East Forces Commander who, he said, was due to arrive there. Thereupon, the generals immediately left the Area Army Headquarters in several automobiles. When evening came they failed to return.

While great concern was being shown over their safety, the Area Army commander's chauffeur came rushing back to report that the generals had been taken somewhere by Soviet planes. However, Major General Seiichi Takeda, the Chief of the Ordnance Section of the Third Area Army, and Major General Hirano, the Commander of the 2d Engineer Unit, had not gone to the airport, the former due to sickness and the latter to ignorance of the assembly. Therefore, General Hirano, assumed the post of acting commander of the Third Area Army. Meanwhile, Colonel Takebayashi, the Chief of the Ordnance Section of the Army, became the acting commander of the Forty-fourth Army. Toward evening the Soviet force demanded that the Area Army Headquarters vacate its building so it could be used to quarter Soviet troops. The headquarters then moved to Oyama Hall.

On 21 August, public disorder in Mukden and its environs worsened. Plundering by Manchurians was rife. When one company of the 1st Special Garrison Unit performing guard duty in front of Mukden Station attempted to suppress the plundering, it was surrounded by a Soviet tank unit which apparently was unaware of the Soviet commander's agreement. The Area Army Headquarters upon learning of the incident notified the Soviet commander, but before action could be taken the Japanese unit was disarmed.

In view of the breach of faith and the trickery of the Soviets in kidnapping the Japanese generals, Colonel Omori, senior staff officer of the 1st Special Garrison Unit, feared for the future of the Japanese force. He recommended to Army headquarters that all elements of the garrison unit be concentrated in Chiyoda Park for battle.

In view of the gravity of the situation, the Army held an emergency conference at Third Area Army Headquarters, and concluded that for the time being, while submitting to minor insults, it should pursue a policy of watchful waiting. Since the Army was disarmed and a battle would be futile, the concentration of troops was opposed.

On the evening of the same day, Third Area Army protested that the disarmament of the special garrison unit was a breach of agreement, but the Soviet commander demanded that the responsibility for guarding the city be relinquished to his troops. He added that one third of the garrison unit could retain weapons for self-defense, but directed that the remainder of the unit be disarmed and assembled near Wenkuantun. Moreover, on that day a Soviet infantry division entered Mukden.

All the warehouses of the zone of communication depots in and around Mukden were placed under the control of the Soviet forces, and their operating personnel relieved. However, the Soviets kept the South Manchuria Arsenal and the Air Depot at Wenkuantun in operation to repair their ordnance equipment.

Meanwhile, in response to repeated requests of Japanese residents to prevent looting and outrages by Soviet troops, the army negotiated with the Soviet command, but obtained no satisfaction. Furthermore, when it was reported that the troops of a Japanese tank company who had been put to work in the vicinity of Tungling, were being driven hard and whipped by Soviet soldiers, repeated negotiations were made with the Soviets through the Third Area Army Headquarters, but without avail.

On the afternoon of 22 August, two Soviet soldiers armed with revolvers entered and looted the Army Headquarters; they were shot to death by our guards. When the Army informed the Soviet command of the incident, Major General Blittora, Soviet Garrison Commander, immediately came to conduct an investigation, but realizing that the soldiers were at fault, he departed without taking action.

On 23 August Army Headquarters moved to the Mukden office of the former South Manchuria Arsenal; Soviet forces of about regimental strength occupied the vacated Oyama Hall. The Army laid telephone lines to the units assembled north of Mukden, but these lines were all severed. Only runners could be used for liaison purposes, and they risked their lives in delivering messages.

On 25 August, Third Area Army and Soviet Army representatives began a joint survey of prospective internment camps for Japanese forces in Mukden and its vicinity, and decided to establish a camp at Peiling.[23]

On the 29th the Soviets ordered all units stationed in Mukden to assemble at the Peiling Internment Camp. The Army, after releasing civilian employees, made preparations for the move. On the 30th the main body of the Army Headquarters and several female civilian employees who wished to stay with it entered the Peiling Camp, and on the 31st the remaining members of the Army Headquarters also entered.

The troops interned in the Peiling Internment Camp numbered about 25,000. In addition to personnel of units previously moved to the Mukden area, this number included stragglers, and soldiers and civilian employees (some of them juvenile workers) of various supply depots.

---

23. The Peiling area is noted as the burial place for prominent Manchurian families.

The camp site had several structures including those of the Manchurian Railroad School and the Kwantung Army Communication Training Unit.

The number of internees at the Peiling Internment Camp increased day by day. By about 5 September, the units stationed in and around Antung, Fushun, and Penchihu began arriving in marching columns. On the 10th about 6,000 residents in Mukden who had been conscripted during the July mass-mobilization and released after the end of hostilities, were interned in the camp.

The Soviets on 14 September began organizing labor battalions. On the same day three trains departed Mukden heading northward, and three each day thereafter. Each train carried about 1,500 men. Each battalion was equipped, in addition to individual equipment, with two trucks, five wagons, and six horses.

Civil Affairs

On 10 August, when the Army was ordered to redeploy to Mukden it also received instructions to evacuate all Japanese residents. The Army immediately convoked conferences at its headquarters, summoning the Liaison Councillor of Hsingan General Province in Liaoyuan and the West Hsingan local councillors who were then assembling in the city to discuss defense measures. Army authorities explained the general situation and requested them to assemble all Japanese residents and land development groups at specified points along the railroads by 12 August and to take steps for their evacuation. The Army stated that it would allocate a certain number of trains for use in evacuation work, adding that those who were late in assembling because they lived for inland or received orders late would be permitted to use troop trains. The Army requested the councilors to act rapidly and, at the same time, communicated evacuation instructions to each subordinate command.

Japanese residents along the Ssupingchieh-Taonan Line were evacuated to Tunghua on 12 August either by the evacuation train or troop train. However, those living in remote areas received their orders belatedly and were unable to utilize these trains; they were evacuated on foot. Some Japanese residents who had been in the vicinity of Hsingan encountered Soviet units while evacuating on foot, and a great many of them supposedly were ravaged. Japanese residents in the remote parts of West Hsingan Province withdrew on foot to Mukden and its vicinity.

The families of the army officers and civilian employees of the 107th Division lived in the vicinity of Arshaan and Wuchakou. With the commencement of hostilities, these frontline families were evacuated by the train together with Japanese residents. The families of members of Army Headquarters lived in Ssupingchieh or Liaoyuan. These families retreated to Tunghua with Japanese residents in Liaoyuan and vicinity; they moved to Fushun after cessation of hostilities.

Manchukuoan Government officials did not on the whole remain loyal to Japan. In several of the insurrections that occurred in various parts of Manchuria after the outbreak of hostilities, there were some officials who were revealed to have secret understandings with the Nationalist Government of China. These refused to take any action, and became completely engrossed in self-preservation. Consequently, these insurrections were not stemmed. However, other Japanese officials remained loyal, especially those councillors who were serving in the Mongolian region; these devoted themselves to such activities as transmitting intelligence, assisting guerrilla activities, and guiding Japanese residents.

Manchukuoan Army tactical units had been gradually reduced in number after the Pacific war worsened. Many units were reorganized into engineer and transport units, and their ordnance equipment transferred to the Japanese Army. With the outbreak of war in Manchuria many Japanese officers assigned to the Manchurian Army were killed. Manchukuoan troops deserted in alarming numbers. The Mongolian Officers School at Hsingan seemed to have been planning a revolt, and when Hsingan was bombed on 9 August, began a rebellion. The rebels took the Hsingan army commander prisoner and fled. With the cessation of hostilities on 15 August, all Japanese officers in the Manchukuoan Army were replaced by Manchurian officers. In South Manchuria, particularly in Chinhsien, the situation was very serious. Although there were no revolts, the antiaircraft artillery unit there deserted en masse. The majority of the Manchurian police deserted to protect themselves as soon as hostilities began. However, the Japanese police were quite active to the very end, especially in maintaining order and furnishing information about the Soviet Army.

Manchurians, Koreans, and White Russians

As a result of the Japanese commandeering of goods, drafting of personnel, and other factors following the adverse turn of events, the Manchurians completely lost confidence in their government. The trend of the popular feeling required close watching. There were many who communicated secretly with the Nationalist Government of China in an attempt to insure personal safety.

With announcement of the cease-fire order on 15 August, the Chinese Nationalist flag was hoisted on almost every house in Mukden. By 17 August public order had begun to deteriorate. Manchurian soldiers either deserted singly or rebelled in groups. Japanese property was looted and the Japanese themselves were subjected to personal attacks. Nevertheless, while the Japanese Army remained there, some degree of public order was maintained. But on 19 August, when the Soviet Army occupied Mukden and gave the weapons of the Japanese Army to the mob, Mukden was suddenly gripped with insurrection. In the vicinity of Peiling, mobs confronted Japanese forces and attacked with rifles, but were driven off with hand grenades. Such was the situation at the time.

The front of the Mukden Station and its neighborhood were in a chaotic state, and after 21 August all refugees and passengers were robbed and assaulted. The deserted Japanese Army barracks, official residences, and the houses evacuated by the Japanese residents were pillaged so thoroughly that not a single article was left. The Manchurian police who harbored malice toward their Japanese superiors arrested and subjected them to torture when the Soviet Army entered the city. When the Japanese Army withdrew to the north of Mukden all communication wires for liaison purposes were severed by the Manchurians. Bandits began to appear in the area between Mukden and Fushun. Of course, there were some friendly Manchurians who protected the Japanese people and accorded them conveniences, but these were few in number.

At the time of the cease fire, the Koreans were afraid of retaliation by the Manchurians, but they hoisted the Korean national flags. When the Soviet Army entered Mukden, the Koreans led the Russian troops in looting the Japanese. Many Koreans became spies of the Soviet Army and informed against the Japanese.

White Russians in Manchuria, as the war situation became unfavorable, gradually began to acquire Soviet Union citizenship due to the maneuvering of that country, and they engaged increasingly in espionage activities. Some who had been cooperating with the Japanese Army fled to Tientsin or Shanghai upon entry of the Russian Army, but most were captured. All members of the White Russians

Bureau, which handled the affairs of White Russians in Manchuria, were executed by the Soviets. Some White Russians actively cooperated with the Russian Army as spies. Most of the White Russians were sent under guard to Russian territory, and nearly all of these must have been executed as traitors.

Monograph No 155-G

CHAPTER VII

The 63d Division[24]

Organization

The 63d Infantry Division was organized near Peiping, China, during June-July 1943, with the 15th Independent Mixed Brigade as its nucleus. Its primary missions were to perform garrison duty and to conduct anti-guerrilla operations against Chinese Communist bandits. To accomplish these missions elements of the division had to be widely deployed. The division's area of responsibility extended throughout the sub-provinces of Peiping (Yenking), Paoting, and northern Shunteh, all in Hopei Province. Division headquarters was in Peiping, and the division was under the control of the North China Area Army.

Since it was organized for garrison duties and guerrilla warfare, the division was not trained or equipped for modern warfare against a well-equipped enemy. Its table of organization differed from that of a "combat" division in several respects. Its largest infantry unit was a brigade (instead of a regiment). It had no organic artillery. Furthermore, since its garrison mission rendered it a

---

24. This section was prepared by Colonel Sadaji Sato, staff officer of the 63d Division until 26 July 1945.

more or less stationary force, it had no mobile supply units.

Organically the division consisted of two infantry brigades (each with four battalions), an engineer battalion, a transport battalion, a signal company, and a field hospital. (See inset, Map No 1). Attached to the division was an independent infantry brigade, stationed in Shihmen.

In March 1945 the division was directed to organize two independent garrison units, one at Peiping, the other at Paoting. When formed, these units were assigned to the division and assisted it in carrying out garrison responsibilities. In May the division began a gradual relinquishment of its garrison responsibilities to the two independent garrison units, and at the same time ordered its organic elements to assemble in the Peiping and Paoting areas for new orders. Meanwhile it undertook a specialized training program in order to prepare its troops for combat operations in Manchuria. Since it was not a "combat" division, it was ordered to organize an artillery battalion (actually only a company equipped with four 75-mm field guns was formed) and a baggage section (ammunition and provisions train) for each battalion. These additions had the effect of transforming the division from a "garrison" to a "combat" division. The brigade structure, however, was retained.

The tactical methods employed by the division during its long assignment to garrison duties in China differed greatly from those a combat division. In view of the wide dispersal of units, furthermore, infantry brigade commanders had never been known to assemble their sub-units to issue orders to their entire commands.

To give its elements experience, therefore, the division, after transferring its garrison duties to the independent garrison units and assembling its organic elements, conducted active mopping-up operations under the commanders of its two infantry brigades. Field training during these operations was conducted with a view towards improving the command ability of all unit commanders, and increasing the level of training of each unit. Emphasis was also placed on training in maneuverability. Division headquarters and its various specialized units also conducted active field training.

Transfer to Manchuria

Early in June the division was relieved completely of its guard duty in North China and ordered to move to the Tungliao area in southern Manchuria. Special efforts were made to maintain secrecy from the beginning of its preparations until its actual departure by rail. The move was executed smoothly, the division passing to the control of the Kwantung Army upon crossing the frontier. It completed the move to the new station in mid-June, and was assigned to the Forty-fourth Army.

Division headquarters was established at Tungliao. Organic elements were deployed mainly at key points (principally inhabited areas) along the railroad lines running east and south from Tungliao. The 66th Brigade's main body was at Liaoyuan, with elements along the

Liaoyuan-Tungliao Railway. The 67th Brigade's main body was at Tungliao, with elements along the northern section Tungliao-Tahushan Railway; one of its infantry battalions was deployed at Kailu, eighty kilometers west of Tungliao. Other divisional elements were stationed in the vicinity of Tungliao or along the Liaoyuan-Tungliao Railway. (See Map No 1)

Late in June the division received operational instructions from Forty-fourth Army, defining its mission as follows:

> The division's main body will occupy positions in the vicinity of Tungliao. Elements will be deployed at Kailu and other principal places along the Liaoyuan-Tungliao Railway, especially in the vicinity of Liaoyuan. The division will crush the eastward advance of the enemy by guerrilla tactics.

Since this was the same substantially as the original deployment of the division, no major redispositions were made. However, as soon as this mission was received all division elements promptly became absorbed in the construction of defense positions, limiting the construction of billeting facilities to the bare minimum.

In issuing instructions regarding the construction of positions the Army stated that it was unable to provide construction materials and directed that they be obtained locally. Since the division was located in a vast tract of desert land, there was scarcely any material available locally. Thus the construction of strong points, such as caves, was delayed. However, adapting itself to the characteristics of the desert, the division began constructing individual

MONOGRAPH NO. 155-G
MAP NO. 1

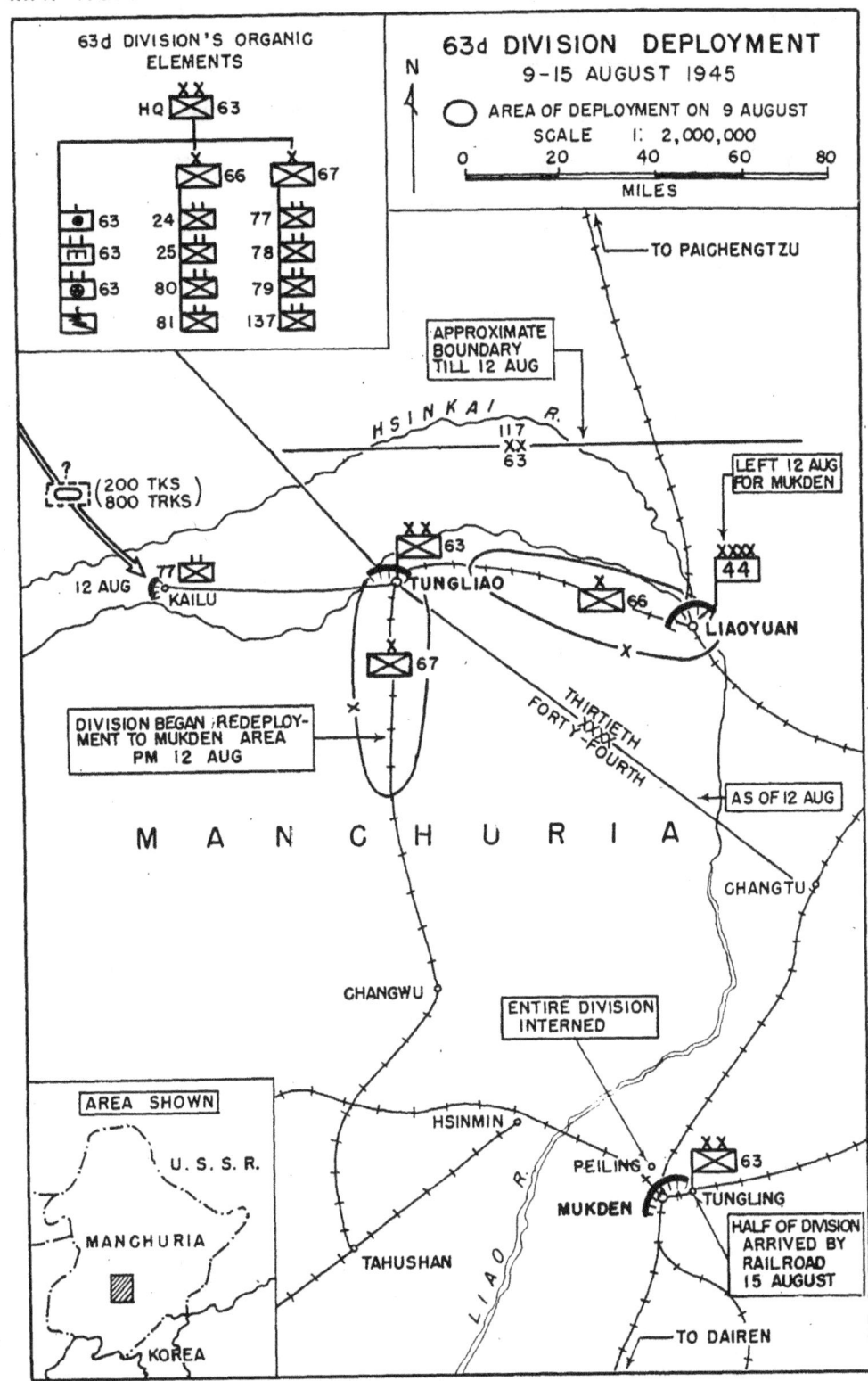

trenches, and planned to develop them into strong points later when materials became available.

The Army was also unable at first to provide operational supplies, such as arms, ammunition, and explosive charges for guerrilla warfare. The shortage was so great for awhile that it was difficult to conduct training. Gradually, however, the division was furnished with some supplies. Meanwhile, the division took steps to strengthen each organization and to improve the condition of equipment.

Training

The division commander, Lieutenant General Kenichi Kishikawa, had always placed great emphasis on training. After the division received its operational mission in Manchuria, this emphasis was continued. The major objective of training was to improve the command ability of officers and noncommissioned officers in guerrilla operations. Since the division had had experience in guerrilla warfare against Chinese Communist bandits in north China, both officers and men were thoroughly familiar with such tactics. Nevertheless, to master these tactics, the division sent selected units, including officers, to the Chilin maneuvers in mid-July, conducted by the 1st (Kinoshita) Mobile Brigade under Kwantung Army sponsorship. The division chief of staff participated in these maneuvers to gain experience in directing and controlling units in guerrilla operations.

Meanwhile, training in the division's area was carried on. All units devoted as much time as possible to it considering the other details they had to perform, such as construction of positions. Close-quarter suicide attacks against tanks were practiced. Since the division has no tanks or armored cars, railway motor cars moving on rails at the speed of tanks were used to simulate targets. The division commander took an active part in this training every day, directing it as well as inspecting it.

Combat Effectiveness

After the division moved to Manchuria the quality of its unit commanders dropped sharply below what it had been since the time of its organization in China in 1943. An infantry battalion that in former days had been commanded by a colonel or lieutenant colonel of the regular army, now was commanded by a captain brought up from the enlisted ranks. Furthermore, the fighting effectiveness of the division for modern warfare was considered to be less than fifty per cent of that of a first-class division.

However, the type of operation planned by Forty-fourth Army against the Soviet consisted solely of guerrilla warfare. It was not to be a conventional operation in which the combined strength of all arms, and the skillful use of strategy and tactics under a superior commander were to be counted on to win the war. Rather, the issue of battle was to be decided by the collective result of each individual guerrilla engagement fought by small unit commanders and their men. In a sense it was to be a primitive operation in which each member of each unit, including headquarters, was to be a combatant in guerrilla fighting.

Such an operation was indeed much favored by the division since it had been fighting guerrilla warfare day and night in North China. Considered in this light, the division's combat effectiveness was believed to be not inferior to that of the first-rate divisions in Manchuria. Moreover, the morale of the division was high. Since first learning in early 1945 of its probable transfer from China, the division had been prepared to sacrifice itself at the front in the decisive battle. It was with such determination that the division moved to Manchuria and devoted every moment to training. Furthermore, before the move to Manchuria the losses sustained in North China were replaced, bringing the division up to authorized strength.

Outbreak of Hostilities

The division had completed all operational preparations by the time war broke out in Manchuria. Upon learning of the enemy's moves in its direction the division prepared to send the 77th Independent Infantry Battalion from its front line position at Kailu to engage the enemy in guerrilla operations, in accordance with pre-arranged plans. Meanwhile, however, the division received orders on 10 August to withdraw to positions near Tungling, east of Mukden, and to defend Mukden jointly with other units.

Without ever contacting the enemy, the division began the move to Mukden by rail on the afternoon of 12 August. Although in general the move progressed smoothly, the simultaneous evacuation of Japanese residents caused considerable difficulty. Elements began arriving in the Mukden area one by one and occupied assigned positions. The division never saw action, however, even in the Mukden area. After half of the division had arrived in Mukden, and while the remainder was still en route, the war ended. Hence, the division's fighting capacity remained unimpaired at the war's end.

Disarmament

The Soviet Army representative arrived in Mukden by plane on 19 August. On the following day, all Japanese generals in the Mukden area, including the 63d Division commander, were ordered "to assemble at the airfield to meet the arrival of the Soviet commander." All reported to the airfield but they were taken captive and transported to the Soviet Union by air. In the meantime, the division was assembled in one area to be disarmed.

Subsequently, the entire division was interned in the Peiling Internment Camp and remained there until mid-October. The Soviets formed labor battalions (1,500 men each) from all personnel up to and including the grade of captain, and one officer battalion of field grade officers. Colonel Hashiba, commander of the 67th Brigade, concerned over the men under his command, volunteered to become a commander of a labor battalion. The division attempted to have one of its field grade officers appointed as commander of each labor battalion but, except in Colonel Hashiba's case, this was rejected by the Soviets. Thereafter, the labor battalions and the officer battalion were transported to Soviet territory.

Monograph No 155-H

CHAPTER VIII

The 117th Division[25]

Transfer from China to Manchuria

In many respects the history of the 117th Division paralleled that of the 63d Division: like it, the 117th Division was a garrison division organized with a brigade, rather than regimental, structure, before being ordered to Manchuria, it was assigned to the Twelfth Army of the North China Area Army with the mission of suppressing guerrillas; in Manchuria it was assigned to the Forty-fourth Army, and in the midst of the war with the Soviets was redeployed. Like the 63d Division in Manchuria, it never made contact with the enemy and never participated in an engagement.

In China, the 117th Division was in charge principally of the defense of the northern part of Honan Province (north of the Yellow River), the division's main body being stationed in the Hsinhsiang area, and division headquarters in Hsinhsiang city itself. However, division elements also carried out suppression operations in Hupeh Province. In fact, when the division was ordered to Manchuria late in May 1945, its Yoshitake Detachment (203d and 389th Independent Infantry Battalions, respectively of the 87th and 88th Brigades)

---

25. This section was prepared by Major Yoshio Tsutsui, staff officer of the 117th Division.

MONOGRAPH NO. 155-H
MAP NO. 1

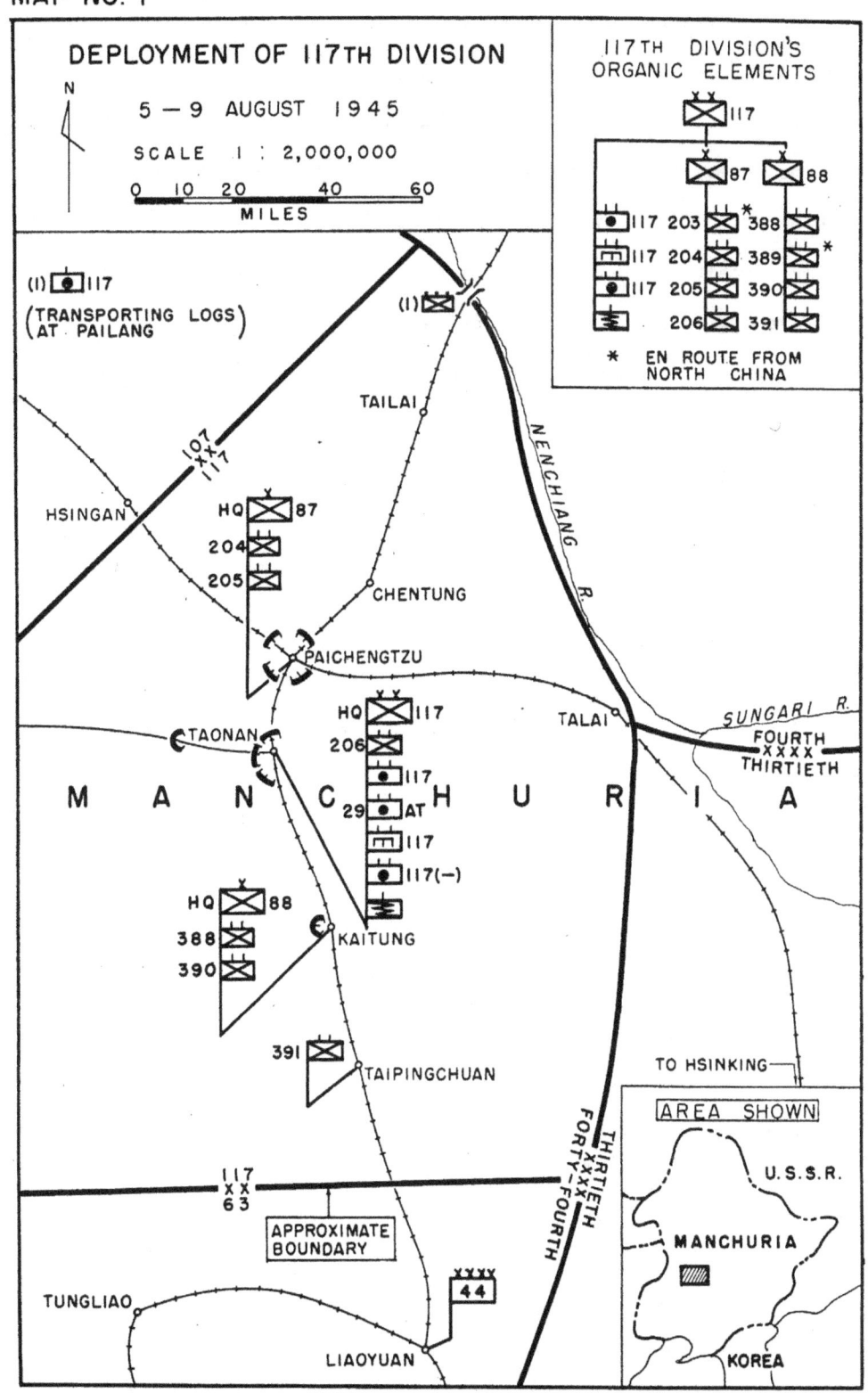

was still participating in operations near Laohokou in Hupeh Province.[26]

The division began moving to Manchuria secretly in the middle of June and virtually completed the move by the end of the month. In Manchuria it took up positions directly north of the 63d Division's positions. The 87th Brigade's main body was deployed in the Paichengtzu area, the 88th Brigade's main body in the Kaitung area, and division headquarters in Taonan (See Map No 1). The two battalions of the Yoshitake Detachment, meanwhile, were disengaging from Laohokou and were to follow later.

On 6 August the division received Forty-fourth Army's operational plan including instructions governing the disposition of forces, and immediately began drafting its own plan. The division commander, Lieutenant General Hiraku Suzuki, scheduled a unit commanders conference for 10 August, at which time he planned to announce the division plan.

Outbreak of Hostilities

Meanwhile, on 9 August war broke out in Manchuria. Forty-fourth Army immediately assigned the 29th Antitank Battalion, which was

---

26. The commander of this detachment, Major General Yoshitake, was the 87th Brigade commander. On 31 March 1945 he was assigned to the staff of the North China Area Army Headquarters. His successor as brigade commander was Major General Sen Shoji. The latter took the main body of the brigade (204th, 205th, and 206th Battalions) to Manchuria. General Yoshitake continued to command the two battalions until they disengaged in China and moved to Manchuria.

deployed in the division's area, to the division. On 10 August the scheduled unit commanders conference was held. After announcing the division's plan, General Suzuki directed all units to give priority to the construction of positions.

On the same day division headquarters received a telephone call from the vice-governor of Lichuan Prefecture to the effect that "according to reports of natives, several thousand tanks are advancing toward Lichuan".[27] To intercept this enemy force the division sent its newly assigned antitank battalion and the 206th Infantry Battalion, with orders to harass the tanks at a point approximately 30 kilometers west of Taonan.

During the afternoon Forty-fourth Army Headquarters ordered the division to redeploy immediately to Hsinking where, upon arrival, it was to come under the command of the Thirtieth Army. Twelve trains, the Forty-fourth Army stated, would be assigned to transport the division on the evening of 12 August.

In preparation for the move the division immediately recalled the 29th Antitank Battalion and the 206th Battalion, and on the following morning moved the 388th Battalion from the Kaitung Area to Taonan.

---

27. This figure, given by civilians, was undoubtedly an exaggeration even if military vehicles of all types were included. Military estimates were that the Soviet force in this area had about 200 tanks and about 800 trucks. The small force sent to intercept it was to harass it only. (See Map No 2.)

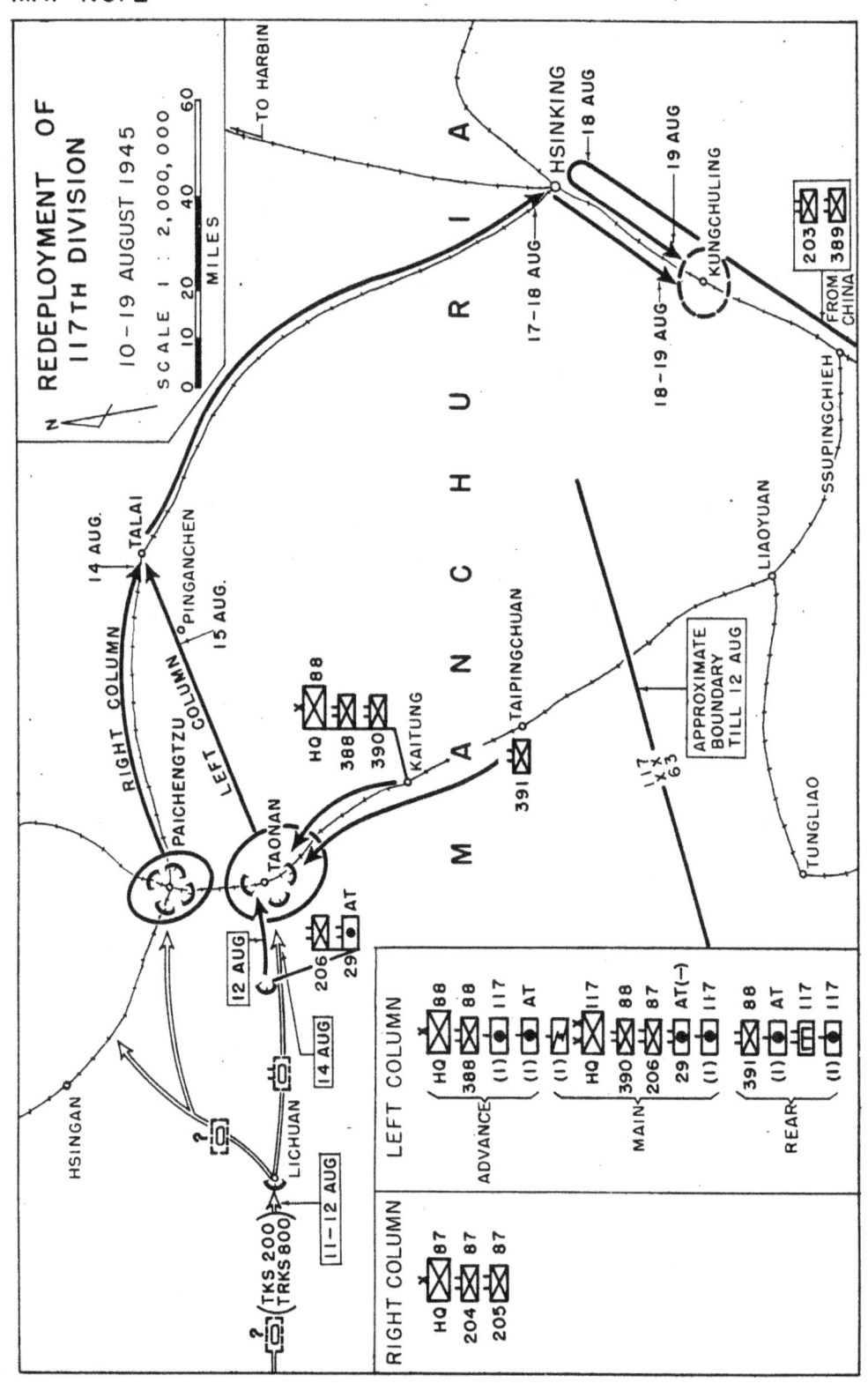

At about 1800 hours on 12 August Forty-fourth Army Headquarters called again stating that since no trains were available the division would have to redeploy to Hsinking on foot. The division immediately revised the movement plan, and started moving elements in two columns, leaving Taonan at midnight. (See Map No 2.)

The commander of the right column managed, apparently through arrangements made directly with Kwantung Army Headquarters by telephone, to obtain rail transportation for his two battalions of the 87th Brigade and for brigade headquarters. Most of this column arrived at Talai on 14 August.

The left column, which consisted of the remainder of the division including division headquarters, was divided into three sections: an advance guard, a main body, and a rear guard. During the march enemy planes circled overhead on 13 August and again during the night of the 14th, and although they dropped some flare bombs, they did not attack the column, discouraged possibly by intermittent rain. After marching 70 kilometers the column reached Pinganchen on the morning of 15 August, and learned from a radio of the Division Signal Unit that a cease-fire order had been issued. The two battalions en route from China to Manchuria learned of the order while at Tientsin.

End of Hostilities

After receiving notification of the cease fire, the division tried to have its main body transported by rail to the Hsinking area.

Meanwhile, however, the division commander with some of his staff proceeded to Kwantung Army General Headquarters in Hsinking, arriving there early in the morning of 16 August, when he was instructed to assemble the division at Kungchuling. Before beginning the rail movement toward Kungchuling, the division was required to leave some elements (the 204th Battalion, an element of artillery, an engineer company, and the signal unit) in Hsinking. Hence, some elements of the division were disarmed in the Hsinking area and some in the Kungchuling area. On 18 August, the two battalions from China arrived in Hsinking, but were sent to Kungchuling on the 19th and disarmed there.

Monograph No 155-I

CHAPTER IX

The 108th Division in Jehol[28]

Organization

The 108th Infantry Division was formed in Jehol Province[29] between 1 and 15 August 1944 with the 9th Independent Garrison Unit as its nucleus. It was assigned to the Kwantung Defense Army and given the missions of maintaining peace and order in Jehol Province, conducting guerrilla operations against Chinese Communist bandits, and preparing for operations against the Soviet Union.

The division was composed mainly of three infantry regiments, (each consisting of three infantry battalions, an infantry gun company, a signal unit, and a mounted platoon), and one field artillery battalion. Service units were less than the normal regimental size: one engineer company, two horse-drawn transport companies, one motor transport company, a division signal unit, and a division medical

---

28. This section was prepared by Major Yutaka Sato, staff officer, 108th Division.
29. Jehol, a province of about 72,000 square miles (mostly mountains and desert), was formerly a part of Inner Mongolia. It was incorporated as part of Manchukuo at the time the latter's "independence" was proclaimed under Japanese sponsorship on 18 February 1932. Japanese military occupation of this province, which is divided from China proper by the Great Wall, did not take place until January-March 1933, about a year after Manchukuo's independence had been proclaimed. The decision to announce Manchukuo's "independence" may have been hastened by the League's appointment on 10 December 1931 of the Lytton Commission to investigate the situation arising out of the Mukden Incident.

unit (consisting of three stretcher companies and one vehicle company). There was no veterinary hospital or ordnance duty platoon. Division headquarters had one staff officer (instead of the normal three) in addition to the chief of staff. None of the headquarters special staff sections had a regular section chief (of full colonel rank). The division commander was Lieutenant General Torajiro Iwai.

Early in 1945 the division was augmented by the attachment of a fourth regiment, the 171st Cavalry. On 23 May an ordnance duty unit was organized by the artillery battalion and was stationed in Jehol, and a veterinary hospital was organized under the guidance of the transport unit and was stationed at Chinhsien.

On 1 August, a raiding battalion was organized, and the artillery battalion was reorganized into a regiment of three battalions. To form the raiding battalion each of the infantry regiments contributed 280 men each, the cavalry regiment fifty men, the engineer battalion forty men, and the transport and medical units thirty men each; the battalion's 1,000 men were young and efficient, but the unit did not have time to achieve internal unity. To expand the artillery battalion to a regiment, local draftees were used for the most part; the soldier qualities of these men were low. The artillery equipment consisted of 75-mm field guns for two of the battalions and 105-mm howitzers for the third.

To replenish the strength of units which had contributed men to form the new organizations, draftees obtained locally during August were assigned.[30] Most of these men joined their units as late as 12 or 13 August, and hence had no time for training. Moreover, all could not be armed since rifles and even bayonets were in short supply. Nor could they be provided with uniforms; many had to wear the clothing in which they were drafted.

Disposition

The division's disposition in April 1945 was principally intended not to meet a possible Soviet invasion from Mongolia, but rather to carry out guerrilla operations against the Chinese (Communist) Eighth Route Army which was active along the Great Wall. For such operations, the 240th and 242d Regiments deployed small elements at several places: north of Kupeikou, at Hsinglung (Hsiaying), Chinglung, Shanhaikwan, Suichung, Chinhsi, Hulutao, and Pingchuan. Headquarters of the 242d Regiment was at Chinhsien, and that of the 240th was at Jehol city as was also division headquarters.

Meanwhile, as a token defense force against a Soviet invasion, the 241st Regiment, with headquarters and two battalions at Fouhsin, deployed small elements at Linhsi and Chihfeng. Several of the

---

30. The August augmentation gave each infantry regiment 600 draftees. (The 241st Regiment had acquired 800 during May). Figures for other division elements are not available.

division's elements were deployed outside of Jehol province, principally along the Dairen-Mukden railway line, because of the shortage of billeting and other facilities. The 171st Cavalry Regiment, for example, was at Haicheng, as was also the division's artillery regiment. Smaller units were also deployed along the railroad. Toward the end of May the division was placed directly under Third Area Army whose Headquarters had just moved to Mukden.

Following the end of the war in Europe, the Soviet Union gradually redeployed large forces to the Far East. Thereafter, the threat posed by Soviet forces in Mongolia began to overshadow that posed by the China Eighth Route Army. It therefore became necessary to plan for the redisposition of division elements. Division Headquarters assumed that the Soviet invasion of its area would be made via Inner Mongolia, a vast stretch of wasteland, and that the Soviet Army would push its main body along the Apaka-Linhsi-Chihfeng axis. For this reason the division decided to deploy the 241st Regiment along this axis with instructions to construct fortifications, and the regiment's main body in the vicinity of Jeshui which was located in comparatively advantageous terrain.

Plans to change the disposition could not be put into effect promptly, however, because of the political situation in Jehol and also because adequate camp facilities were not available in forward areas. Although some time was lost, steady progress in redisposition was made during June.

No changes were made at Chihfeng or at Linhsi where the 2d Battalion, 241st Regiment, had its main body and its 5th Company, respectively. At Jeshui, however, the remainder of the 241st Regiment arrived from Fouhsin, and also the 108th Engineer Battalion from Yingkou, and promptly began to construct fortifications. At Yehpaishou the 108th Artillery Regiment moved into positions, and at Lingyuan the Raiding Battalion. Thus by early July the Linhsi-Chihfeng-Yehpaishou line and adjacent areas had been strengthened. This redisposition was complicated by several factors, however, the most important of which was that while preparing for a Soviet invasion from Mongolia, the division had to contend with the China Eighth Route Army. The redisposition was destined to be short-lived.

Following the Soviet redeployment of large forces to the Mongolia area, the Chinese Communists became more active, apparently in response to Soviet orders. The Chinese threat became so great that the division was compelled to redispose its forces anew. Up to that time, the Eighth Route Army had kept its main body well south of the Great Wall, and had harassed the division by sending small bands of guerrillas to operate in Jehol Province. Division Headquarters believed, however, that the Eighth Route Army was preparing to enter a new phase by launching a major offensive during August in conjunction with a Soviet invasion. The plan of the Chinese, it was believed, was to send its main body along the

Pingchuan-Kuangtoushan axis with the object of establishing contact with the Soviet Army which would be advancing from the Chihfeng area.

The Southwest Defense Command and Operations Against the Eighth Route Army

Although the division's major mission was to prepare for operations against the Soviet Union, in view of the threat from China it had been assigned the additional mission of suppressing the Eighth Route Army, and for this purpose was designated the Southwest Defense Command. This designation was made at about the time the Kwantung Defense Army was converted to the Forty-fourth Army, and several defense commands established in the area taken over by the Third Area Army.

As the Southwest Defense commander, Lieutenant General Torajiro Iwai had under his command, besides his own division, the Fifth Army District of the Manchukuoan Army. Commanded by Lieutenant General Ho-Muhsia, a Manchurian, the Fifth Army District was composed of eight regiments, each deployed north of the Great Wall. It was not considered a dependable force. In fact, the Eighth Route Army had always managed to remain one step ahead of it. The Chinese intelligence network was well organized, and the enemy seemed always to have prior information of operational actions of the division. For suppressing guerrilla activities of the Chinese Communists, General Iwai up to this time used mainly Manchukuoan Army units, reserving his own division for use against a Soviet invasion.

In view of the powerful Chinese offensive expected in August, however, General Iwai decided to throw the main bodies of all his divisional infantry regiments against the China Eighth Route Army, with the object of dealing a mortal blow to it before the Soviet Army launched its offensive. Furthermore, to assist it in this expedition the division acquired two independent infantry battalions from the 63d Division, the Oda Battalion and the Magara Battalion. These two battalions, each consisting of about 800 men, arrived at the end of July. They were initially stationed near Jehol City; later one was assigned to the 240th Regiment, the other to the 241st.

In addition to his division, the Manchukuoan Army regiments, and the two newly acquired infantry battalions, General Iwai also had some assistance in guerrilla suppression from Japanese Army elements of the China Expeditionary Army south of the Great Wall. The most notable of these was the Hara Unit (8th Independent Mixed Brigade) which consistently worked closely with the division. Also of assistance south of the Great Wall was the Isshin Unit, a Manchurian police force composed of some 2,000 officers and men, and commanded by a Japanese civilian official named Minagawa. A few of the top officers of this police force were Japanese. It achieved good results. By using simple equipment it attained a high degree of mobility. It was very effective in gathering intelligence, aided by the fact that the nationality of its members was the same as that of local inhabitants. Furthermore, it carried out operations

MONOGRAPH NO. 155-I
MAP NO. I

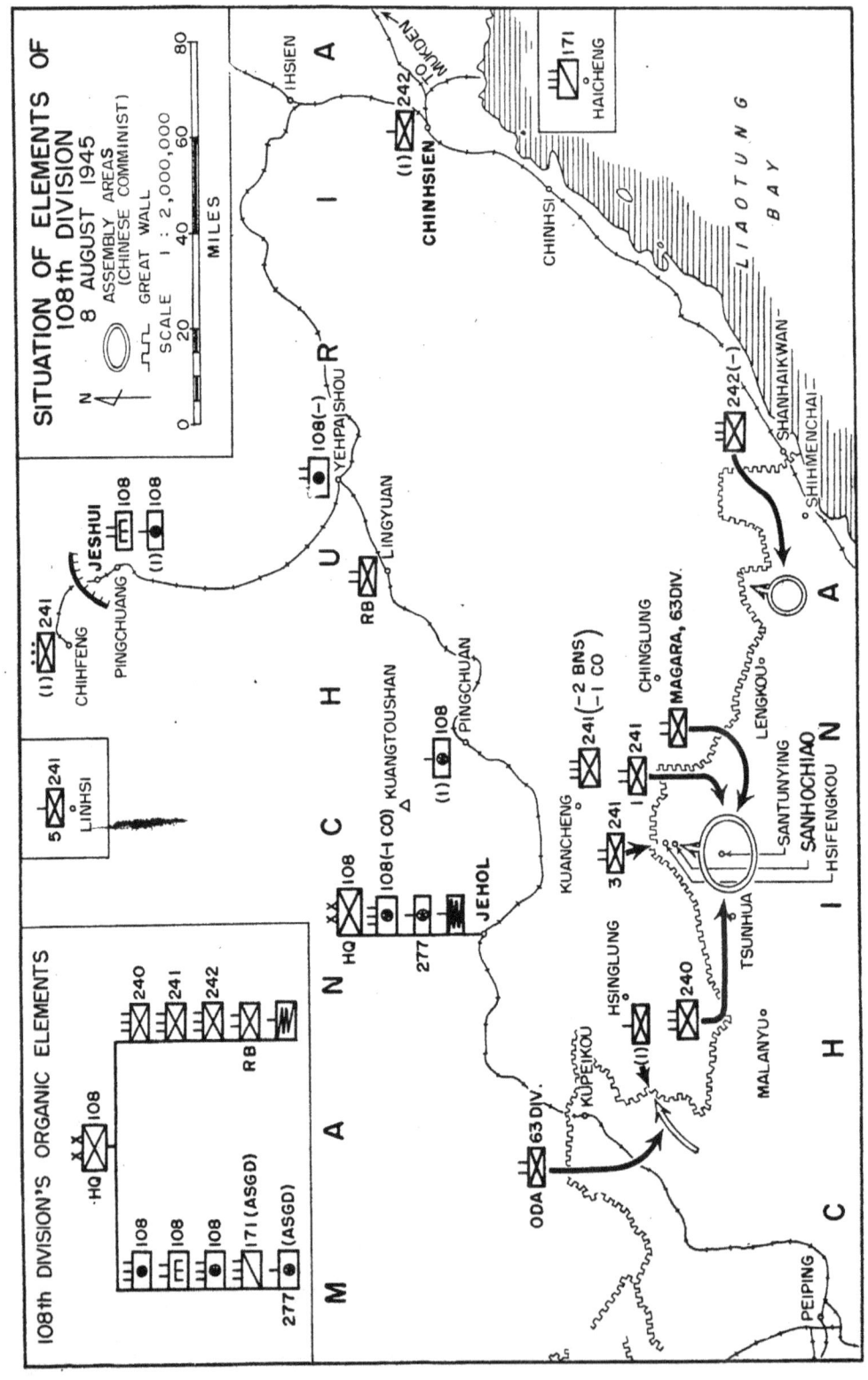

systematically, according to plans laid down by the Southwest Defense commander.

Since the Chinese underground in Jehol had become more active, and the danger from China was immediate, the division pulled out the main body of the 241st Regiment from the Jeshui area, leaving only one platoon there, and sent it to join the expedition to smash the Chinese along the Great Wall. This naturally delayed the construction of positions near Jeshui. (See Map No 1)

The division's plan to counter the Eighth Route Army was to use the 240th and 241st Regiments to smash the enemy's main body in the Sanhochiao area, with the 242d Regiment as a supporting force in the area from Sanhochiao eastward to Shanhaikwan. Operations were launched secretly between mid and late July.

The main force pushed its operations to encircle the enemy's main body, presumed to be concentrated near Sanhochiao. Though these operations were continued until 9 August, no major engagements were fought. The enemy proved to be quite elusive, and it was difficult to catch him in the vast area. Meanwhile, the Chinese underground continued to be very active; some infiltrating spies were arrested. The direction of our widely deployed forces was hindered by the fact that the only means of contact was by wireless telegraph. The expedition to cripple the China Eighth Route Army had not achieved notable results by the time the Soviets entered the war.

Status of Preparations for Operations against the USSR

In almost every respect preparations for full-scale operations against the Soviet Army had been incomplete at the time the Soviet invasion began.

Fortifications that could be completed in the Jeshui area by the 241st Regiment and the division engineers before the former was transferred to the Great Wall front were minimal. They consisted mainly of communications trenches, concrete emplacements for machine-guns, and concrete structures for command post installations. At Yehpaishou the construction of a concrete ammunition dump by the engineers was begun but could not be completed. The construction of simple billets at Yehpaishou, Lingyuan, and Pingchuan to accommodate artillery, engineer, and transport units was also begun but the work had hardly gotten under way.

Supply and transportation facilities and installations were wholly inadequate. The only supply installations of the division were a branch freight (general supplies) depot and a branch motor transport depot at Chinhsien, and a freight depot branch at Jehol. Plans to establish freight depot branches at Pingchuang and Yehpaishou, and storage facilities for ammunition and fuel in Yehpaishou could not be implemented. Transportation demands made necessary by operations against the Eighth Route Army taxed the Jehol Railway to its full capacity, and left no room for establishing new depots or dumps. A major problem was the transportation of feed for several thousand Manchurian horses commandeered for use in constructing the Chihfeng airfield. Even this demand could not be met satisfactorily. Furthermore, the scheduled transfer of ammunition for the artillery regiment after it moved to Yehpaishou was scarcely begun. Although the 277th Motor Transport Company was assigned to the division to supplement organic units, it was impossible to meet all the demands for transportation throughout the vast mountainous province even had it been possible to use all of the divisional transport companies. In short, the supply and transportation situation was considered to be very serious.

The traffic network along which the Soviet Army could be expected to invade consisted mainly of one operational road along the Yehpaishou-Chihfeng axis, passable to all types of vehicles. However, there were so many smaller dirt roads that could be used by horse-drawn vehicles that the enemy could invade from nearly every point without much difficulty. In the south, on both sides of the Great Wall, the road network was comparatively well organized. There were several automobile roads connecting Kupeikou, Malanyu, Hsifengkou, and Lengkou around steep mountains, which could be used by the enemy as well as by ourselves.

The greatest concern regarding traffic in Jehol Province was the tendency of rivers to overflow during the rainy season. In the dry season river beds served as roads; bridges were unnecessary. But in the rainy season traffic was completely disrupted. Even heavy

MONOGRAPH NO. 155 – I
SKETCH NO. 1

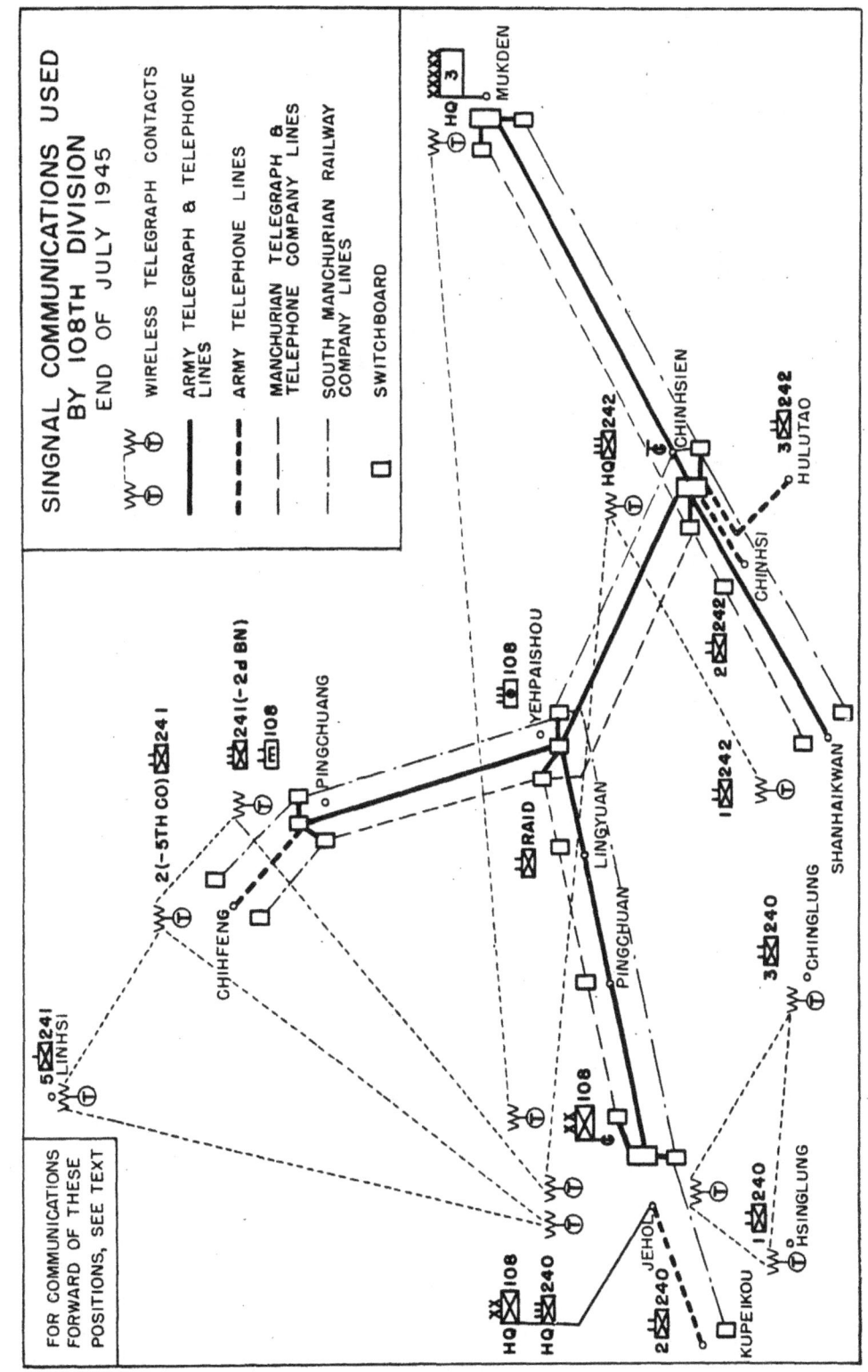

rains of short duration frequently caused traffic to be suspended for some time.

The communications nerve center, both military and civilian (Manchurian Telegraph and Telephone Company), was at Chinhsien, where 242d Regimental Headquarters was located. Military and commercial lines from Mukden passed through Chinhsien on to Shanhaikwan to the south, on to Yehpaishou to the west and from there north to Chihfeng, and to Jehol in the west. From Chihfeng to Linhsi, and between Chihfeng and Jehol city only wireless telegraph communication was available. Wireless telegraph communication was also available between the points connected by telephone lines as well as directly between Third Area Army Headquarters at Mukden and 108th Division Headquarters in Jehol city. For units located at other points, for example those deployed immediately north of the Great Wall, wireless telegraph had to be used almost exclusively. Although the telephone lines of the Manchurian Telegraph and Telephone Company were not dependable to any great extent for operations, those of the railway company were quite valuable and were used as an auxiliary means of communication. (See Sketch No 1) Besides these facilities, Government administrative communications (telephone and wireless telegraph) existed both along the border and in the interior, and were used by police units and lookout sentries for air defense. These agencies were given top priority for the transmission of information to the air defense center maintained at division headquarters.

For the conduct of operations against a Soviet invading Army, division headquarters felt that its command post should be located at Yehpaishou, and made plans to modify the communication net accordingly. But the invasion began before the plan could be put into effect.

Thorough training in anti-Soviet combat techniques was given to troops of each of the combat arms. Special emphasis was placed on carrying out surprise raids and on antitank operations. For the latter, the supply of explosives was almost nil until just immediately prior to the outbreak of war when a small percentage of requirements was received. Until then every effort was made to produce explosives locally.

The combat effectiveness of the division was relatively low. This resulted partly from the transfers from the older units to form new units and partly from the fact that a great many recruits were brought in to the division. In some cases the strength of a company was less than 100 men. The fighting capacity of the recently organized artillery regiment was estimated to be less than that of two battalions. Furthermore the combat effectiveness of the division was reduced by shortages of equipment, particularly rifles, explosive charges, and artillery shells.

The collection of intelligence regarding Soviet Russia was very inadequate. Some of it was obtained from the Apaka Special Service (Intelligence) Agency or from the 5th Company of the 241st Regiment

MONOGRAPH NO. 155-I
MAP NO. 2

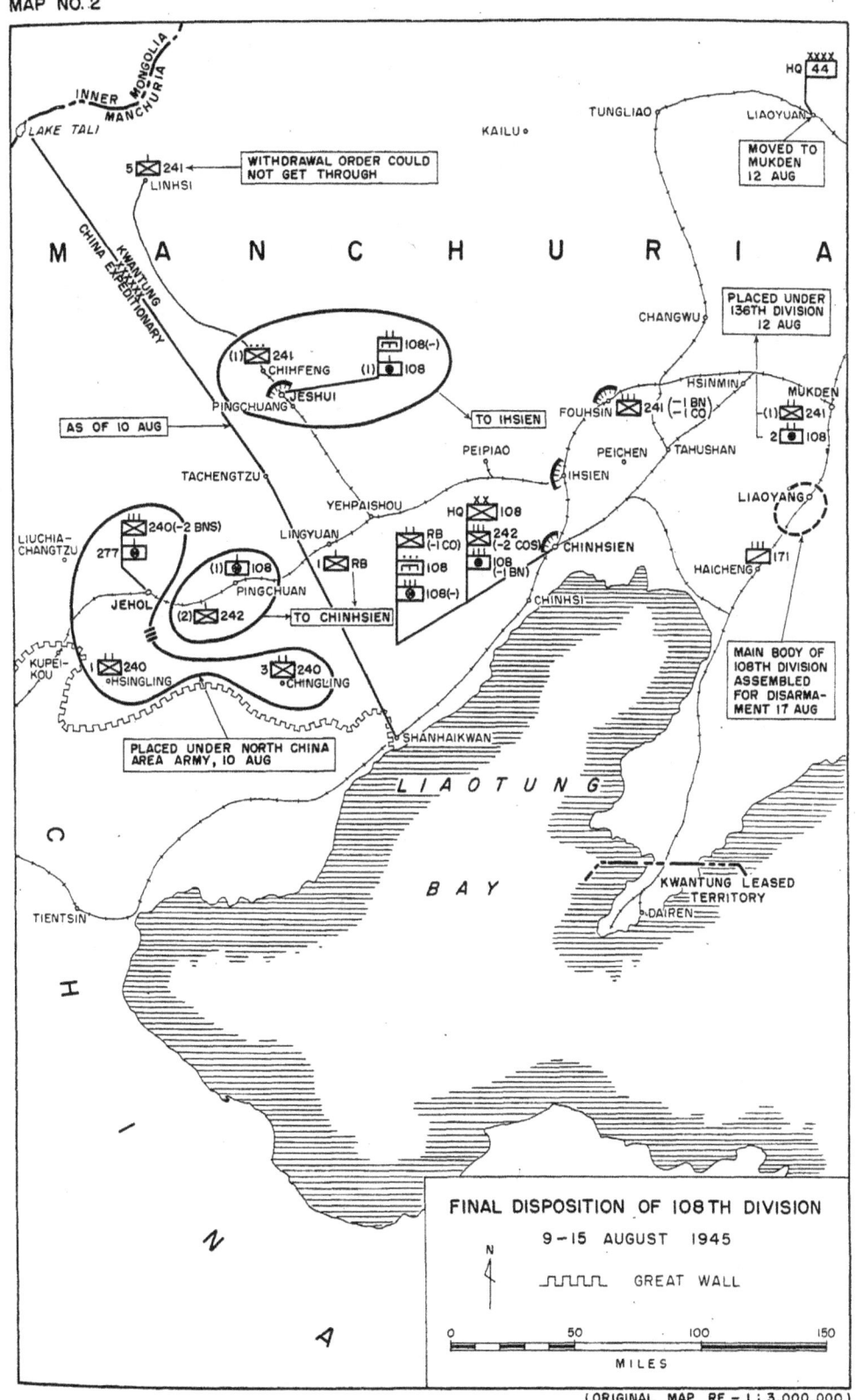

at Linhsi. For most information, however, the division had to rely on higher headquarters.

Border defense was not stressed. No border defense installations had been constructed since operations across the desert areas of Inner Mongolia were considered to be of little value. It would have been extremely difficult to defend the length of the Inner Mongolia border, depending as it would on long supply lines. Moreover, the division did not have an adequate number of units to deploy along the border, and had to concentrate its main body against the Eighth Route Army in the south.

Opening of Hostilities   (See Map No 2).

On 14 June Kwantung Army distributed its outline of the new operational plan, providing for delaying operations throughout Manchuria and a final withdrawal to the redoubt in the Tunghua area. After studying this outline, General Iwai unofficially suggested to Third Area Army that the division be redeployed to the area generally east of Chinhsien city. This area was more suited to defensive operations, and several elements of the division were already stationed in Chinchou Province. Although this would in effect abandon most of Jehol Province, the division's mission in Jehol was principally one for peacetime--the maintenance of peace and order. The division's suggestion was based on a wartime deployment, and was in accord with Kwantung Army's plan for final withdrawal to the redoubt. Third Area Army rejected this suggestion, however, apparently attaching greater importance to the peacetime mission because of the political importance of Jehol Province, situated as it was amid the three states of Manchuria proper, Inner Mongolia, and China. Consequently the division continued to follow the Area Army's policy which did, however, provide for the division's withdrawal to the area east of Chinhsien as a last resort.

On 9 August, while engaged in suppressing guerrilla activities of the Eighth Route Army, the division received reports of the Soviet Union's entry into the war.

On 10 August Kwantung Army announced a change in its boundary with the China Expeditionary Army. The new boundary, which had been decided upon by Imperial General Headquarters on 13 July, was established along the line from Shanhaikwan, through Tachengtzu, to the eastern end of Tali Lake. Kwantung Army placed 108th Division elements in the vicinity of Jehol City under the North China Area Army, and ordered the division to withdraw its main body to the Fouhsin-Chinhsien line, and prepare for a defense along that line. This was substantially what the division had recommended earlier to Third Area Army. On the same day the division was assigned to Forty-fourth Army.

The division received orders also from Forty-fourth Army on the 10th directing it to send one infantry and one artillery battalion to Mukden to help the 136th Division in the defense of that city. The division promptly dispatched one battalion from the 241st Regiment and the 2d Battalion of the artillery regiment, both under the command of Captain Mizunuma, the infantry battalion commander. (These battalions left Chinhsien on 12 August. They never rejoined the division. At the end of the war they were disarmed in Mukden, organized into labor battalions, and sent to Soviet Russia.)[31]

After it received Kwantung Army orders, the division prepared its own orders for subordinate commands. Beginning with a summary of the situation and a brief resume of Kwantung Army's plan, the division orders continued with the following salient points:

> The division will withdraw to the railway line extending from Fouhsin, through Ihsien, to Chinhsien, and will secure the area east of this line and check the enemy's advance.
>
> The 240th Regiment will hold its present positions and will be placed under the command of the North China Area Army. Attached to the regiment will be: the 277th Independent Motor Transport Company, the Jehol Military Hospital, the 5th Special Garrison Battalion, the Jehol Freight Depot Branch, and the Fifth Army District of the Manchukuoan Army.
>
> Each unit will begin to move immediately to the places indicated (railway transportation instructions will be issued separately):

---

31. This was the last of the modifications that complicated the organizational structure of the 108th Division and that were without parallel elsewhere in Manchuria. These modifications were of two types--additions and subtractions. The additions were: 1) one cavalry regiment, 2) two infantry battalions of the 63d Division (later returned). Subtractions were: 1) one infantry regiment near Jehol city was assigned to the China Expeditionary Army (actually only one battalion joined), and 2) one infantry battalion and one artillery battalion sent to help the 136th Division in Mukden.

Chinhsien: Division headquarters, 242d Regiment, main body of raiding battalion, 108th Field Artillery Regiment, 108th Engineer Unit, 108th Transport Regiment, and the division Medical Unit and Veterinary Hospital.

Fouhsin: Main body of the 241st Regiment

Ihsien: Elements of the 241st Regiment

The raiding battalion will leave one company at Lingyuan to check the enemy's advance. This company will later withdraw to Chinhsien.

Instructions on the disposition and duties of units at the new positions will be issued later.

The Oda and Magara battalions will return to Mukden to rejoin their parent units.

Assembly of Division along the Fouhsin-Chinhsien Line

By 12 August the following units had arrived at Chinhsien: Division headquarters, the 242d Regiment (minus the 5th and 9th Companies), the 108th Artillery Regiment (less its 2d Battalion), the Raiding Battalion (less the 1st Company), about 100 men (including the commander 2d Lieutenant Kuroki) of the Engineer Unit, the Veterinary Hospital, and the Transport Unit (less the 3d Company). The total strength was 8,000.

After arriving, each unit began to dig antitank ditches around Chinhsien. They were determined to defend the city to the last. Japanese and Manchurian residents in the area cooperated day and night in constructing defense installations.

At about 2000 hours on 14 August the senior staff officer of the division received a telephone call from Colonel Suehiro, operations staff officer of Third Area Army, stating that the Empire had decided to surrender unconditionally to the Allies. All members of the headquarters were stunned by this news and were at a loss as to what to do next. Shortly thereafter, however, another telephone call was received from Area Army Headquarters, correcting the earlier message and calling it a grave mistake arising from a misunderstanding on the part of Kwantung Army. Everyone was encouraged by this.

Still later a call from Army Headquarters revealed that His Majesty, the Commander in Chief, would make an important broadcast at noon of 15 August, and that all should listen to it. It was believed that the broadcast would announce renewed determination to fight to the very end, and all awaited the broadcast in pathetic anticipation. To the great surprise of the listeners, His Majesty broadcast the declaration of surrender. The troops were discouraged and dumbfounded.

At the time, the tactical situation of the division was quite serious. An enemy mechanized unit, after crossing the Hsingan Mountains, was advancing from Tungliao toward the vicinity of Hsinmin and Tahushan, and threatened to isolate the division by cutting the Mukden-Shanhaikwan line. On the night of 15 August, the division received a new movement order by telephone direct from Third Area Army (at Chinhsien, communications with Forty-fourth Army had not yet been satisfactorily established):

> The 108th Division will promptly withdraw to
> Liaoyang to prepare for subsequent operations.

> Transportation arrangements will be made directly with the Chinhsien Branch of the Continental Railway Force.

The next day, the division moved most of its troops in four military trains. Captain Maeda and a number of other personnel of division headquarters were left in Chinhsien with instructions to give guidance to units withdrawing from Jehol, and then to follow the division to Liaoyang. In moving to Liaoyang the division took only side arms, leaving large guns and horses in Chinhsien, since the most urgent requirement was to transport troops. Meanwhile, the 241st Regiment at Foushin and Ihsien, like the main body in Chinhsien, had begun defense construction, but upon learning of the withdrawal of the division's main body to Liaoyang, it withdrew almost simultaneously.

Back at Chinhsien, meanwhile, Captain Maeda gained several units. The largest of these was the 3d Battalion of the 240th Regiment, which earlier had been directed to join the North China Area Army. This battalion explained that after the opening of hostilities it had tried to join regimental headquarters at Jehol, via Pingchuan, but turned back upon learning of the situation at Jehol. It then marched from Chinglung along the Great Wall, repulsing on the way revolts of natives and attacks by the Eighth Route Army, before reaching Chinhsien.

The 5th and 9th Companies of the 242d Regiment did not arrive at Chinhsien until about 20 August. On the same day, elements of the transport unit also arrived. The 1st Company of the raiding battalion arrived at about the end of August; during its withdrawal it encountered a revolt by Manchurians, and its commander, 1st Lieutenant Ishikawa, was killed.

The only unit of the division to engage in action--the 5th Company of the 241st Regiment--also arrived, but not until mid-September. The cease-fire order had not reached this company. At the outbreak of war it had engaged elements of the Outer Mongolian Army at the Linhsi positions, retreating after sustaining heavy losses. The company commander and about fifty men arrived at Chinhsien; other survivors had withdrawn to Peichen via Peipiao. The total number of troops assembled by Captain Maeda in Chinhsien came to approximately 2,000.

Situation in the Jehol Area

After the end of the war all units which were supposed to have passed to the control of the North China Area Army, with the exception of the 1st and 3d Battalions of the 240th Regiment, assembled in Jehol. The 1st Battalion, however, crossed the Great Wall near Malanyu and became part of the China Expeditionary Army. (At the end of the war the China Expeditionary Army surrendered to Chiang Kai-shek. Its members were more fortunate than their compatriots who surrendered to the Soviets or to the Chinese Communists to be formed into labor battalions and sent to the Soviet Union or Mongolia. Chiang Kai-shek repatriated the China Expeditionary Army to Japan. The members of the 1st Battalion of the 240th Regiment who crossed the Great Wall were repatriated late in 1945.)

The regimental commander therefore had only the 2d Battalion besides regimental headquarters and attached units at Jehol. He sent two companies to escort the military delegates of the Soviet Army (presumably to the airfield northeast of Jehol city). One company was commanded by Lieutenant Hyakutake, the other by Lieutenant Ioi. Although the Ioi Unit's journey was uneventful, the Hyakutake Unit before returning to Jehol was assaulted by Manchurian rioters who killed about ten men. Lieutenant Hyakutake was listed as missing.

While disarming Japanese units, Soviet troops shot some members of the 5th Company at Liuchiachangtzu who attempted to escape.

Post-disarmament Period

The main body of the division reached Liaoyang on 17 August and was billeted in barracks and primary schools. The division took command of the units in and near the city. Since there were no immediate prospects of full repatriation, the division began preparing for winter by storing as much food and clothing as possible for the use of Japanese civilians as well as military personnel.

Meanwhile, the Soviet Army was reported to be gradually moving southward, disarming Japanese forces. Kwantung Army had issued instructions that the division was to be placed "as is" under Soviet control. However, division staff officer Sato, liaison officer to the Forty-fourth Army Headquarters, being able to observe Soviet disarmament procedures in Mukden, reported these proceedures to the division by telephone. This enabled the division to get an early lead in carrying out disarmament procedures.

Staff officer Sato also reported that after Japanese forces in Mukden were disarmed, Manchurian mobsters ravaged the city, looting Japanese properties. For awhile it appeared that this looting might spread to Liaoyang but, except for some looting of the canteen warehouse of the garrison, this threat did not materialize. In general, the life and property of Japanese residents in Liaoyang was not endangered.

By the time Soviet forces reached Liaoyang on 23 August, the division had completed disarmament procedures. On the evening of the 24th, all Japanese units in Liaoyang were ordered to march to Haicheng. The 60 kilometer day and night march by more than 10,000 officers and men, destitute of fighting spirit and arms, presented a pitiful sight. Escapes were numerous because of the lack of vigilance on the part of the Soviet escort force. The units arrived at Haicheng on 27 August.

The unity maintained up to this time began to crumble at Haicheng, and the semblance of an army organization gradually disappeared. Orders were not effectively carried out; everyone seemed totally engrossed in self-preservation. Morale among the soldiers was non-existent.

The units assembled at Haicheng and placed under the division's responsibility were:

>Liaoyang Officer and Noncommissioned Officer Training Unit
>372d Infantry Regiment
>Haicheng Military Police Squadron
>Tashihchiao Railway Station Command
>Tashihchiao Airfield Battalion
>Hsiungyuehcheng Airfield Battalion
>Kwantung Army Dog Unit.

Later, the Japanese units at Port Arthur and Dairen moved northward and also assembled at Haicheng, coming under division control. Among them were the Port Arthur Officer and Noncommissioned Officer Training Unit and the Dairen Branch of the Air Depot. Also at Haicheng were the Haicheng Military Hospital and the Port Arthur Military Hospital. These remained in the area after the division was moved to Soviet territory. They left some of their patients and medical personnel behind, but most of the hospital personnel were moved to Soviet Russia.

At Haicheng the main body of the division and the units under its control were organized into fifteen labor battalions of 1,000 men each, and one officer battalion. Soviet intentions were still obscure, but responsible Soviet officers officially stated that return to Japan might be possible by January. The majority of the internees sincerely believed this, and as though in confirmation, the first two or three battalions were transported south. Nearly all of the remaining battalions were transported north, however. Internees were nevertheless still firmly convinced of their imminent repatriation, believing in the propaganda that they would be sent home from Vladivostok Via Harbin and Mutanchiang. Thus, dreaming of repatriation to the last moment, they entered Soviet Russia.

The Situation at Chinhsien and at Jehol

Units assembled at Chinhsien were placed under the command of Lieutenant Colonel Inoue, Commander of the Airfield Battalion and concurrently commanding officer of the district. Like the units at Liaoyang, these units were also formed into labor battalions and sent to Soviet Russia. Prior to the arrival of the Soviet Army, the city had been in turmoil, and the life and property of Japanese residents had been endangered.

The Eighth Route Army, against which the division had engaged in guerrilla warfare, took severe measures in dealing with the troops assembled at Jehol, sending the main staffs to the Jehol prison. The Chinese later organized the Japanese units into labor battalions which were transported principally to Ulan Bator.

Japanese Residents, Families, and Land Development Groups

With the retreat of the Japanese Army, some Japanese residents withdrew to Chinhsien and some to Mukden. Approximately 500 remained at Jehol, and of these the women were reported to have suffered numerous injuries at the hands of the Eighth Route Army. Turmoil and uneasiness prevailed in Chinhsien because of the acts of the Eighth Route Army and the Manchurian rioters, but peace was gradually restored. The families of military personnel withdrew to Liaoyang, and later assembled at Haicheng.

Manchukuoan Government Agencies, Army, and Police

Because of the role of the Jehol Province Public Office in the guerrilla operations against the Eighth Route Army, it was taken over by the Chinese after the war. Prior to this, the deputy chief of the Office, Mr. Kishitani, together with his family, committed suicide. Other high ranking Japanese officials were taken prisoner.

The Fifth Army District of the Manchukuoan Army seemed to have collapsed with the surrender of Japanese forces. General Ho-Muhsia and his men, in an effort to reverse the tide, entrenched themselves in the mountains, but when their resources were exhausted the commander committed suicide. Japanese in the Manchukuoan Army disguised themselves as civilian residents, and fled to Mukden.

Two infantry regiments of the 1st Division of the Manchukuoan Army, stationed at the north barracks in Chinhsien, (although not under the command of the 108th Division) revolted immediately after the war ended and may have joined the Chinese Nationalist Army. (The other elements of this division, including its headquarters, had been transferred to Poli during June and July 1945) The fate of the police force is unknown. It was believed that it either disbanded or surrendered. Since it was a wing of the force used against the Eighth Route Army, it may have been subjected to reprisals.

Monograph No 155-J

CHAPTER X

The 136th Division[32]

Organization

The 136th Infantry Division was organized at Penchihu during the mass-mobilization of July 1945. Recruits obtained during this period provided the bulk of the division's strength, while the Penchihu Guard Unit served as the nucleus. Organization of the division was completed on 31 July.

Commanded by Lieutenant General Toru Nakayama, and deployed principally in Penchihu-Kungyuan area, the division consisted of the following components:

        Division Headquarters
        371st Infantry Regiment
        372d Infantry Regiment
        373d Infantry Regiment
        136th Field Artillery Regiment
        136th Engineer Regiment
        136th Transport Regiment
        Division Raiding Battalion
        Division Ordnance Duty Unit
        Division Signal Unit
        Division Veterinary Hospital
        Division Medical Unit*
        Division Gas Control Unit*
        1st Field Hospital*
        4th Field Hospital*
        Division Purification Unit*

   * Authorized but not formed

The manpower strength of the division on 31 July was only 9,000,

---

32. This section was prepared by Lieutenant Colonel Kensuke Nikaido, staff officer, 136th Division Headquarters.

or less than 60 per cent of the authorized 16,000. The division was not supplied with adequate quantities of horses, transport vehicles (wagons), motor trucks, engineer materials, nor of weapons, particulary rifles, heavy and light machineguns, and artillery guns. The number of rifles was so few that hand spears had to be issued as substitutes. Perhaps most distressing, in view of anticipated antitank operations, was the shortage of explosive charges.

Training in basic subjects was given even while the division was being organized. This was followed by training in antitank close-quarter attacks and bayonetting. To standardize training the division drafted a set of training instructions, but was unable to have it printed prior to the outbreak of hostilities.

As for fortifications, the division was directed by Third Area Army to survey sites in the Penchihu and Kungyuan sectors with a view to improving semi-permanent fortifications there, and to draw up plans accordingly. These surveys were made and plans submitted. But the Area Army, although it shipped some construction materials, was indecisive about approving the plans.

Opening of Hostilities

At 0600 on 9 August, the chief of staff, Colonel Sueharu Ijichi, learned from a radio broadcast that the Soviet Union had entered the war. At 0800 the division was ordered by the Third Area Army Commander to move its main body to Mukden for the defense of that city. The division commander promptly sent an advance party to

MONOGRAPH NO. 155-J
MAP NO. 1

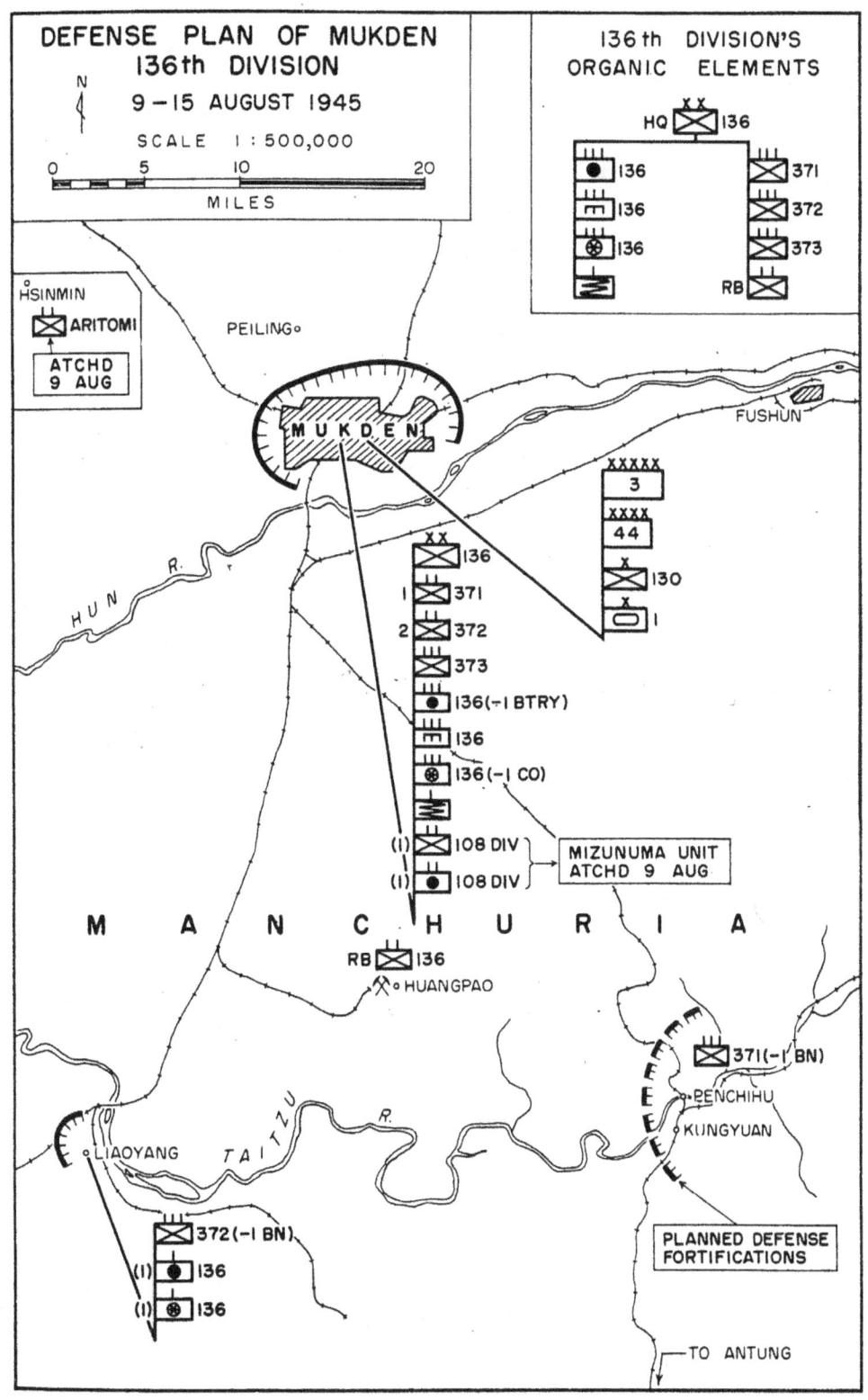

Mukden, and alerted the main body of the division. At the same time he ordered the raiding battalion to move to Huangpao, and the 372d Regiment (less the 2d Battalion) with supporting units to proceed to Liaoyang, about 60 kilometers south of Mukden. On the evening of the 9th, units began leaving Penchihu and Kungyuan, and by the morning of the 10th the moves were completed.

Meanwhile, on 9 August, Third Area Army reinforced the division by attaching the Aritomi Raiding Unit and the Mizunuma Unit. The Aritomi force was an infantry battalion directly under the Area Army and commanded by Lieutenant Colonel Aritomi; after attachment to the division, it remained at Hsinmin, about 50 kilometers west of Mukden. The Mizunuma Unit consisted of an infantry battalion and an artillery battalion of the 108th Division; it joined the division's main body in Mukden on 10 August. (See Map No 1)

The Area Army plan was to meet the Soviet forces along the Hsinking-Mukden segment of the Dairen-Hsinking Railroad. Therefore, the division at once undertook the construction of field fortification around Mukden, but in doing so ran into some problems relative to the type of fortifications. The Area Army's fortification plan for Mukden in effect up to this time was called "Nago," and stipulated that defenses be constructed of concrete and steel. Upon the outbreak of hostilities, the Area Army, in view of the urgency of the situation, hastily revised this plan and prescribed that the fortifications be constructed of wood instead of the more durable materials in order to hasten completion. The division commander requested that the original "Nago" plan be implemented, but the Area Army commander rejected his request on the grounds that this would be impracticable under the urgent circumstances. It was finally decided to start work in accordance with the revision and to reduce the radius of the fortification area.[33]

The construction of antitank obstacles along the main roads leading to Mukden was begun on 11 August, as was also the construction of firing positions in the suburbs and the open areas of the city. Third Area Army gave the division commander the additional duty of commander of the Mukden Defense Sector, and for this purpose placed all units and military offices in the Mukden area under his jurisdiction. On 12 August the Area Army assigned a second staff officer to General Nakayama's staff in view of the additional load.[34]

On 13 August, Third Area Army decided that the Penchihu sector should be defended after all, and ordered the division to start works on the fortifications in that sector according to earlier plans. The division immediately sent the 371st Regiment (less the 1st Battalion) back to Penchihu. There, the regiment was assisted by the employees of the Penchihu Steel Works and the local inhabitants in the preparation of defense positions.

---

33. The Area Army Commander also had a disagreement with the commander of the 148th Division regarding fortifications in the Hsinking area. See sub-Monograph No 155-C.
34. See note on staff officers in Chart No 1, Monograph 155-B. (following page 19)

End of Hostilities

At about 1600 hours on 14 August the division received a cease-fire order from the Area Army, and transmitted the order first to the Aritomi Raiding Unit in Hsinmin and then to other elements. At about 2100 hours, however, it received a telephone message countermanding the previous order and directing the resumption of fighting. After transmitting the second message, the division learned that an important broadcast concerning the cease-fire would be made at noon on 15 August. The division headquarters listened to this broadcast, in which the Emperor announced Japan's surrender, and immediately suspended all operational actions. In the immediate post-hostilities period it discharged, in two increments, all personnel who had been drafted in Manchuria.

At about 1700 hours on 19 August, elements of the main body of the division, beginning with division headquarters, surrendered their weapons to the Soviet forces. Earlier, Soviet army representatives had declared that each unit would be permitted to retain one-third of its weapons in order to maintain order. At the time weapons were being turned over, however, the Soviet reduced this percentage to between one-fifth and one-tenth.

At noon of 20 August, the division commander was taken to the Mukden airfield under the pretext that he was to meet a certain Soviet general. Other Japanese generals in the Mukden area were also taken there. All disappeared into Soviet territory.

The Soviet Army ordered all units in Mukden to move to an area about 30 kilometers north of the city on 20 August. The division began moving during the afternoon, and by the following afternoon had assembled in the vicinity of Kuchengtzu. There it remained for about fifteen days. Meanwhile the shortage of provisions began to be felt, and the number of deserters increased. On about 10 September, the division was moved to the Internment Camp in Peiling.

The Soviet authorities at Peiling directed that Japanese units be formed into labor battalions of 1,500 men each. In mid-September the 32d, 33d and 34th Labor Battalions were formed from the main body of the division and were transferred to Soviet Russia. Field grade officers of division headquarters and Major Harada, commander of the transport regiment, were formed into a separate unit and sent to Morshansk Camp, about 250 kilometers southeast of Moscow. They were detained there, engaged in labor tasks, until 10 May 1948.

The units in Liaoyang were placed into labor battalions formed at Haicheng, and were likewise sent to Soviet Russia. The commander of the 372d Regiment and field grade officers, plus some of the men, were placed in an officer battalion formed in Haicheng, and were also sent to the Morshansk Camp.

Monograph No 155-K

CHAPTER XI

The Fourth Army[35]

Assumption of Responsibility for Northern Manchuria

Early in 1945 Kwantung Army Headquarters began considering a change in the strategical plan for Manchuria. In March it rushed a plan to Imperial General Headquarters, providing for delaying operations in the border areas, and a last-ditch stand in the mountainous area astride the Manchuria-Korea border--an area more or less enclosed by the Hsinking-Tumen and the Hsinking-Dairen railway lines. Meanwhile, pending approval of the plan, Kwantung Army ordered a re-disposition of major subordinate commands.

The re-disposition was carried out during May. Third Area Army which while responsible for northern Manchuria had maintained its headquarters at Tsitsihar, moved south to Mukden to take up its new responsibilities in southcentral and southwestern Manchuria. Fourth Army which while under Third Area Army had been responsible for the area adjacent to the Amur River and had maintained its headquarters at Sunwu, was given responsibility for most of the northern provinces formerly under Third Area Army, and moved its headquarters south to

---

35. This section was prepared by Colonel Kenjiro Kaneko, senior adjutant of Fourth Army.

MONOGRAPH NO 155-K
MAP NO. 1

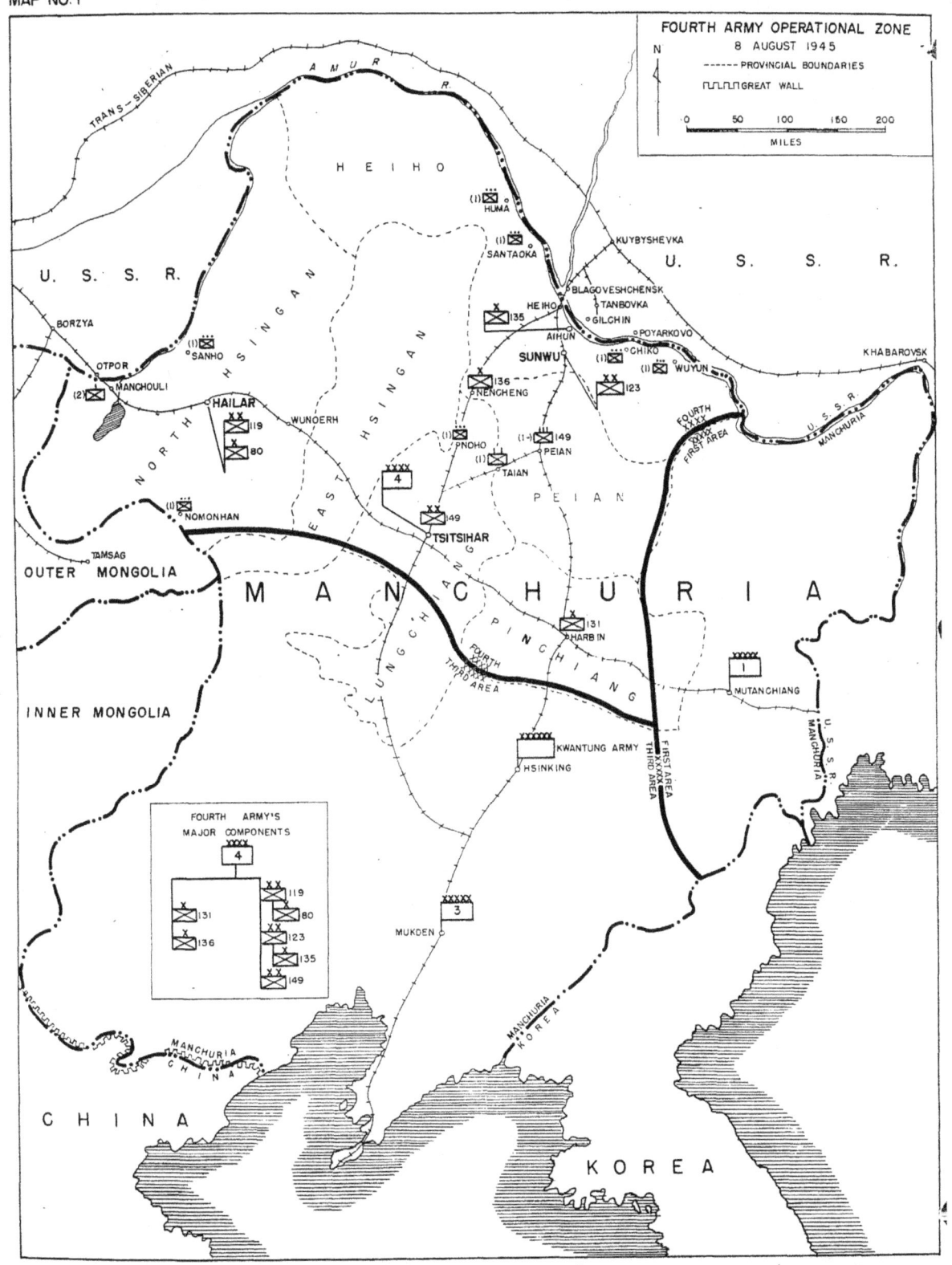

Tsitsihar in mid-May. Specifically, Fourth Army retained responsibility for Hieho Province and Peian Province, and was given jurisdiction additionally over almost all of North Hsingan Province and East Hsingan Province, the northern half of Lungchiang Province, and the greater part of Pinchiang Province. Thus, to the Amur River front which Fourth Army formerly held, was added responsibility over northern part of the Greater Hsingan Mountain Range in the northwestern provinces. (See Map No 1)

At the same time, the strength of Fourth Army was augmented and it was placed directly under Kwantung Army, becoming one of the three major subordinate commands in Manchuria. It was commanded by Lieutenant General Mikio Uemura.

Geographical Characteristics

The most predominant terrain features in northern Manchuria are the Greater Hsingan Mountains (1,200 to 1,700 meters) on the west and the Lesser Hsingan Mountains (600 to 800 meters) on the east. These two ranges join in the far north to form an inverted V. The mountainous areas are densely forested with pines, birch, and willow. Where the inverted V opens, the great central plain begins. To the west of the Greater Hsingan Mountains, Manchuria forms a salient into Outer Mongolia; the terrain of the salient is characterized by a desert-like plateau.

The strategic points of entry into northern Manchuria from Siberia were Heiho and Manchouli, the railroad termini in Manchuria in the northeast and northwest, respectively, both of which were linked with Soviet lines. In the interior, the major cities are Hailar, Tsitsihar, Harbin (the largest), and Peian, each an important rail and communication center. The strategic trans-Manchurian rail line ran through Fourth Army's area, as did also two north-south lines which converged at Heiho near the northern border.

Fourth Army thus had the area with the longest uninterrupted border contiguous to Soviet territory. It had two major geographical salients into Soviet territory, one in the north and one in the west, and each of these salients was vulnerable to penetration at points of entry on both sides of the salients' necks.

The Defense Plan

Fourth Army viewed the defense of its area in two parts: the Amur River front and the Greater Hsingan Mountain Range front. On the Amur River front, an enemy penetrating the Heiho area could advance southward along the two railroads and the parallel road routes. The plan called for the garrison units disposed along the river bank to obstruct the enemy crossing of the river. Thereafter, the enemy advancing along the Heiho-Peian axis was to be checked at defense positions near Sunwu, and the enemy advancing along the Heiho-Erhchan-Nencheng-Tsitsihar axis was to be checked to the Erhchan area and again in the Nencheng area.

On the western front where the enemy was expected to advance along the Manchouli-Hailar-Wunoerh-Pokotu axis, a force deployed

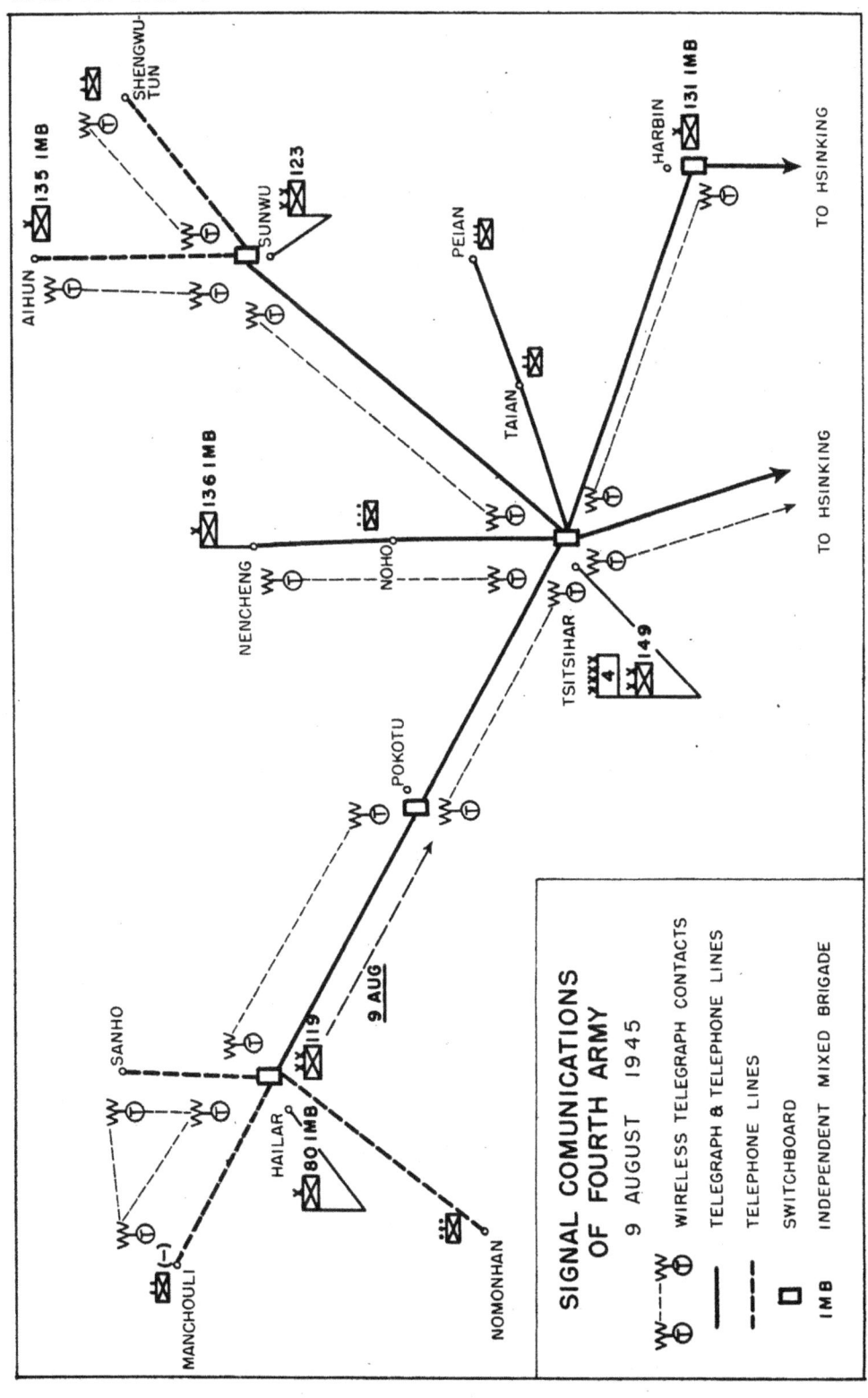

in positions in the Hailar area was to check the enemy advance as long as possible; thereafter, a defense in depth was to be carried out in the mountain fortifications near Wunoerh, with the Pokotu sector as the rear line. (Sketch No 1 shows signal communication network of Fourth Army).

Fortifications

Most of the operational preparations made in earlier years had been intended for offensive or holding operations, and were not adequate for delaying operations with reduced troop strengths. This was especially the case with fortifications. Therefore the Army planned to construct new fortifications and to remodel certain of the old fortifications to meet the needs of the delaying plan. Work on this was to start in the middle of May.

On the Amur River front, a revision in the organization of positions in the vicinity of Sunwu was planned so that the sector north of Sunwu could be defended independently by one division. Other planned construction on this front included new positions in the vicinity of Erhchan for two infantry battalions and one artillery battalion.

On the western front, positions at Wunoerh had been under construction by the Kwantung Army since 1943. Since these were huge positions designed for use by about three divisions, plans were made to reduce their size so that they could be used by one division, and to increase them in depth. In the interior, positions were to be constructed for troops deployed in the vicinities of Tsitsihar and Nencheng.

Work on these construction projects did not progress according to schedule. Principally responsible for the delay was the shortage of materials, aggravated by the reduced capabilities of construction crews--which included officers and NCOs--resulting from reorganization of some units and the transfer of others. After the Soviet build-up in the Far East began, the Army Commander attempted to accelerate the construction program, but by the time the war started only field fortifications had been constructed. In the areas occupied by units organized in July, furthermore, only preparatory reconnaissance of terrain had been made.

Intelligence

Intelligence gathering agencies were instructed to seek principally information of the following types:

> Activities of Soviet forces, changes in disposition, and especially indications of an offensive.
>
> Traffic situation along the segment of the Trans-Siberian Railway that paralleled the Amur River.
>
> Modifications in Soviet fortification installations.
>
> Changes in the attitude of the local population.

To gather intelligence, three principal means were employed: ground observation (by military units at Sunwu, Hailar, and along the border, and by Manchurian border police units); investigations (by special service agencies at Heiho, Hailar, and Tsitsihar, and military police units at Sunwu, Hailar and Tsitsihar); radio listening posts (including the deciphering of wireless messages) of the Sunwu and Hailar branches of the Kwantung Army Special Intelligence Unit.

Within Manchuria, the main intelligence sought related to the surveillance of the speech and behavior of inhabitants in the border zones, and the search for spies particularly in the vicinities of Peian, Manchouli, Pokotu, and Chalantun.

Furthermore, each front was assigned specific intelligence gathering missions. The Sunwu front was directed to report the volume of traffic on east-bound trains of the Trans-Siberian, including movements over the Blagoveshchensk and Tambovka branch lines, and also to keep under surveillance the fortification installations in the vicinities of Blagoveshchensk and Poyarkovo, changes of troop strength in those vicinities and near Gilchin, and any concentration of river-crossing equipment. The Hailar front was directed to report on concentration of troops in the vicinities of Borzya and Nomonhan, changes in the installations in the vicinity of Otpor, rail operations over the Mongolian (Borzya-Tamsag) Branch Line, and any troop concentrations along the Outer Mongolia border.

Furthermore, Fourth Army cautioned all border garrison units to avoid acts that might provoke the Soviets. As the danger of Soviet intervention became more and more imminent, the Army tightened border defense measures, and sent intelligence officers to the border areas with instructions to alert the units to report even the slightest indications of Soviet intentions.

Training

Training was limited to those subjects directly relating to military operations. Special emphasis was placed on improving the leadership abilities of junior leaders. Since the combat effectiveness of all units had declined as a result of reorganizations and transfers, the Army attempted to restore the fighting capabilities of its units by conducting unit training and by holding field exercises in close-quarter fighting. Furthermore, it established a special training center at Tsitsihar to give training to personnel of rear units, since even they could expect to engage the enemy.

Reorganization

During June and July, numerous changes were made in the organization of Fourth Army. Some units were transferred, some disbanded, and several new units were organized. In early June the 125th Division at Shanshenfu was transferred to Tunghua, and on the 18th the 12th Field Transport Headquarters and the 82d Independent Motor Transport Battalion were transferred to the Seventeenth Area Army in Korea.

The following units were disbanded in order to form larger tactical units: the 5th and 6th Border Garrison Units, the 104th Guard Unit Headquarters, and the 76th Line of Communications Guard Unit. New units organized during July were:

        149th Division
        131st, 135th, and 136th Ind Mixed Brigades
        Kwantung Army 3d Special Guard Unit
        12th Raiding Unit
        102d Guard Unit Headquarters
        One special guard battalion
        Eleven special guard companies
        Two special guard engineer units

Status of Preparations

In almost every command, the unit commanders up to and including those of battalion level were draftees, with little or no combat experience. Many of the battalion commanders were too young for their commands. Most of the troops also were draftees, mobilized in Manchuria; many of them were old or physically unfit. Since the training period was short, their fighting capabilities had not been developed.

At the time the war started the division and the brigades formed in July had about two-thirds of their authorized strength; some of the draftees were still en route to join their units.

Fourth Army's units were in no better shape as regards supplies and equipment. In general, Fourth Army's stocks of provisions and ammunition (except antitank explosives) were adequate, but the stockpiling of these supplies in fortified positions where they were most needed lagged behind schedule.

The 149th Division and the 131st, 135th, and 136th Brigades, organized in July, were extremely short of arms and equipment; the 149th Division, for example, did not have a single artillery piece.

MONOGRAPH NO. 155-K
MAP NO. 2

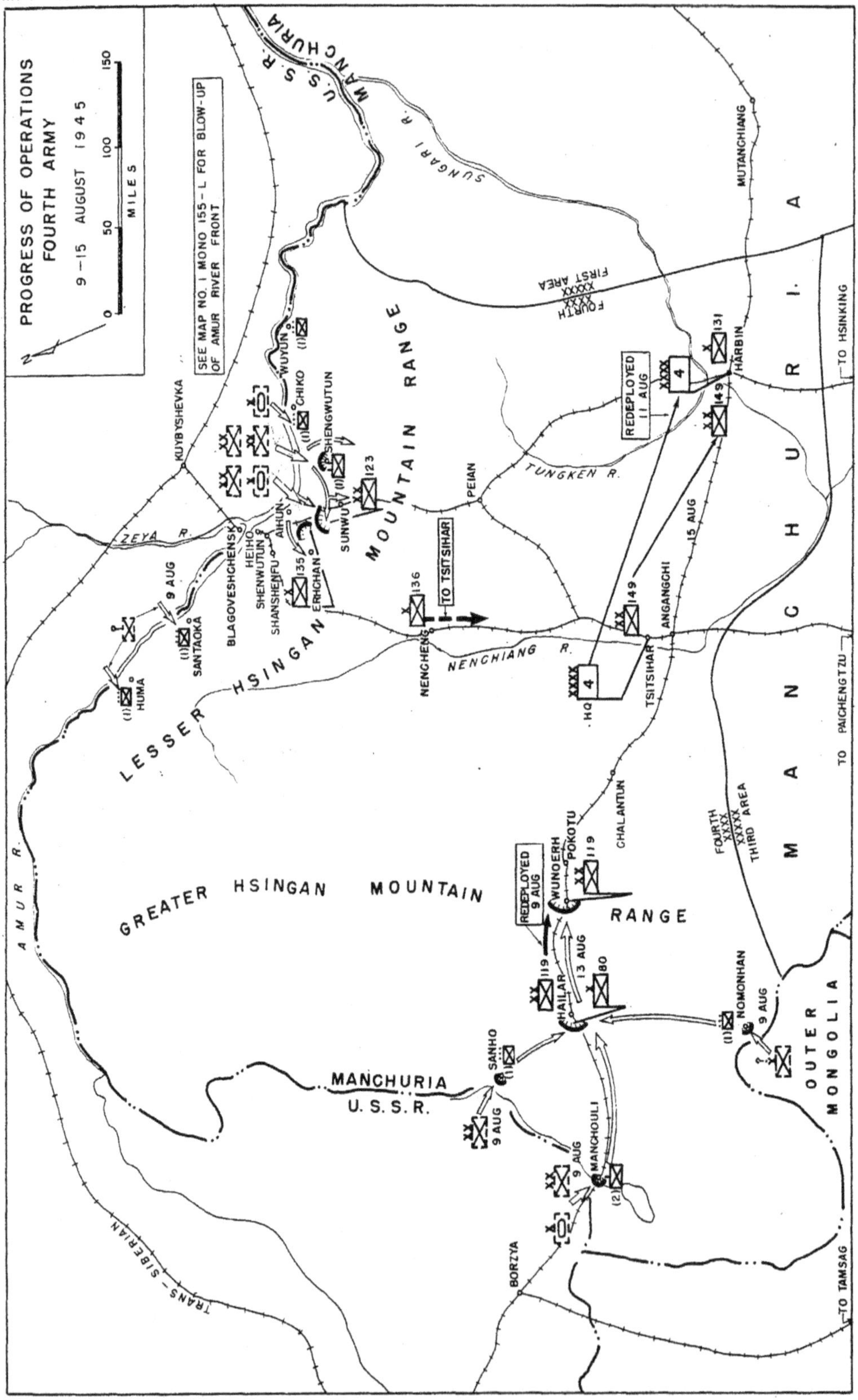

(ORIGINAL MAP RF – 1: 4,000,000)

The comparatively older 119th and 123d Divisions, however, had almost their complete authorizations of arms and equipment, although they lacked infantry heavy weapons and grenade launchers. The shortages of weapons had the effect of reducing the fighting capacity of each division to that of an infantry regiment.

Although operational preparations were started in earnest about the middle of May when Fourth Army's jurisdictional area was expanded, by the beginning of August they were still inadequate. The Army commander attempted to accelerate these preparations, anticipating an imminent Soviet invasion, but progress was repeatedly hindered. The major hindrances in all areas were the frequent transfers of personnel and units, the dispositional changes that had to be made each time new units were organized, the shortages of fortification equipment and materials, the inadequate transport facilities, and the decline in the quality of officers and noncommissioned officers. Even in the vicinity of Sunwu, where the progress of fortifications work was most remarkable, by the beginning of August, only field fortifications had been completed, and underground construction had just been begun.

Outbreak of Hostilities   (See Map No 2)

Before dawn on 9 August, Army Headquarters was notified by Kwantung Army of the Soviet invasion of Manchuria. The Army commander immediately notified all subordinate commands, ordering them to put their pre-arranged emergency plans into effect. At the Army

Headquarters, a check of personnel showed that about one-fourth of the officers were on duty at the time. (Headquarters had been operating during the preceding week on an around-the-clock schedule, fearing that war was imminent.)

Reports from the border indicated that Soviet armored units had carried out simultaneous invasions of the Manchouli area and along the Outer Mongolia border in general before dawn of 9 August, and were advancing toward Hailar. In the Amur River area, reports indicated, the Soviets had not yet begun to cross the river.

A log of some of the actions taken by Army headquarters from the beginning to the end of the war follows:

9 August

1. Command post established in the elm grove within the headquarters compound.
2. Preparations made to receive and quarter families expected to withdraw from the Hailar area.

10 August

1. Preparations made to move command post to site of former ordnance depot northwest of Tsitsihar, in view of enemy bombings.
2. At night, headquarters received Kwantung Army's orders to move to Harbin.

11 August

1. Headquarters made preparations to move to Harbin.
2. Headquarters decided to permit families to accompany personnel during move.
3. Loading started in the evening for rail transportation. Entraining hindered by enemy aircraft carrying out night bombings.

12 August

1. Entraining continued during morning.
2. Army commander and key staff officers departed for Harbin by plane during morning.
3. Army headquarters established at Pinchiang (Province) Defense Headquarters (131st Independent Mixed Brigade Headquarters) in Harbin.

13 August

1. Pinchiang Defense Command directed by Army Headquarters to organize positions to defend Harbin.
2. Army Headquarters moved to site of former division headquarters in Harbin.

14 August

1. Signal communications with front-line units and with Kwantung Army Headquarters deteriorated.
2. Main body 149th Division ordered to move to Harbin (it arrived at 1600 on 15 August). The 136th Independent Mixed Brigade was ordered to leave Nencheng and go to Tsitsihar.
3. Army Headquarters ordered each unit under its direct command to organize a raiding force to cope with the advancing enemy.
4. Reserve officer candidates who had been training at Hsinking arrived at Harbin en route to parent units. About 700 or 800, unable to return to their units, were attached directly to the Army. (See below for movement order to Meihokou).

15 August

1. Army headquarters learned of the termination of the war at noon through a broadcast by His Majesty the Emperor.
2. Four sentries and one NCO of Army Headquarters committed suicide. Five other soldiers and one officer also committed suicide. Similar incidents reported in various units.

Situation in Forward Areas (See also Monographs 155-L and 155-M)[36]

On the night of 9 August, a powerful enemy infantry element of about battalion size carried out preliminary assaults across the Amur River at Huma and Santaoka, where small elements of the 135th Brigade were deployed for defense. The enemy quickly overran these positions.

The major enemy crossing of the Amur began on the night of the 10th and continued until the 11th. With approximately three enemy infantry divisions and two armored brigades massed north of the river, the enemy made three major crossings: at Aihun, Shengwutun, and Chiko. The crossing at Aihun was followed on the night of the 11th by attacks against the permanent fortifications which had been prepared by the 6th Border Garrison Unit before its disbandment. The main body of the 135th Brigade, then manning this area, repulsed this attack. Without continuing this assault on the Aihun positions the enemy's main force, with a strength of approximately one infantry division and one armored brigade, advanced on the Erhchan sector. Meanwhile, however, it sent approximately one regiment to hammer at the southwestern front positions of the 135th Brigade continuously from the 12th until the 14th. The brigade successfully repulsed

---

36. No detailed monograph is available on operations of the 80th Independent Mixed Brigade and the 119th Division in the Manchouli-Sanho-Hailar-Nomonhan (northwest) area.

these attacks.

Because of the disruption of communications with Sunwu, the cease-fire order did not reach the brigade until the 20th when it was delivered by a liaison officer of the 123d Division. The brigade terminated operations on the 21st.

The enemy crossing at Shengwutun was opposed by one battalion of the 123d Division. This battalion resisted stubbornly until the night of the 14th, when enemy tanks succeeded in getting through gaps in its positions. Meanwhile, the 123d Division's main body, which had taken up positions on the northern side of Sunwu, was attacked on its southeastern sector on 15 August by the enemy tank force that had penetrated the Shengwutun defenses. The division prepared to launch a night attack against the enemy concentrated in the vicinity of Sunwu airfield, but the cease-fire order intervened.

Meanwhile, in the vicinity of Nencheng, the main body of the 136th Independent Mixed Brigade (organized at the end of July) had taken up defense positions. On the 14th, Army Headquarters ordered this brigade to withdraw to Tsitsihar. The war ended while the brigade was enroute.

On Fourth Army's western front, the garrison unit at Manchouli was taken by surprise by the Soviet invasion on 9 August. It fought desperately as it retreated toward Hailar, meanwhile, suffering heavy losses.

At the permanent fortifications in the Hailar sector the 80th Independent Mixed Brigade fought an all-out engagement with the enemy advancing from the Manchouli and Sanho sectors.

The 119th Division, which had been deployed in the Hailar positions, immediately upon the outbreak of hostilities began withdrawing its main body by rail to the Wunoerh positions. On the 13th, the enemy confronted outpost positions in this sector, and, when the war ended was engaging the defenders.

The units in the Harbin area at the end of the war were, besides Army headquarters, the main body of the 149th Division, the 131st Brigade, an artillery unit under the Army's direct command, and various rear echelon units. None of these units engaged in battle.

Estimated losses in the Shengwutun sector were 500 killed, and in the Aihun and Erhchan sectors about 500 killed or wounded. In the Manchouli Area, about 200 were killed. In the Hailar area about 1,000 troops were killed in action and in the Wunoerh area about 1,250.

Meanwhile, on 14 August, Fourth Army received orders from Kwantung Army to redeploy its main body to Meihokou to take charge of the defense of the redoubt in the mountains astride the Manchurian-Korea border. The Thirtieth Army, previously designated as the redoubt defense force, had been pulled out by the Third Area Army commander on the 10th to defend Hsinking. Kwantung Army's instructions relative to Fourth Army redeployment were neither coherent nor realistic. Elements in the Hailar, Wunoerh, and Sunwu areas, which were then being engaged by the enemy, were to remain in place. Kwantung Army failed to clarify measures regarding the control of these units, and it would be difficult for Fourth Army (almost 1,000 kilometers away) to do so by remote control, especially in view of poor communication facilities.

Termination of Hostilities

Although Army Headquarters heard the broadcast of the Imperial Rescript on 15 August, it still had not received cease-fire orders from Kwantung Army. Consequently, it took no steps to stop hostilities. However, it did decide to move the Headquarters to Meihokou, in accordance with Kwantung Army orders. Soon after departing Harbin, while at the Pingfang railway station, headquarters received orders to return to Harbin; it returned on the afternoon of the 17th. Headquarters personnel observed numerous red flags displayed along the railway, and could hear intermittent rifle fire.

On 18 August a Soviet delegation led by a lieutenant general arrived at the Harbin airfield in two planes. They were met by the Fourth Army Commander, chief of staff, and senior staff officer; cease-fire negotiations were opened immediately. Also attending were the governor of Pinchiang Province and the chief of the Harbin Special Service Agency, Major General Akikusa.

The Soviet negotiators required that the various units of Fourth Army be assembled at Hailar, Chalantun, Tsitsihar, Aihun, Sunwu, Peian, or Harbin, for disarmament. Army Headquarters was ordered to move to the suburbs of Harbin and occupy the barracks of the railway regiment. The 149th Division was to assemble at the Lichiatun barracks, and other units in the outskirts of the city.

The Soviet lieutenant general departed for Khabarovsk in the evening, leaving his party at the Yamato Hotel, where negotiations were continued.

Meanwhile, the Soviets detained General Akikusa at the Yamato Hotel for interrogation, and required that Japanese officers conversant with the Russian language be furnished as interpreters.

On the 20th Soviet authorities began to commandeer Japanese motor vehicles, and on the same day transported all general officers in the Harbin area to Soviet territory by plane. On the 21st, disarmament began.

On 23 August troops in the Harbin area began moving to internment camps. The first echelon, consisting of personnel of Army Headquarters and of the main body of the 149th Division, was transported by rail via Acheng to Hengtaohotzu. From there the troops were marched toward Hailin. En route they were robbed by Soviet soldiers. After arriving at Hailin on the 27th, they were interned at the ordnance depot there.

In the internment camp at Hailin were assembled about 40,000 men of Fourth and Fifth Army units, plus between 20,000 and 30,000 Japanese civilians. Because the camp had earlier been set afire only a few facilities remained to provide shelter against the elements. The administration of the camp and negotiations with Soviet authorities were handled by Fourth Army Headquarters personnel.

During the move to Hailin, and after the arrival there, many persons who had misgivings about their future escaped; quite a number were shot by Soviet sentries while attempting to escape.

In mid-September, several labor battalions of 1,000 men each were formed and sent to Soviet territory. The remaining prisoners were moved to Mutanchiang on 13 October. During the early part of November, additional labor battalions were formed and sent to the USSR. Officers were organized into two battalions and sent to European Russia. The aged and sick were formed into two rehabilitation battalions of 700 to 800 men each, and were interned at the former Mutanchiang Hospital.

Civil Affairs

In general, Japanese residents actively cooperated with the Army before the termination of the war. In the face of the unexpected defeat and with the loss of protection by the Army, they were stunned. As they had never met the bitter experience of defeat, many did not foresee the miseries to come, and hence felt their destitution keenly.

At Harbin and Tsitsihar Japanese residents fared somewhat better. Relatively large numbers of them had lived there for many years, and in the early post-war days they formed "residents' associations" and were able to lead comparatively peaceful lives. At other places, however, Japanese civilians were reduced to a miserable plight.

Japanese land development groups, who had settled in remote areas and along the borders, had difficulty evacuating. Their situation was aggravated by the fact that they consisted mainly of women and children since nearly all men in their prime had been drafted. These helpless groups lost many of their aged and their children during the evacuation, and were also attacked by Manchurians. Many who succeeded in reaching Harbin and other cities in the interior eventually succumbed to starvation or disease.

The pitiful condition of refugees in the areas of Harbin, Hengtaohotzu, Hailin, Mutanchiang, and intermediate areas, was particularly unbearable to witness. Their miseries, as reported by refugees interned in Hailin, were simply appalling. Some of the land development people in the border areas were either unable to evacuate, or abandoned any idea of doing so. One incident was reported of a woman in Heiho who killed two Soviet soldiers with a bamboo spear and then committed suicide together with her two children.

Manchukuoan Government agencies cooperated fully with the Army. These agencies included the Tsitsihar Municipal Office, the Pinchiang Provincial Government (at Harbin), various other municipal officers, and also the railway authorities. A number of Japanese officials serving with these agencies committed suicide at the end of the war.

The Manchukuoan Army showed great unrest from the moment the Soviets entered the war. It was kept under close surveillance, but units at Harbin, Hulan, Shuangcheng, and Angangchi, revolted. The Manchukuoan police force was more cooperative than the army.

Manchurian civilians generally remained indifferent until the cease-fire order, after which they abruptly became pro-Russian and strongly anti-Japanese. However, after the behavior of the Soviets was increasingly manifested during the occupation by acts of looting and raping on the part of both officers and men, the Manchurians, remembering the relatively equable conduct of the Japanese Army, developed a hatred of the Soviets. This was typified in the fact that they called a Soviet captain "Wangpatan" (Chinese for "wicked fool"), instead of "Kapitan."

Korean civilians for the most part were strongly anti-Japanese. They contributed to the general post-war demoralization by freely spreading rumors. However, many Koreans knew the truth about the Soviet forces, and these harbored friendly feeling towards the Japanese forces. Korean soldiers serving in Japanese units were generally malicious.

Although nothing unusual had been noted in the attitude of the Russians living in Harbin at the beginning of the war, as soon as the Soviet occupation began, they suddenly unmasked themselves to show their anti-Japanese attitude. However, many Russians in the vicinity of Hengtaohotzu and in the areas along the Harbin-Mutanchiang railway were generally friendly.

Monograph No 155-L

CHAPTER XII

The 123d Division[37]

Organization

The 123d Division was organized on 10 March 1945 at Sunwu in Heiho Province, with the 78th Independent Mixed Brigade as its nucleus; recruits fleshed out the division and provided the bulk of its strength. The maximum strength reached by the division was 18,000. It was commanded by Lieutenant General Teijiro Kitazawa, and was assigned to the Fourth Army which at the time was responsible only for the Amur River front.

Components of the division, and their commanders, were:

>268th Regiment, Colonel Takasuke Yamanaka
>269th Regiment, Colonel Sampei Goto
>270th Regiment, Colonel Kiichi Ota
>123d Field Artillery Regiment, Lt Col Kensuke Machida
>123d Transport Regiment, Major Takeo Abe
>123d Engineer Regiment, Major Fumio Hirokawa
>Raiding Battalion,[38] Major Jinzo Tsuyuki
>Division Signal Unit, Captain Yoshio Hasegawa
>Ordnance Duty Unit, Captain Goichi Shimizu
>Veterinary Depot, (Chief) Captain Yoshinari Kashimoto

Training

Before being beset by transfers and replacements, the division was able to carry out an extensive training program. Based on its

---

37. The information in this chapter was furnished by Colonel Yutaka Tsuchida, chief of staff, 123d Division.
38. The raiding battalion was not organized until late June. It had a strength of 1,113.

anticipated defense mission, it conducted training in defensive warfare, with emphasis on fighting from prepared positions, on antitank close-quarter fighting, on hand-to-hand fighting, on infantry heavy weapons firing, antitank artillery firing, as well as on training in communications and in fortifications work.

For training in defensive operations from prepared positions the division permitted units to enter the fortified zone forward of Sunwu, theretofore an off-limits zone. Each unit conducted realistic training in the positions which they were to use during actual operations.

Some phases of training were stipulated by Fourth Army Headquarters, which ordered the 123d Division, together with the 125th Division, to hold demonstrations in platoon defensive operations, antitank operations, and meeting engagements. These exercises were conducted principally for the benefit of officers of both divisions, and were highly instructive, particularly to officers of poor quality.

Close-quarter antitank training was given to all personnel; the division commander himself participated in it. During this training the commander periodically inspected each unit. His presence greatly stimulated the program.

Training in hand-to-hand fighting was also prescribed by higher headquarters as a result of the battle lessons of the war in the Pacific. Special emphasis was placed on bayonetting, with swords as well as bayonets. Both the Army and the division, in compliance with instructions from Kwantung Army, held fencing and bayonetting tournaments and obtained highly satisfactory results from this type of training.

The weakest aspect of the division's training was in communications and in the firing of infantry heavy weapons. To remedy this the division consistently stressed communications, holding frequent inspections to assure the attainment of skill in this field. Moreover, because of the importance of employing artillery as antitank weapons, thorough training was given in this subject, particularly as regards artillery-infantry teamwork.

Training in the construction of fortifications work was an important item of the division's operational preparations, and one that was to consume much time. Since a general knowledge of this work was lacking, the Army built a model defense position in the Sunwu vicinity, which served as an instructional aid. Utilizing this model, the 123d Division trained its own troops so thoroughly that when fortifications construction was actually begun, hardly any difficulty was encountered.

For about a month and a half after its organization, the division was able to make substantial progress in achieving organizational unity and in its training program. Thereafter, however, it was continuously beset with problems incident to transferring personnel to newly formed units in Manchuria, and training recruits who arrived as replacements. The result was that the division's unity was repeatedly weakened, and it gradually became more and more difficult to control units, to conduct training, and to construct fortifications. Furthermore, the efficiency of the officers and men, and the fighting capacity of the division as a whole declined.

Operational Preparations

With the transfer of Fourth Army Headquarters from Sunwu to Tsitsihar in the middle of May to assume control of all of northern Manchuria, the division's responsibility was expanded. It was given control over Fourth Army's ordnance depot and supply depots in the Sunwu area, and its volume of work increased sharply.

The frequent changes in personnel prevented the division from formulating an operations plan; consequently, it tentatively adopted the plan of the former 78th Brigade. This included the use of fortifications along the Amur River, which consisted of field fortifications in the vicinities of Chiko, Shengwutun, Aihun, and Shenwutun, and concrete permanent-type fortifications north of Sunwu. These fortifications, however, had been constructed for offensive operations and were to be manned by a force much larger than a division. Hence they were not suitable for the delaying operations plan of Kwantung Army nor for the reduced strength; besides, they were outmoded.

The principal traffic network in the division's area consisted of the Heiho-Sunwu-Peian railroad, and the dirt road paralleling it. No provision had been made for the defense of these arteries against air attack, although for defense against ground attack concrete pillboxes had been constructed near the main bridges. However, during peacetime these pillboxes were not manned.

In June and July the division's responsibility was again expanded. After the departure of the 125th Division to the Tunghua area in early June, the division was given responsibility for the Shenwutun area. In July, the 135th Independent Mixed Brigade was organized at Aihun[39] with the 6th Border Garrison Unit as its nucleus, and was assigned to the division. Thus the defense sector of the division was considerably enlarged; it extended along the Amur River from the area north of Heiho to the area east of Chiko. To facilitate control, the division commander made the brigade responsible for the Shenwutun area vacated by the 125th Division in addition to the Aihun area. Upon receiving these orders, the brigade promptly dispatched one infantry battalion to guard the sector north of Heiho.

Meanwhile, the division ordered the 269th Regiment at Peian to move up to Sunwu, and made several other redispositions to conform to the objectives of Fourth Army's operational plan, which called for initial resistance in the river bank area, principally at the

---

39. The city of Aihun enjoyed a brief period of fame in the nineteenth century. By the Treaty of Aihun (Aigun), 1858 China ceded to Russia the north bank of the Amur River.

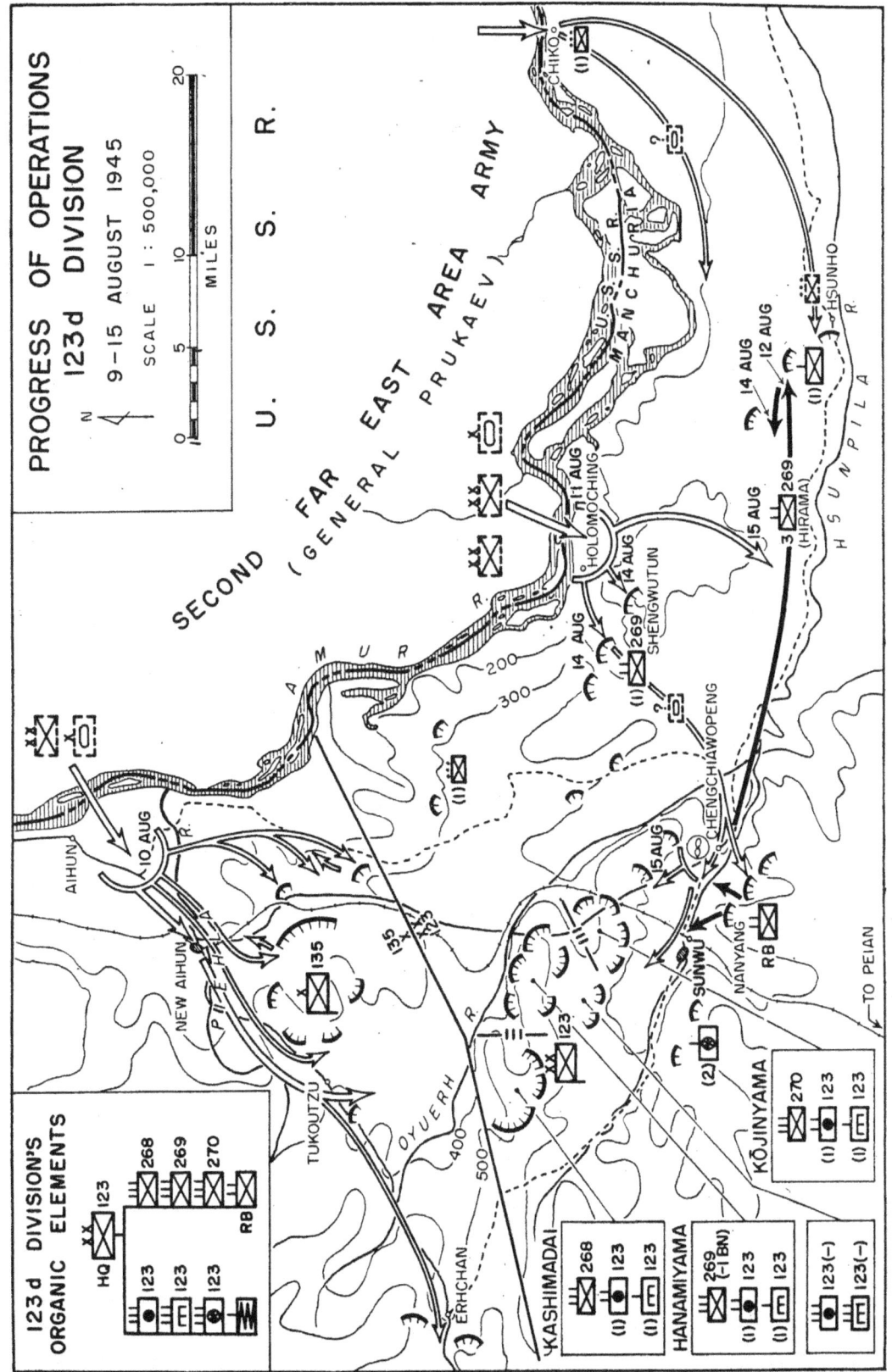

positions south of Aihun and at Shengwutun, and major resistance in the main positions in the hilly Sunwu area to the rear. The river guard units east of Chiko were reduced to lookout posts; at Chiko itself only one platoon was retained. The force at Hsunho was increased to company size, less one platoon. The strength of the Shengwutun garrison (one battalion of the 269th Regiment which moved up from Peian) was not reduced, since this was considered an important advance defense position. This regiment consisted principally of regulars, and transfers in or out of it were avoided in the hope that it would become the elite unit of the division.

The Sunwu positions, where the division was to put up major resistance, were divided into three sectors. On the left, around a hill called "Kashimadai," the 268th Regiment was deployed. In the center, at "Hanamiyama," was the 269th Regiment (less one battalion), with artillery and engineer headquarters to its rear. On the right, at "Kojinyama," was the 270th Regiment. Each of these positions had one artillery battalion and one engineer company as supporting units, and hence each in effect had a regimental combat team. (See Map No 1)

New Operational Plan

By June the division was able to draft a new operational plan. Since at that time the 135th Brigade had not then been organized the command relationships between the two were not established until later. The plan is summarized below:

Policy. The policy of the division will be to secure the prepared positions in the vicinity of Sunwu and to crush the enemy there. In the event that the enemy's main body by-passes our positions, the division will harass the enemy rear in order to facilitate the operations of Fourth Army's main force. In any event, the division must hold out at prepared positions for about three months, and wait for the arrival of reinforcements.

Outline of Tactics. Units deployed at forward positions along the Amur River will repel any attempt by the Soviet Army to cross the river. The river guard units, including lookout posts, will then gradually withdraw to main positions, meanwhile maintaining contact with the enemy. The withdrawal of the lookout posts will be carried out at their own discretion; the withdrawal of river guard units will be carried out on orders from the division. During these withdrawals, raiding parties will be left behind at key points to throw confusion into the enemy ranks. To delay the enemy advance the above units, before withdrawing, will destroy the main traffic net.

All other units will hold out at their respective position. Each unit is ordered to send out raiding parties to carry out surprise attacks on enemy headquarters and on artillery and tank units, in order to facilitate the operations of the division.

Japanese Populace. Japanese residents, military dependents, and other nationals, will be accommodated and protected. If, however, there are some who desire to participate in operations, they may be used for receiving the dead, nursing the injured, hauling ammunition, and similar functions.

Supply. Three months' provisions, and ammunition for at least one general engagement (three months), will be stockpiled by each unit in its position before the start of operations.

Communications. The communications network center will be established at division headquarters. Wire communications will be established with each front-line unit, the wire being laid underground in view of the possibility of bombings. Wireless telegraph equipment will

be provided, with the major transmitting set to be
placed in an area near headquarters where detection
by enemy radar will not be likely. Communication
between rear units and Fourth Army will be by permanent wire installations, and after operations begin
will be carried out principally by wireless telegraph.

Fortifications. The construction of field fortifications
will be completed by the end of June; underground installations capable of withstanding the continuous firing
of large guns will be completed by the end of July.

Fortifications in the Sunwu Area

In accordance with the plan's provisions for the construction of fortifications, new positions were begun about the middle of June in the vicinity of the major defense area at Sunwu. The division had intended to construct rather strong field positions in great haste. However, in accordance with an Army directive, it was required to construct positions in two stages. Initially light field positions were to be constructed and were to be completed by the end of June. Thereafter, these positions were to strengthened.

In carrying out this work, units with time and materials to spare constructed additional subterranean installations, generally about 10 meters underground. In addition, the division intendance and ordnance departments constructed underground installations to store arms, ammunition, and provisions. Furthermore, some existing positions were repaired, especially those that could be utilized for defense. Also, fields of fire were cleared, and the communications network was repaired.

Earlier, before the transfer of the 125th Division to the south, the Army, counting on the availability of two divisions in the Sunwu area to carry out its defense mission, had directed the 123d Division to prepare positions for two divisions. Even after the 125th Division's transfer, however, the scale of positions prescribed by the Army was not reduced. In addition to this work, the division was also directed to construct positions in the vicinity of Erhchan for a force whose nucleus was to consist of two infantry and one artillery battalions. These positions were needed to protect the Aihun-Erhchan-Nencheng-Tsitsihar road.

Rifle pits for infantry positions were dispersed as widely as possible in anticipation of vigorous enemy artillery attacks, air bombings and straffing, and tank attacks. Ambush pits for close-quarter attacks on tanks were dug at many points in front of and within infantry positions. Infantry heavy weapons were disposed in and out of the position so as to effect flanking fire. Several alternate positions were also constructed.

Positions for the main force of the artillery, which was attached to the front-line infantry battalions for antitank operations, were also dispersed, and were so constructed as to conceal them within the infantry positions. Antitank ditches with triangular sections were constructed directly in front of the positions, with the artillery pieces deployed so as to provide flanking fire. Remaining elements of the artillery force were placed near the center of the division's position, under the direct command of the artillery regiment commander. The division's four 240-mm howitzers remained in emplaced positions in the rear.

Other preparations made by the division included the laying of underground wires, and the construction by each unit of ammunition and provisions dumps within its position. In cases where time permitted, caves were dug deep underground or on the hillsides. Furthermore, in the valley to the north of the division's positions, preparations were made to inundate the area from nearby streams.

To construct positions in the Erhchan area, a unit from Aihun was dispatched, with an element of the division engineers attached. Even under strong pressure, this construction force was barely able to complete field positions by the end of the July. What ammunition and provisions it was able to store in the positions were wholly inadequate.

Status of Preparations

Meanwhile, because of the great attention devoted to construction, training suffered. Each unit utilized spare moments in the morning and evening for firing exercises, practice in close-quarter fighting, and bayonetting. Such training was carried out right on the construction grounds, and was intended to raise proficiency as well as morale.

Collection of intelligence was continued during this period of intense construction. Communication facilities for the transmission of intelligence reports in the expanded divisional area were improved, and closer contact was maintained with the Heiho Special Service Agency as well as with military police units. After the move of Fourth Army Headquarters to Tsitsihar, the division began to receive intelligence reports direct from observation units stationed along the bank of the Amur.

In late July, the Sunwu military police detachment was reorganized, into a battalion of the Kwantung Army's 3d Special Guard Unit. Despite the assistance given by the division, the organization of this battalion progressed slowly and was not completed by the outbreak of hostilities. The commander was Major Koreshige Tanaka.

With respect to the status of supplies, the shortage of antitank explosives was the greatest concern of the division. Although the division manufactured small quantities, which it promptly distributed to each unit, the quantity was wholly inadequate to meet requirements.

Just prior to the outbreak of hostilities, most of the 100-mm cannons and ammunition in the Shengwutun area were transferred to other sectors. Only one cannon and a small quantity of ammunition were left in Shengwutun.

Situation at the Outbreak of Hostilities

The fighting effectiveness of the 123d Division at the time of the Soviet entry into the war was only about that of one regimental combat team, as was also that of the 135th Independent Mixed Brigade. The latter was by far superior to the division in the matters of unity, fortifications, and training.

At the outbreak of hostilities the division had, besides the brigade, the following units stationed in Sunwu which were attached without definite orders: an element of the Kwantung Army Special Intelligence Unit, the Sunwu branch of the Kwantung Army Water Supply and Purification Depot, and a battalion of the Kwantung Army's 3d Special Guard Unit. Included among the division's personnel were Koreans some of whom had been called up for military service for the first time and others of whom were reservists.

By the end of July positions in and around Sunwu had been almost completed. With a view to strengthening them as much as time permitted, the division initiated the construction of comparatively deep underground facilities, principally living quarters and ammunition dumps. By the time war broke out, some of these underground facilities were in readiness for operations, but efforts to store ammunition and provisions in the underground shelters had lagged, mainly because of the muddy roads caused by a long rain during this period.

When hostilities began all units were engaged mainly in fortification work in their respective defense positions. Hence, they had little difficulty going into a combat disposition. Some changes, however, were made in the disposition of front-line forces. Newly attached units took up positions as follows: the element of the

Kwantung Army Special Intelligence Unit, near division headquarters; the Water Supply and Purification unit, in the low ground of the Sunwu position; the 18th Field Ordnance Depot, just outside and to the rear of the main positions. There had been some discussion prior to hostilities as to whether to redeploy during hostilities the battalion of the 269th Regiment at Shengwutun to Hill Nanyang, across the Hsunpila River opposits the main Sunwu position. However, fearing that the tactical situation might not permit this, the division instead ordered the Raiding Battalion to occupy Hill Nanyang, and to use it as a base of operations.

Continuous rain from late July to early August caused vehicles in the Sunwu area to mire in the mud and slowed down transport operations. Rain and swollen rivers also hampered traffic, in other areas, particularly along the road linking Sunwu with Peian and Harbin. Furthermore, the inundation of the Tungken River (See Map No 2 Monograph No 155-K) hampered railway movements, even during operations. Washouts at several points limited trains to movements within the unaffected areas, and passengers in order to make connections had to negotiate the washed-out areas on foot.

Intelligence Estimate

Since May, Soviet troops had been observed conducting periodic maneuvers north of the Amur River, opposite the division's defense sectors. They were also observed constructing what appeared to be unloading platforms along a railroad siding near Chiko, the eastern extremity of the division's positions, but this was concluded to be part of the maneuvers. In early August, furthermore, five or six Soviet soldiers were observed studying maps on the river bank opposite Chiko. Such observations were invariably reported to Fourth Army. Colonel Maki, Fourth Army staff officer, sent to conduct an aerial reconnaissance of the division's zone along the Amur River, reported the enemy across the river to be extremely quiet.

Observations along the border, however, were indicative only of local intentions, and the division during this period received no information from the Army concerning the general war situation or Soviet activities in other areas. Lacking intelligence reports upon which to make an estimate of the general situation, the division relied more or less upon newspaper reports, and assumed from them that it would be some time before the Soviet Army invaded Manchuria. It believed, furthermore, that if an invasion did come, it would come in the spring of 1946, the original expiration date of the neutrality pact between Japan and Soviet Russia.

Opening of Hostilities

The division first learned of the invasion at about 0500 on 9 August, when Fourth Army informed it that Soviet forces had launched an invasion across the east and west borders of Manchuria. The division's immediate action was to disseminate the report to units under its command, ordering them at the same time to take up battle stations, reinforce positions, and particularly to accelerate the movement of arms, ammunition, and provisions to defense positions.

The Fourth Army Commander, fearing that enemy mechanized units would make a direct push toward Tsitsihar, on the 9th expressly ordered the division to direct the 135th Brigade to redeploy its main body to the Erhchan area and to leave only an element in the Aihun area near the river. Neither the division commander nor the brigade commander favored such a disposition, however, because only light field defenses had been completed at Erhchan, and hardly any ammunition and provisions had been stocked there. Both believed that stiff resistance could hardly be expected from the Erhchan position.

Before transmitting the order to the brigade, the division commander made repeated attempts to persuade the Army Commander to reverse his order, stating that committing the main body to Erhchan would greatly diminish the fighting capacity of the division and eventually prove disadvantageous to the Army itself. The Army Commander, however, refused to alter his order, and the division commander then transmitted it to the brigade commander.

Upon learning that the division's pleas had been rejected by the Army commander, the brigade commander disregarded the order, and left his main body at Aihun, and only one element at Erhchan. This disposition was retained during operations.

The guard units and lookout posts stationed along the banks of the river were under orders to maintain close watch and report immediately any signs of enemy attempts to cross the river. They reported that the day was quiet, except for the occasional appearance of a medium sized steamship plying the Amur River between Shengwutun and Chiko, near the opposite bank. Meanwhile, at 1800 hours, division headquarters moved to a prearranged command post within the Sunwu positions, burning the headquarters building in Sunwu city before departing.

Expecting the enemy to cross the river that night or the following morning, the division urged all its units to continue to move ammunition and provisions to their positions. Because the roads had been washed out by continuous rains, however, the transporting of these supplies bogged down.

At night a battalion-size enemy force began crossing the river just below Huma, the northwestern extremity of the division's front. The guard unit along the river bank was never heard from; it was believed to have been annihilated. The division, believing that a full-scale crossing might be undertaken in this area, alerted all units.[40]

On the 10th no further word was received about the landings near Huma. In other areas, quiet prevailed except for several enemy

---

40. According to the 135th Brigade's monograph, an enemy force crossed the river near Aihun on the night of 9 - 10 August. (See Monograph No 155-M).

reconnaissance flights. On this day, Fourth Army called to active duty all reservists in northern Manchuria and sent them directly to join their units in defense positions.

On 11 August the enemy launched two major crossings simultaneously--one near Aihun, the other near Shengwutun. These crossings, which were continued into the night, were followed by attacks on the Aihun and Shengwutun positions. In both crossings armored units accompanied infantry units. The size of these enemy units had not yet been determined.

The division's plan was to have the garrison at Shengwutun (a battalion of the 269th Regiment, commanded by Major Murakami) fight only a light engagement at its security positions and then withdraw to the main positions at Sunwu. But because the main positions had not been adequately stocked with ammunition and provisions, it ordered the Murakami unit on 12 August to continue offering strong resistance until further orders in order to gain time. In the meantime, the division exerted greater efforts to expedite the accumulation of supplies. Under pressure, and in spite of the bad roads, each unit and particularly the transport regiment made desperate efforts to move supplies forward.

In the evening Fourth Army Headquarters recommended that the division take advantage of the fact that the enemy was still crossing the river by launching a division counter-offensive against the force crossing at Shengwutun and to throw the entire weight of the division into the engagement. However, the division did not respond favorably to Fourth Army's recommendation. The considerably larger enemy landings at Aihun posed a greater threat since elements there had made substantial progress advancing southward. Furthermore, since the enemy force near Shengwutun included strong mechanized elements, the division would need air or tank support to repel it, and it could be assured of neither.

At night the presence of an enemy mechanized force in the Aihun area was confirmed by a report sent to division by the Kwantung Army Special Intelligence Unit. This same unit also reported that another tank force had broken through Chiko and was advancing on Hsunho. To check the latter drive the division sent the 3d Battalion (less one company) of the 269th Regiment, commanded by Major Hirama, with instructions to occupy positions along the Sunwu-Hsunho road, linking with the right flank of the Shengwutun unit.

The enemy force that had crossed or was in the process of crossing the river in the Shengwutun and Chiko areas on the 12th was estimated to consist of two infantry divisions and one mechanized brigade; that crossing in the Aihun area was estimated at less than one infantry division plus one mechanized brigade.

In anticipation of the enemy's advance upon the major positions at Sunwu, the division started to burn barracks, warehouses, and other buildings likely to be used by the Soviets.

On the fifth day of operations, 13 August, the enemy river

crossings and attacks on our units appeared to slow down somewhat, and were not as vigorously pushed as on preceding days.

By the 14th, supplies being assembled in the Sunwu positions were near requirements. Ammunition to last at least one engagement, and provisions for a similar period were on hand. With these positions now well stocked, and with the enemy drive in the Shengwutun area gaining momentum, the division commander issued orders for the Hirama unit to begin withdrawing to its former positions at Sunwu at 2400 hours, and the Murakami unit to follow.

At nightfall, before these withdrawals could be carried out, the enemy intensified his attacks on the Shengwutun positions. The main body of the force that had landed in this area penetrated deeply into the gap between the positions of the Murakami and the Hirama units. At the same time his tanks broke through the Shengwutun-Sunwu road and rushed toward the Sunwu area. Meanwhile, the mechanized unit that had crossed the river at the division's extreme right flank near Chiko was advancing toward Shengwutun along the river bank.

By this time the Hirama unit had begun its scheduled withdrawal to the Sunwu positions. En route near the confluence of the Hsunpila and Oyuerh Rivers, it encountered an enemy tank unit pushing southward from Shengwutun in a dense fog. In the engagement that followed, Major Hirama was killed, but the rest of the unit crossed the Hsunpila River and assembled in the vicinity of Hill Nanyang. It was later learned that the enemy unit whose approach toward Hsunho on the 12th, reported by the Special Intelligence Unit, had caused the division commander to dispatch the Hirama battalion, consisted of only one infantry platoon.

The Shengwutun positions, meanwhile, were penetrated by a tank unit at about midnight, the tanks continuing southward along the Shengwutun-Sunwu road. The division, upon learning of the enemy's approach, promptly ordered the engineer regiment to destroy bridges along this road, and at the same time ordered the raiding battalion as well as front line elements to carry out raids on the enemy's lines. Meanwhile, communications with the Murakami unit at Shengwutun were cut off. Wireless telegraph transmissions went unanswered. Later, a noncommissioned officer from this unit came to division headquarters and stated that although the transmitter had been damaged and the code books burned, the receiving set was still operative. Thereupon, the division repeatedly transmitted retreat orders in plain language. Eventually, small elements of the unit were able to retreat and join the division; the main body, it was learned after the war, had escaped to the Peian.

In the Aihun area, the enemy on the 14th was engaged by advance elements of the 135th Brigade. These elements gallantly attacked the enemy and delayed his approach to the main Aihun positions.

On the 15th, Soviet forces, after repairing the bridges on the Shengwutun-Sunwu road, continued advancing and assembled in the vicinity of the emergency landing strip at Chengchiawopeng.

Artillery elements of this force reached the vicinity of the military officers club at Sunwu city, and occupied positions nearby.

On this day the division's main defense positions at Sunwu were attacked for the first time when a number of infantry patrols infiltrated. Concurrently, rumors reaching division headquarters stated that enemy tanks and cavalry had appeared in front of the positions. The division thereupon made plans for a night attack in the vicinity of the airstrip, and ordered the 269th Regiment to make preparations for such an attack. But cease-fire orders were received before it could be executed.

Shortly after 1500 hours, the division received a message from Fourth Army stating: "Listen respectfully to the important broadcast at noon of the 15th." As that hour had already passed we missed the broadcast. At about 1700 hours, however, the division was notified by the Kwantung Army Special Intelligence Unit that Japan's surrender had been broadcast. This news shocked the division commander and his staff. In consideration of the morale of troops, division headquarters withheld announcing the news until confirmation could be obtained.

After the report was confirmed from radio broadcasts emanating from various parts of the world, division headquarters assembled all unit commanders at 2000 hours, announced Japan's unconditional surrender, and passed on instructions prepared by the division commander exhorting all personnel to avoid any rash acts that might aggravate the situation. The latter instructions could not be transmitted to the 135th Brigade because of the breakdown of communications.

On the 16th the division commander at the Sunwu positions sent Staff Officer Katayama under a flag of truce to propose a cease-fire to the Soviet commander. He returned about noon with the Soviet Army's terms, which are summarized below:

> The Japanese Army will suspend all hostile acts by 1700 hours today.
>
> The Japanese Army will collect its arms within the respective positions of units by 1700 hours, 17 August, and will assemble all troops in the official residence zone of Sunwu city.
>
> The use of all communication facilities will be prohibited. All such facilities will be turned over to the Soviet Army.
>
> The destruction or burning of any buildings, installations, arms, or materials is prohibited.
>
> Should any of the above provisions be violated, the Soviet Army will immediately attack and annihilate the Japanese force.

The division designated five points within the Sunwu positions as collecting points for arms, and made arrangements for the arms, together with certifying documents, to be turned over to a Soviet Army officer.

The division commander decided to accept the Soviet terms without any revision, and sent Staff Officer Katayama back to continue negotiations. The Soviet Army commander proposed a meeting with the division commander at noon of the 17th, in the vicinity of the crossroads at the west end of Sunwu. The division commander agreed to this proposal.

That night each unit familiarized its troops with the objectives of the cease-fire order. In spite of some agitation, the arms were collected, and preparations were made to move to designated assembly areas. The colors were burned by 1500 hours.

The 123d Transport Regiment was disbanded by order of its commander, Major Abe. Its men went their respective ways in groups of two or three.

On 17 August divisional units assembled according to the schedule set by headquarters. Although division strength at the outbreak of war had been approximately 27,000 (including reservists called to duty after hostilities had begun, and members of the volunteer corps), the number of men who gathered at the assembly area on this day did not exceed 15,000.

The conference between the division commander and Lieutenant General Mojuhin, commander of the Soviet Second Army, took place as scheduled; afterwards, the division commander joined his troops in the assembly area.

Meanwhile, fighting continued in some sectors. The units occupying positions in the vicinity of Aihun and Erhchan, and the raiding battalion, whose elements were widely scattered, continued fighting gallantly. The division tried to disseminate the cease-fire order by runners and by every other means possible, but was unable to reach all elements.

On 18 August the Soviet Army began interrogating members of the division. The investigators, mainly officers of the Soviet Army Headquarters, questioned the division commander and officers of all ranks closely and persistently. The interrogation continued until 25 or 26 August. Initially, it took the form of questions relative to the troop strength of the division, and included making a close check of the arms turned over. Later, more detailed questioning was begun regarding operational plans, organization and equipment, training, and fortifications, each investigator apparently being assigned certain subjects to investigate.

Losses

Two things in particular made it difficult to determine Japanese losses accurately. Operations had been carried out mainly by forward elements and raiding units. Detached, these units could not report their figures regularly. Furthermore, at the cessation of hostilities the Soviets took control of the communications network and prohibited anyone from approaching the fighting areas.

It was known that the number of men who were assembled after the fighting stopped was 12,000 less than the number at the opening of hostilities. However, the majority of these had deserted their units and fled to the Peian area. The number actually killed in action was estimated at 500. Presumably not a few of those who had escaped from Sunwu were attacked and killed enroute to Peian by Manchurians, Koreans, or Soviet troops. Furthermore, of those who succeeded in reaching Peian, many were ultimately captured and detained.

Soviet losses were even more difficult to ascertain. However, it is believed that heavy casualties were inflicted on the enemy during the fighting in the Shengwutun and Aihun positions. In addition, several Soviet tanks were believed to have been damaged in the Erhchan positions.

Post-Hostilities Situation

The Soviet force which had engaged in operations against the division occupied the vicinity of Sunwu for about a week and then moved southward to the Harbin area. It was replaced by a garrison unit under the command of a lieutenant colonel of the Internal Peoples' Commissariat, which undertook the maintenance of public peace.

During the internment period the division drew upon its own stores to supply its troops and Japanese civilians. Soviet authorities permitted the consumption of a normal quantity of rations, but the division, in view of the uncertain future, decided to use only 70 per cent of the normal amount.

At the end of August the division was still interned in the official residence zone of Sunwu city. At about that time, the Soviet Army began forming units of about 1,000 men each, calling them construction units, and, after cunningly falsifying destinations, led them into Soviet territory. By 10 September, the main body of the division had departed. There still remained a number of officers and hospital patients, but these too were transferred to Soviet territory shortly afterwards.

Civil Affairs

There were relatively few Japanese residents in the Sunwu area. At the outbreak of hostilities, these residents, together with the families of military personnel and of civilian employees, were quartered principally in the barracks of the 268th and 270th Regiments. While operations were under way, however, it was decided to evacuate them to Harbin, and starting on 12 August, they were withdrawn to the Peian area.

Residents and dependents in the Aihun area initially joined the defenders within the defense positions, grimly determined to withstand the siege. After fighting started, however, they realized the disadvantage of their presence and withdrew to the Sunwu area during the night of 12 August. Their evacuation to Peian was prevented by the disruption of railway traffic between Sunwu and Peian. Hence they were compelled to remain in the military official residence area of Sunwu until the war ended. Some of the Japanese nationals in the division's area were young student-farmers of the agricultural development groups. A number of these were evacuated to the Peian area, but most of them remained in the Sunwu positions and helped with logistical tasks.

Also accommodated in the division's positions were a number of Japanese officials of the Manchurian Government. Some of these participated in defensive or guerrilla actions in the Peian-Sunwu sector. Governor Matsumoto, of Heiho Province, arrived at division headquarters during the early stages of hostilities, and in compliance with his wishes, was given written authorization to go to Hsinking to report the situation in Heiho to the Manchurian Government.

The largest Manchurian Army unit in the division sector was a regiment near Ssuchan, engaged in constructing positions for the defense of the Aihun-Tsitsihar road. It was reported that this regiment rebelled, killed its Japanese officers, and that its members thereafter dispersed. A smaller unit was engaged in construction work near Erhchan, but its movements during and after operations were not learned.

Among Manchurian and Korean nationals there was considerable unrest, particularly near the fighting zones; but there was no evidence of positive steps by them against the interests of the Japanese Army. However, instances were reported wherein our deserters were assaulted and killed, the war dead stripped of their arms and equipment, and furniture and other articles stolen from official residences or other vacated houses. Furthermore, Japanese residents and dependents of military personnel who were evacuated from Sunwu to Peian were robbed of everything but the clothing they wore.

Monograph No 155-M

CHAPTER XIII

The 135th Independent Mixed Brigade[41]

Organization

The 135th Independent Mixed Brigade was organized in July 1945, with the 6th Border Garrison Unit as its nucleus. The 6th Border Garrison Unit, in turn, had been formed in November 1938 to defend the permanently fortified area in the vicinity of Aihun, and in early 1945, when Kwantung Army adopted the delaying operational plan, had been converted into a semimobile force to carry out operations of movement utilizing terrain freely. In conjunction with this transition, the permanent fortifications in this area had been seriously weakened by the dismantling of many emplaced weapons and the removal of huge quantities of arms and materials for use in the homeland and in the Pacific theater or to supply new units.

The strength of the brigade after its organization was completed was approximately 6,000.[42] It consisted of the following components:

```
Brigade headquarters
Four independent infantry battalions
One raiding battalion
One artillery Unit (12 medium trench mortars)
```

---

41. The information in this chapter was furnished by Major Masami Sugata, staff officer of the 135th Brigade.
42. Compare with strength given in Table No 1, furnished by the Demobilization Bureau.

>   One engineer Unit
>   One signal Unit
>   One transport Unit
>   One independent antitank gun battalion (attached)

Shortly after its formation, the brigade was assigned to the 123d Division, and was given the mission of guarding the sector north of the division's Sunwu positions. The brigade commander, Major General Junosuke Hamada, deployed his main body in the Aihun defense positions. He deployed elements as follows: a reinforced infantry battalion at the Erhchan positions, an infantry battalion at Shanshenfu, and two reinforced companies in the Chaoshui positions. In addition, the brigade maintained lookout posts along the Amur River. Of the brigade's elements, the most important was the detachment at Erhchan, which prior to hostilities was engaged mainly in constructing positions to block the enemy's passage along the road between Aihun and Nencheng.

Outbreak of Hostilities

At 0600 on 9 August, three Soviet planes bombed river lookout positions in front of Aihun, and at 0630 bombed the Aihun defense positions. Anticipating a Soviet invasion, the brigade alerted all its elements to take up their battle stations and to make preparations for operations. Meanwhile, it took immediate steps to get back twelve artillery pieces (six 105-mm howitzers, four 100-mm cannons, and two 150-mm howitzers) that had been dismantled from the Aihun positions and were then at the Aihun Railway Station

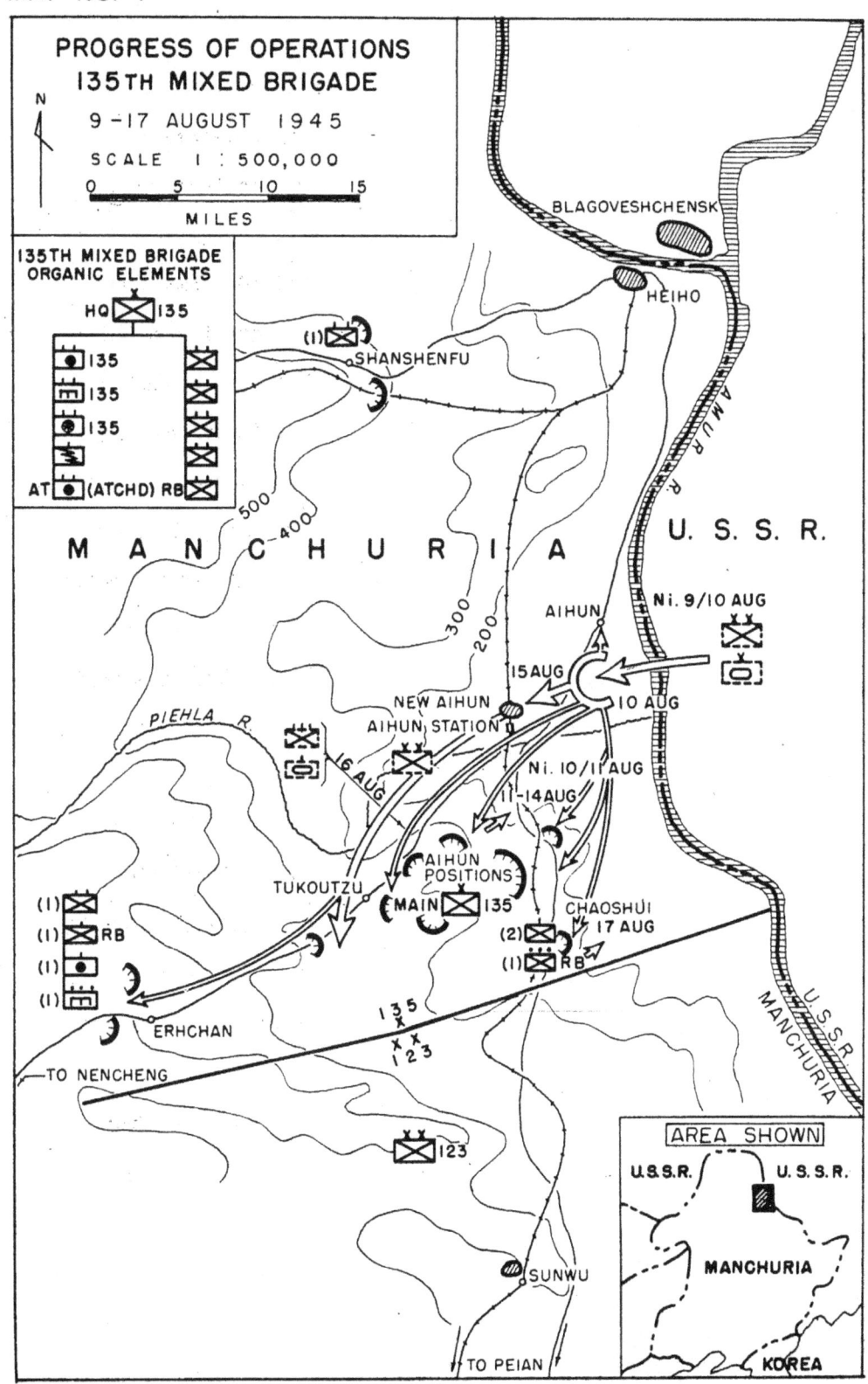

awaiting shipment to other areas. At the same time the brigade made arrangements to accommodate Japanese residents and dependents of military personnel and civilian employees in barracks in the positions at New Aihun. The brigade's operational preparations were completed at about noon.

Progress of Operations   (See Map No. 1.)

During the night of 9-10 August, enemy elements crossed the Amur River just south of Aihun, and in the morning sixty vehicles and about eighteen 100-mm guns were observed to have been put ashore on the Manchurian bank of the river. The brigade's 100-mm cannons immediately began shelling this force. Meanwhile, the brigade commander ordered elements of the raiding battalion to prepare to carry out raids after dark. From all indications the river lookout unit near Aihun had defended its assigned post to the very end.

An element of the enemy force that had crossed the Amur on the night of 9-10 August continued southward, and put a unit of about 300 men and approximately 12 tanks across the Piehla River south of New Aihun during the night of 10-11 August. At about 2200 hours this unit made its first attempt to penetrate the main Aihun positions, but by midnight had been repulsed in hand-to-hand fighting. At daybreak of the 11th, the 105-mm howitzers in the brigade's main position began shelling this unit and destroyed two of its tanks. Meanwhile, enemy river crossings continued, and the 300-man unit in front of the Aihun positions was gradually reinforced.

As a result of the artillery duel, communications between Sunwu and Erhchan were severed. On this day, the 11th, the battalion at Shanshenfu, which at the outbreak of hostilities had been placed directly under Fourth Army, was ordered to withdraw to the Nencheng area.

On the 12th, the artillery in the Aihun positions continued shelling the enemy to its immediate front, and apparently forced him to detour along the left flank of the Aihun position. During the night this enemy element of about 300 men advanced in a flanking movement toward Tukoutzu, and attacked the brigade's main position from the southwest. It was thrown back. On the 13th and 14th, the enemy carried out repeated attacks both from the north and southwest, following the pattern of the preceding days, but was repulsed each time.

By the 15th the Soviets had put a substantial number of troops across the river. The largest of these was a force of approximately division strength which reached the barracks area in New Aihun. Brigade artillery shelled it, and inflicted heavy losses. Throughout the day, the brigade's signal unit received by commercial radio several messages that sounded urgent but were unintelligible. Having received no change in orders, however, the brigade continued operations.

On the evening of the 16th, the Soviet division-size force in the New Aihun area also began a southwestward drive to outflank the brigade's main Aihun positions, and advanced in the direction of the 123d Division's main positions at Sunwu, meanwhile sending some elements to Erhchan. Among its equipment were observed more than eighty tanks and about ninety guns. This appeared to be the main force the enemy was sending southwestward to Sunwu.

Presumably in support of this drive, the enemy unit near Tukoutzu which had been attacking since the 12th, resumed its attack against our company defending this southwest approach to the brigade's main positions. During its attacks of the preceding days it had consisted of only about one company. Now it was approximately regimental size, and its weapons included about twenty tanks and more than ten guns. Our company, carrying out close-quarter attacks against enemy tanks, fought a desperate engagement to protect the rear avenue of approach to the brigade's main Aihun positions. Eventually, however, nearly all the men of this company, including the commander, were killed or wounded.

On the 17th, sporadic action continued in each sector. Enemy gunboats on the Amur began to bombard the Aihun positions. On this day, our Chaoshui position was attacked by an infantry unit supported by tanks, but our garrison put up stubborn resistance and repulsed the enemy, although about one of its platoons was annihilated. Meanwhile, in the Tukoutzu position an element of the brigade engineers went to the aid of the company gallantly resisting the enemy's drive.

Localized engagements, marked by artillery duels, continued from the 18th until the 20th. The main Aihun positions remained secure, and the morale of officers and men was excellent. At about 1800 on the 20th, however, Major Mori and 2d Lieutenant Nakamura of the 123d Division arrived with cease-fire orders. The brigade commander decided to stop operations that night, and at 0600 on the following morning opened negotiations with the Soviet commander, a colonel, at the bridge on the Piehla River south of New Aihun.

The Soviet commander directed that the brigade be disarmed in position at 1600 hours and that it later assemble at Sunwu. Following disarmament, the brigade commander and staff officers left immediately for Sunwu. On the 22d and 23d the brigade assembled at Sunwu, where it was later interned. Approximately 480 Japanese residents and dependents were likewise interned at Sunwu. There, a few details of the situation of the Erhchan garrison were learned: it had been engaged by elements diverted to Erhchan by the Soviet division driving toward Sunwu; although it had fought gallantly, it had been weakened by the fact that the incompletion of positions and the inadequate supply of ammunition and provisions, had compelled it to divide its forces during its engagement.

Casualties

Brigade casualties totalled about 510. Most of these were sustained by the main body in the Aihun positions, where about

240 were killed and about 180 wounded. In the Erhchan area about 70 were killed and in the Chaoshui area about 20.[43]

---

43. Compare with KIA figures in Table No 1, furnished by the Demobilization Bureau.

Monograph No 155-N

CHAPTER XIV

The 149th Division[44]

Organization

At Tsitsihar, where the headquarters of the 149th Division was located, the road and railroads from Heiho in northeastern Manchuria joined those from Manchouli in the northwest. Tsitsihar was the most northerly of the major communication centers in Manchuria, and was in the general area where dense population began.

The 149th Division, created to give Fourth Army a reserve, was the last unit to be formed by the Kwantung Army. Its nucleus was the 74th Line of Communication Garrison Unit. It completed its organization on 30 July 1945, (with only two-thirds of its authorized strength, however) and was immediately assigned to Fourth Army. It deployed its main body in the Tsitsihar area, with elements at Peian, Taian, and Noho. Division components were:

    Division Headquarters
    274th Infantry Regiment
    386th Infantry Regiment
    387th Infantry Regiment
    149th Field Artillery Regiment
    149th Engineer Regiment
    149th Transport Regiment
    Division Raiding Battalion

---

44. The information in this section was furnished by Colonel Kiyoshi Innami, chief of staff of the 149th Division.

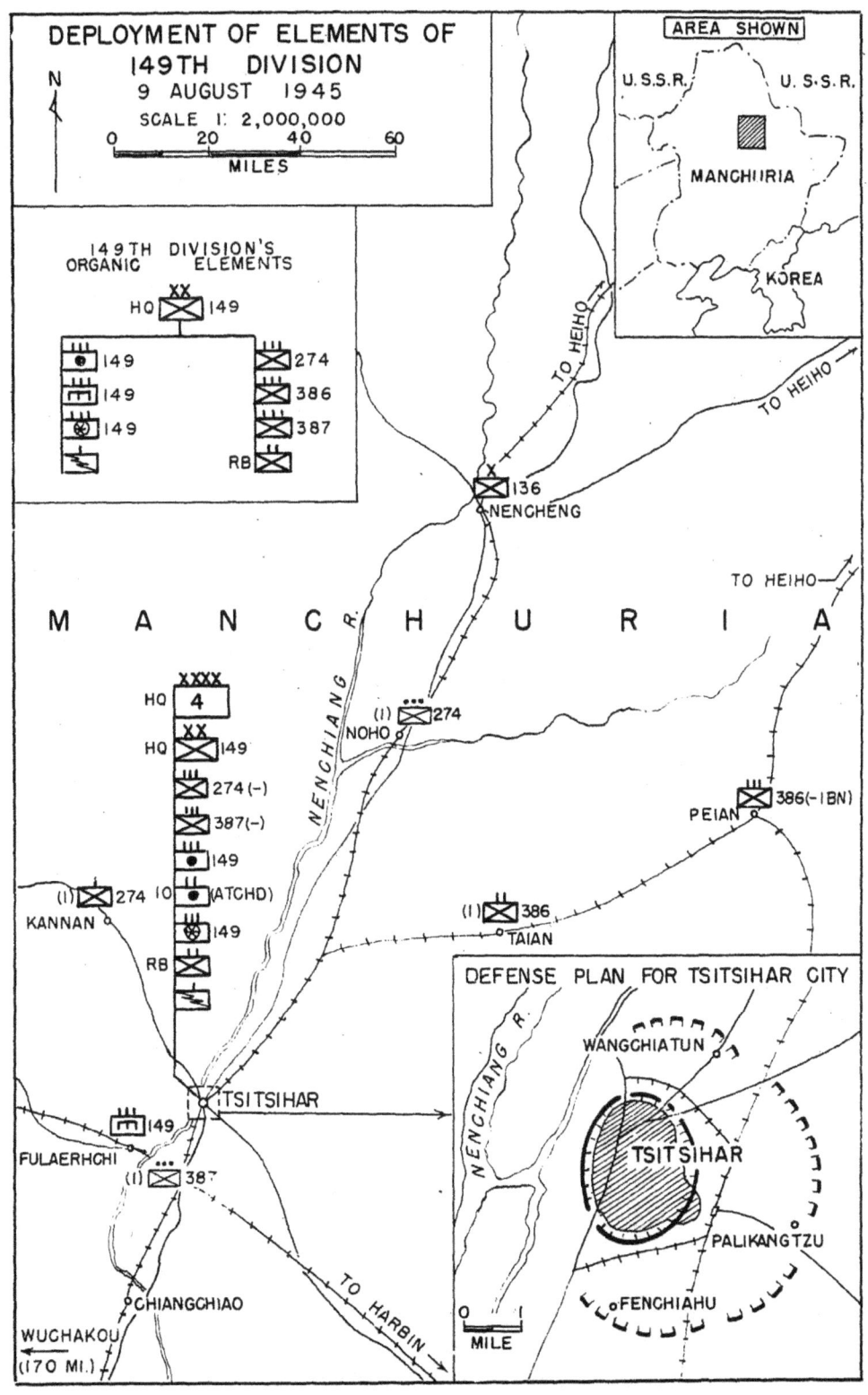

>   Division Signal Unit
>   Division Ordnance Depot
>   Division Veterinary Depot
>   10th Independent Field Artillery Battalion (attached)

The elements deployed outside the Tsitsihar area were the 386th Regiment (less one battalion) at Peian, one battalion of the 386th at Taian, and one platoon of the 274th at Noho. (See Map No 1)

The great majority of the men assigned to the division were old and untrained, the division having been organized largely from reservists or recruits in Manchuria, including some untrained Koreans. To remedy this weakness, the division carried out training on an emergency basis, stressing only necessary military subjects such as antitank attacks, rifle firing, and bayonet practice. Since recruits arrived in successive stages, this training had to be repeated for each group.

Most of the division's company grade officers and some of its field grade officers were elderly reserve officers only recently called to active duty. The majority of noncommissioned officers, like the bulk of the men, were either recently recalled reservists or recruits drafted in Manchuria.

The division was fairly well equipped, although it lacked some of its authorized guns for the artillery regiment and some heavy weapons for the infantry regiments. However, equipment was generally of inferior quality.

Operational Preparations

In preparation for operations, the division, on instructions from the Army, formulated a defense plan for the city of Tsitsihar, where Fourth Army Headquarters was also located. The defense plan provided for the construction of two fortification belts around the city, the inner belt at the city's outskirts, the outer belt at a radius of about two miles. Defense works of the inner belt were to be constructed by police units, and some of this work had been begun. The outer ring was to be divided into three segments: the segment in the north-northeast of the city centering around the Wangchiatun suburb was to be constructed by Manchukuoan Army units; the segment east of the city, centering around the Palikangtzu suburb and the segment south-southeast of the city, centering around the Fenchiahu suburb, were both to be constructed by the division. However, none of the work on the outer belt could be initiated before hostilities began. West of the city, two rivers provided natural obstacles and served as the western segment of the outer defense ring. (See Inset, Map No 1)

Division headquarters had a dual role. As the Tsitsihar District Defense Command, it had control over the military police and Manchukuoan police force in the district. Hence it was able to gather some intelligence from these sources. However, for the bulk of intelligence information, the division depended mainly upon Army Headquarters.

Opening of Hostilities

No major changes in disposition had been made by the time the war started. The combat effectiveness of the division was low, possibly not more than 15 per cent of that of an elite division. The division had no time to train its units adequately.

Immediately upon the outbreak of hostilities, division headquarters, in its role as the Tsitsihar District Defense Command, ordered an emergency disposition of antiaircraft observation posts within the defense district. Furthermore, it assumed control of all units in Tsitsihar, and ordered them to prepare for a complete defense of the city. At the same time it summoned the commander of the Manchukuoan Army unit and requested him in particular to retain effective control of his troops. The division intelligence section, meanwhile, intensified its activities, enlisting the help of Japanese students in the city of Tsitsihar.

At the same time, the division commander, Lieutenant General Toichi Sasaki, decided to defend Tsitsihar at the outer belt. This decision was based first upon the inadequate strength of the division, (slightly over 12,000), and second on the limited time available for throwing up hasty defense works. He also ordered each unit to begin preparing defenses immediately.

Also at the outbreak of war, the division sent one company (with two machine guns) of the 274th Regiment to the village of Kannan to prevent enemy infiltration and to quell disturbances among the inhabitants, but more particularly to protect Japanese land development groups in that area. In addition, it dispatched one platoon of the 387th Regiment to defend the road bridge over the Nenchiang River near Fulaerhchi, and assigned another platoon of the same regiment to guard the army clothing warehouse in Tsitsihar city itself.

Other measures taken by the division at the outbreak of hostilities were as follows: it ordered the 149th Engineer Regiment to defend the railroad bridge at Fulaerhchi; one infantry platoon to patrol, aboard an armored train, the Noho-Tsitsihar-Chiangchiao railroad segment; the military police to remain on the alert for possible disturbance among the people, and especially to keep under surveillance the actions and movements of the Manchurian Army unit; the Manchurian police to take precautions against disturbance among the people, and to gather information on a possible invasion by enemy mechanized units from the Hsingan area in the southwest.

During the first day of hostilities, an unescorted Soviet bomber made two or three flights to Tsitsihar. Apparently on a mission of intimidation, it dropped one or two bombs each time in the outlying sections of the city, and then disappeared.

Through Army Headquarters, the division was able to receive timely reports on the enemy situation in the Hailar and Wuchakou areas. Most feared by the division was a possible invasion of its area by enemy mechanized forces from the Wuchakou area. Such an invasion would threaten the division's southern flank. Hence, utmost precautions were taken against such a possibility.

In view of the danger to civilians, division headquarters summoned the mayor of Tsitsihar, and key Japanese officials, including the president of the Japanese Association, and advised them to evacuate Japanese non-combatants. At first, they stubbornly refused to do so, insisting on remaining in Tsitsihar. It was not until the 13th that they consented to the evacuation of women and children on the voluntary basis. The evacuation order covered specifically the dependents of Japanese and Manchurian military personnel, of Manchurian Railway Company employees, and of Japanese and Manchukuoan government officials, in addition to all Japanese women and children. Earlier, on the 10th, the division had provided for the reception of evacuees from the Hailar area, and for accommodating them in the city hall and other buildings.

On 11 August, Fourth Army prepared to move its headquarters to Harbin. It placed several elements of the division under its direct command and directed them to accompany it to Harbin. The principal elements involved were the 387th Regiment, one battalion of the 149th Field Artillery Regiment, and the 10th Independent Field Artillery Battalion, and the main body of the signal unit. The move was made on the 12th. The division thereupon ordered the Engineer Regiment, sent to Fulaerhchi on the 9th to guard the railroad bridge, to return to Tsitsihar, and sent one railway guard platoon to take its place.

On 14 August the division's main body was also ordered to proceed to Harbin. It departed by train on the same day, with the division commander in direct command of the move. The units remaining in the Tsitsihar area were the engineer and transport regiments, the ordnance and veterinary depots, the company at Kannan, and the platoons guarding the road and railway bridges at Fulaerhchi. Before the departure, the division commander, anticipating a protracted war, ordered all personnel to wear their best uniforms and to take as large a quantity of clothing, including winter clothes, as the loading capacity of the train permitted. General Sasaki also appointed Major General Tsuchiya, commander of the 136th Independent Mixed Brigade at Nencheng to assume the post of Tsitsihar District Defense Commander. Pending the arrival of General Tsuchiya at Tsitsihar, however, the command was placed in the hands of the commander of the Tsitsihar Military Police.

At about 1400 hours on 15 August, while the train was at Chaotung station (about 60 kilometers out of Harbin), the division learned of the cessation of hostilities. The train continued to Harbin.

Situation at the End of the War

Since the division did not participate in any engagements, it sustained no casualties and inflicted none on the enemy. Neither the division's numerical strength nor its fighting capacity had diminished, except that on orders from Fourth Army all Korean soldiers were released from duty.

Negotiations with the Soviet Army at Harbin were conducted by Fourth Army Headquarters. The division did not come in contact with the Soviets until 23 August. In the early morning hours, a Soviet officer accompanied by a Japanese officer-interpreter came to the Lichiatun Barracks on the outskirts of Harbin and alerted the division for movement. He stated that Japanese forces would be returned to Japan soon after assembling in Hailin (near Mutanchiang). With a ray of hope of returning to their homeland, but half in doubt, all officers and men quietly and speedily prepared for the departure. Meanwhile, on the same day, the division commander was taken to Khabarovsk by plane.

Guarded by the Soviet Army, the main body of the division (about 5,000 men) was moved by train from Harbin via Acheng to Hengtaohotzu. From there the troops went on foot to Hailin. During the march the personal belongings of troops were looted by Soviet soldiers (other than the guards). Along the way our troops observed many Japanese refugees, principally the families of land development groups. Their plight was miserable.

Upon arrival at Hailin on the 27th the division's main body was interned. By that time the number of troops had dwindled to about 4,480, mainly as a result of desertions, despite the precautions taken by the division since it departed Harbin to prevent such acts.

Japanese military personnel at the Hailin Internment Camp numbered between 30,000 and 40,000. Besides division personnel, these consisted of the majority of Fourth Army's forces, and some of Fifth Army's. In addition there were between 20,000 and 30,000 civilian personnel.

Between mid-September and mid-October, the Soviets formed labor battalions at Hailin. From the division were formed three battalions of approximately 1,000 men each, one battalion of about 640 men, and one battalion of officers and men. A total of about 4,200 personnel were formed into these battalions. Where the Soviets sent these battalions is not known.

On 13 October the remaining officers and some noncommissioned officers and men (one orderly was allowed each unit commander) were transferred to the Mutanchiang Internment Camp. On 6 November, they were taken by train into Soviet territory. On 1 December, they arrived at the Rada Internment Camp in Tambov Province, about 460 kilometers southeast of Moscow. During July 1946 they were transferred to the Erabka Internment Camp.[45] During October 1947,

---

45. The conditions in these internment camps and the treatment of personnel are not revealed in any of these monographs. The editor has had a resumé of internment life prepared, based on published accounts in five books and on letters of inquiry to repatriates. See Appendix II.

repatriation to Japan began.

Civil Affairs

Relatively few Japanese residents (businessmen, railway employees, miners, etc.) were actually evacuated from the Tsitsihar and Hailar areas. Those that remained behind, when last heard from, seemed to be in good spirits. At Harbin, Japanese refugees congregated from all points of the compass, so that there was much overcrowding and low morale.

Land development groups near and beyond Tsitsihar had been ordered to assemble in Tsitsihar, but because of transportation difficulties were not able to arrive there until after the departure of division headquarters. Hence their subsequent actions were not known.

Families of military personnel and of civilian employees, with few exceptions, were evacuated to and beyond Harbin. Most of them gathered in Harbin. The division afforded them direct protection until it was disarmed. Afterwards, it assigned to civilian employees to render assistance to them.

Officials of the Tsitsihar Provincial Government Office of the Manchukuoan Government rendered full cooperation to the Japanese Army.

Although the Manchukuoan Army unit near Tsitsihar remained generally calm, its commander took a passive attitude in rendering cooperation. The movement of the Manchukuoan engineer unit in Angangchi remained a mystery until the end of hostilities when it was learned that it had risen in revolt. The attitude of Manchurian police was generally favorable.

Manchurian civilians in the Tsitsihar area remained relatively undisturbed, although even before the outbreak of hostilities rumors of the defeat of Japan were rampant among them. It was said that after the end of hostilities, some of them became anti-Japanese and behaved outrageously, but as a general rule they were believed to be sympathetic to Japan.

Most Korean civilians took flight to rear areas with their belongings at the outbreak of hostilities. However, Korean land development groups stationed on the river bank west of Hailin deeply sympathized with the Japanese Army, and during the movement of troops to Mutanchiang under Soviet guard gave generous assistance to the Japanese troops.

Monograph No 155-O

CHAPTER XV

The Thirty-fourth Army Headquarters[46]

Transfer from China to Korea

As a result of a Kwantung Army request in early 1945 for an additional army headquarters which was needed in northern Korea, Imperial General Headquarters directed the China Expeditionary Army on 28 May to alert the Thirty-fourth Army Headquarters for this purpose.

By orders issued on 17 June 1945, Imperial General Headquarters dissolved the Thirty-fourth Army, assigning its units to the Sixth Area Army in China, and its headquarters to the Kwantung Army. At the same time it ordered the Thirty-fourth Army Headquarters, then in Hankow where it had been organized on 22 July 1944, to proceed to its new station in Hamhung, northern Korea.

Lieutenant General Senichi Kushibuchi and some of his staff officers immediately flew to Hsinking, arriving there on the 19th. After studying the operational plans of Kwantung Army for several days, General Kushibuchi and his party went to Seoul for conferences, mainly on logistics, with the Seventeenth Area Army Commander, finally

---

46. The information in this chapter was furnished by Colonel Hiroshi Ogi, staff officer of Thirty-fourth Army Headquarters. See also Monograph 138 references to this Army.

reaching Hamhung on 12 July, where they immediately began operational preparations. Meanwhile, the rest of the headquarters departed Hankow in late June and, travelling by train (Hankow-Peiping and Peiping-Mukden Railways), arrived in Hamhung in late July.

The order of battle issued to Thirty-fourth Army on 17 June consisted of the following components.

> Thirty-fourth Army Headquarters
> 59th Division
> 137th Division
> 133d Independent Mixed Brigade
> 11th Independent Field Artillery Battalion
> Mutanchiang Heavy Artillery Regiment
> 15th Mortar Battalion
> Yonghung (Eiko) Bay Fortress Garrison Unit (regimental size)
>   Artillery Unit
>   462d Specially Established Garrison Battalion
> 56th Signal Regiment
> 115th Independent Motor Transport Battalion
> 107th Specially Established Construction Duty Company
> 127th Specially Established Sea Duty Company
> 179th Line of Communications Hospital.

Not all of these units were in Korea at the time the order of battle was issued. Some, like the 59th Division, were en route from China. Others, like the Mutanchiang Heavy Artillery Regiment, the 133d Independent Mixed Brigade, and the 15th Mortar Battalion were deployed in other areas. (These three units actually never joined). Furthermore, some units had not yet been formed.

By mid-July the 59th Division was in transit from China, the 137th Division was still being organized, as were also most of the units under the Army's direct command. For all practical purposes, therefore, in the middle of July the Army had only the Yonghung Bay

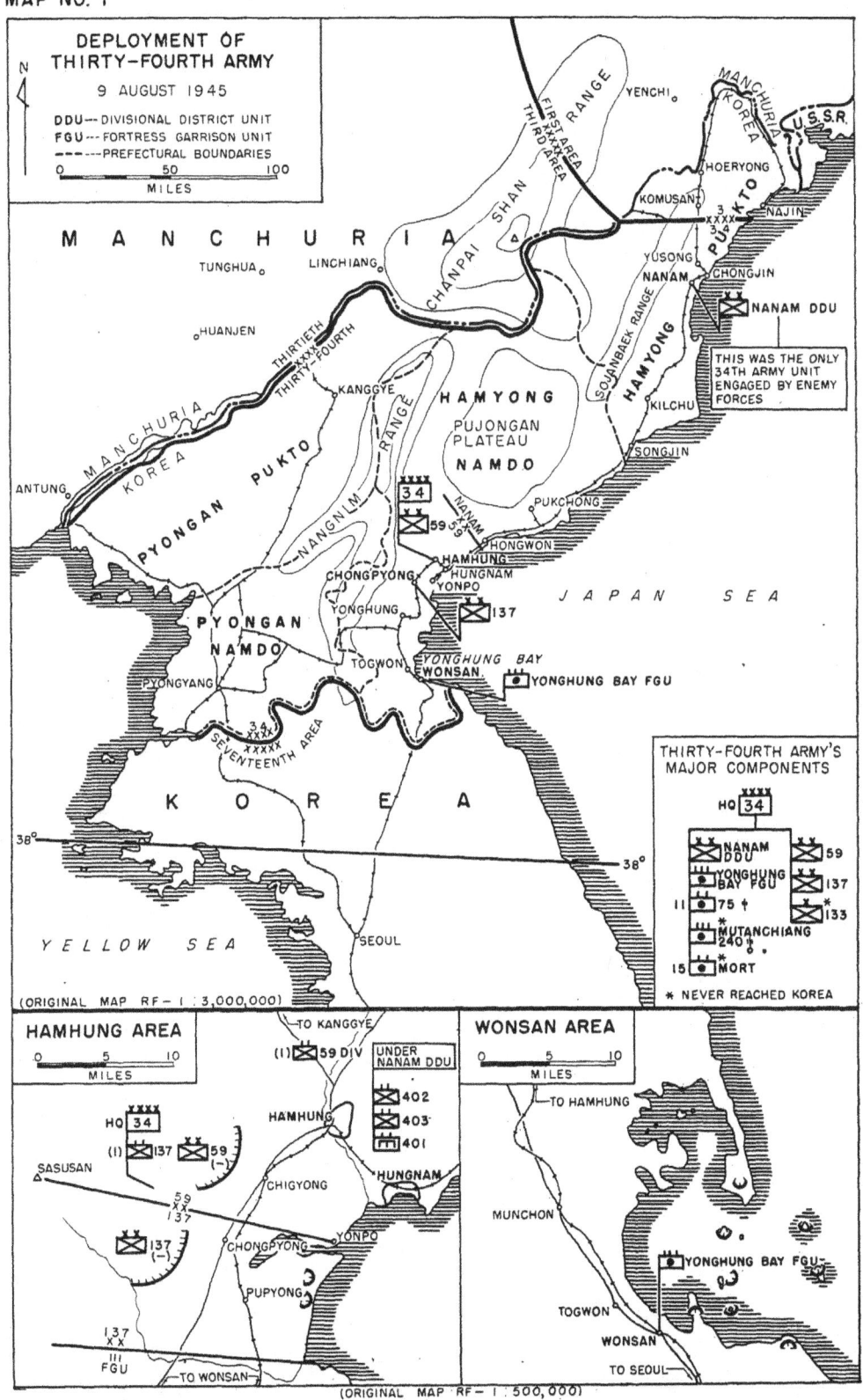

Fortress Garrison Unit.

The 59th Division crossed the China-Manchurian border on 19 July and reached its station at Hamhung several days later; its strength was approximately 15,000. In China it had acquired some combat experience. The 137th Division was assigned on 30 July; its strength was somewhat less than 10,000, consisting mainly of recruits obtained during the final mass mobilization in Manchuria. It was not until a few days before hostilities began--possibly by 2 or 3 August--that the Army got tactical control of its main body.

The quality of personnel was generally low. Except for the 59th Division, none of the commands had had any experience, and except for the Yonghung Bay Fortress Garrison Unit, all units had been recently organized.

As for equipment there was a serious shortage of weapons of all kinds, particularly artillery guns. The 137th Division, for example, had no pieces whatever. Logistical units, recently organized, were of very poor quality, and this was aggravated by the poor logistical situation. These units were never assured of daily supply, and were at times in such dire straits that they had to depend upon the branch freight (food and provisions) depot attached from the Seventeenth Area Army.

Operational Preparations   (See Map No 1.)

The missions given Thirty-fourth Army by the Kwantung Army were to secure strategic points in the vicinity of Hamhung against the enemy expected to advance southward from Hamyong Pukto Province, and to check an enemy advance to Seoul and Pyongyang. The Army was also directed to protect the Kanggye area with some of its elements.

To secure the strategic points in the Hamhung area, Thirty-fourth Army deployed the main bodies of the 59th and 137th Division in the hills southwest of Hamhung. (These hills, between ten and fifteen miles inland, more or less paralled the east coast. Through the coastal plain ran a railroad and a good dirt road.) The hill positions, if attacked, were to be defended to the end. In the event the enemy decided to by-pass them and advance southward toward Wonsan through the coastal plain, the Army was to launch an offensive to prevent the enemy's passage. Although the Army deployed no elements in the Kanggye area, it kept one battalion of the 59th Division in readiness north of Hamhung under its direct command, and planned to send it to the Kanggye area in the event the enemy expanded hostilities to that sector. The Army also assigned operational missions to the Nanam Divisional District Unit. (See Monograph No 155-Q)

Because Korea was considered imperial territory, the problem of the chain of command there had been a perplexing one for some time. This was particularly true in northern Korea where the boundary of the expeditionary Kwantung Army was contiguous to that of the imperial forces in Korea. The problem was aggravated by the gradual extension, beginning on 18 September 1944, of Kwantung Army's responsibilities into northern Korea.[47] Briefly, the Korea Army had been reorganized on 6 February 1945 into the Seventeenth Area Army, a tactical command, and the Korea Administrative Defense Army, a peace and order command. Simultaneously, the Seventeenth Area Army had been directed to give primary attention to operational preparations in southern Korea. Although this had the effect of leaving operational preparations in northern Korea in the hands of the Kwantung Army commander-in-chief, and led to the deployment of Thirty-fourth Army there, it did not totally eliminate Seventeenth Area Army's jurisdiction. The exact limits of the jurisdiction of each command were not clear, although Kwantung Army had authority to issue orders to the commander in Korea in matters relating to operational preparations in northern Korea. In any event, Kwantung Army had always felt that should war break out with the USSR it should be given tactical control of all forces in Korea.[48]

Early in August 1945, Kwantung Army recommended that the following chain of command apply in northern Korea: the Thirty-fourth Army should be placed under the tactical control of the Seventeenth Area Army, while continuing to be supplied principally

---

47. See Monograph No 138, pp 107-108 and 148-151.
48. For a record of the Korea Army (Seventeenth Area Army and Korea Administration District Army) see Monograph No 22.

by the Kwantung Army; the Nanam Divisional District Unit should be placed under the tactical command of Thirty-fourth Army. It further recommended that the zone of responsibility of Thirty-fourth Army consist of the four northern provinces of Korea (Hamyong Pukto, Hamyong Namdo, Pyongan Pukto, and Pyongan Namdo), except the northern part of Hamyong Pukto (including the port of Najin) earlier assigned to the Third Army's 79th Division. These recommendations remained in abeyance until the war started, at which time Imperial General Headquarters placed Seventeenth Area Army completely under Kwantung Army's control.

As soon as Thirty-fourth Army began to assume actual control of its main forces in late July it directed that the construction of fortifications be begun. Because of the shortage of equipment and materials, however, progress was slow. To help in this construction work, Kwantung Army ordered two of its construction battalions to proceed to Korea, but these did not arrive until the war's end. What work was done was designed mainly as a protection against tank and artillery attacks. In this connection, in selecting positions for first line defenses, all units were instructed to avoid if possible the rising ground where the plain joins the hills, because of the vulnerability of such areas to enemy observation.

As for communications, army headquarters had no difficulty maintaining contact with units directly under its command, the principal method being wireless telegraph.

To foster training in the short time available in view of the mounting tension, Army headquarters issued a supplement to the combat manual, stressing raiding tactics, antitank fighting, the effective use of a small force to check a large force, thoroughness of fortification construction, and self-sacrificing patriotism.

End of the War and Negotiations with the Soviets[49]

Upon learning of the Imperial Rescript on 15 August, Army headquarters ordered all its subordinate commands to cease hostilities. Actually, since no elements of the Army had engaged in operations, other than the Nanam Divisional District Unit this order, for all practical purposes applied only to the Nanam Unit which was fighting in the vicinity of Chongjin and did not halt operations until the 18th.

To conduct cease-fire negotiations with Soviet forces, the Thirty-fourth Army commander, at the direction of Kwantung Army flew to Yenchi on 21 August, accompanied by a party of eight, including his senior staff officer, Colonel Ogi. There negotiations were opened with the Soviet Twenty-fifth Army's chief of staff, a lieutenant general.

Particularly noteworthy about the Yenchi conference was the fact that a conflict developed between Soviet and Japanese negotia-

---

49. The author of this monograph failed to include an account of operations. However, see the monograph on the Nanam Divisional District Unit. (Q)

tors regarding the place designated for the assembly of Japanese troops: While the Soviets demanded that all Japanese forces in Korea north of latitude 38 degrees be assembled at Komusan as prisoners of war, the Japanese representatives insisted on assembling at other places, less remote to transport and supply routes, and eventually made the Soviets agree to this. The reason for insisting on this point was that Komusan, a small hamlet, had no reserve supplies, and the railway line to the north where provisions were stored had been destroyed. This meant that assembling large forces in Komusan would inevitably result in logistical hardships and possibly lead to starvation.

The areas proposed for assembly by the Japanese representatives were Nanam (for the majority of the Nanam Divisional District Unit), Hamhung and Wonsan (for Thirty-fourth Army and divisional district units in the vicinity of Hamhung), and Pyongyang (for units in Pyongan Pukto and Pyongan Namdo provinces). Upon completion of these negotiations at Yenchi, the Army commander and his party returned to Hamhung on 22 August, accompanied by a Soviet lieutenant colonel, a major, and a captain.

In direct contravention to the agreement reached at Yenchi the Soviet lieutenant colonel on 24 August directed that all Japanese forces north of latitude 38 be assembled at Komusan. Army headquarters, pointing out that the Twenty-fifth Army chief of staff had agreed at Yenchi to assembly at the three points requested by the Japanese, insisted that the Thirty-fourth Army assemble in the

Hamhung vicinity. The Soviet officer rejected this flatly. Nevertheless, Army headquarters adhered to the Yenchi agreement, and repudiated the lieutenant colonel's directive. Subsequently four conferences were held--at noon and at 1800 of the 24th, and at 0900 and noon of the 25th--but no satisfactory solution was found. Finally, at 1600 hours of the 25th, when General Chushchakov, commander of the Soviet Twenty-fifth Army, arrived at Hamhung by plane, Army headquarters took up the matter with him. He reaffirmed the agreement reached at Yenchi, but it was apparent that neither he nor the Soviet lieutenant colonel had had any knowledge of the details of the Yenchi negotiations.

Disarmament of Japanese troops began on 26 August. On that date, the problem of where to assemble Japanese forces again erupted. This time, however, the problem concerned only troops of the Thirty-fourth Army, and arose out of Soviet instructions to assemble at the Pupyong maneuver area, about thirty kilometers south of Hamhung. Since Pupyong could accommodate only about 2,000, and had poor facilities, it would be difficult to subsist there, particularly in the cold season. Army headquarters requested that units be interned at the twelve places, between Hamhung and Pupyong, at which they were then stationed. The Soviets did not agree to this. Particular objection was raised by the lieutenant colonel who had created the earlier problem. He strongly insisted on internment in one place.

Army headquarters explained to Soviet officials the difficulties in matters of food, clothing, and shelter that would arise from internment at one place, emphasizing that if many troops became sick or died from malnutrition or inadequate sanitary conditions caused by internment at one place, the Soviet Union would be subject to attack by world opinion for its inhumanitarianism. Finally, the Soviet Army's assistant chief of staff, a major general, approved internment at the twelve places designated by Japanese representatives. As a result, Japanese troops were able to live with little anxiety about food and clothing during their two months of internment life in Korea.

Meanwhile, Soviet authorities directed that control of all Japanese forces in the Hamhung area be consolidated under the commander of the Thirty-fourth Army. Accordingly, Army headquarters took charge of the air units at Yonpo and Togwon, the naval units at Wonsan, and naval personnel who had supervised powder production at the Korean Nitrogen Company in Hungnam. However, because of the disruption of signal communication, both the army and navy units at Wonsan could not be controlled. Furthermore, naval personnel at Hungnam deserted.

The Army commander and all other general officers of the Army were taken by plane to the Maritime Province at the end of August. Most of the other officers were interned at the Chongpyong Primary School. They were nominally under the control of Colonel Tamura, chief of the Hamhung Railway Branch, who was the senior officer, but actually took directions from the staff officers of Thirty-fourth Army.

Civil Affairs

After the cease fire, Koreans openly oppressed the Japanese; governmental organs had become totally impotent even prior to the arrival of Soviet occupation forces. Immediately after the war ended, the Army, fearing Korean rioting, had posted troops of two infantry battalions at about ten key points in the Hamhung vicinity. The Army did not feel, however, that this action would be adequate to protect Japanese residents. As an additional measure, therefore, it released all draftees who had relatives in Korea and Eastern Manchuria so that they could go home and protect their families.

Monograph No 155-P

CHAPTER XVI

The 137th Division[50]

Organization

The 137th Infantry Division was organized during the July 1945 mass mobilization that virtually exhausted Japanese manpower in Manchuria. The initial phase of organizing the division, carried out at Antung, was the responsibility of the commander of the Kwantung Territory Guard Unit. From his own unit this commander provided personnel for the headquarters of battalions and higher components. Latter phases were in the hands of the commander of the Nanam Divisional District Unit, which at Nanam provided the remainder of personnel as well as clothing, weapons, and equipment. In addition, some assistance was provided by the 79th Division.

The division commander was Lieutenant General Yoshisuke Akiyama. Most of the officers, noncommissioned officers, and men assigned to the division were draftees. Many of them had been deferred during earlier mobilizations because of the importance of their civilian positions to Manchukuo's economy or government.

The division did not complete its organization until early August, at which time its strength was less than 10,000. The equipment it

---

50. The information in this chapter was furnished by Colonel Shichiro Mihara, chief of staff, 137th Division.

248

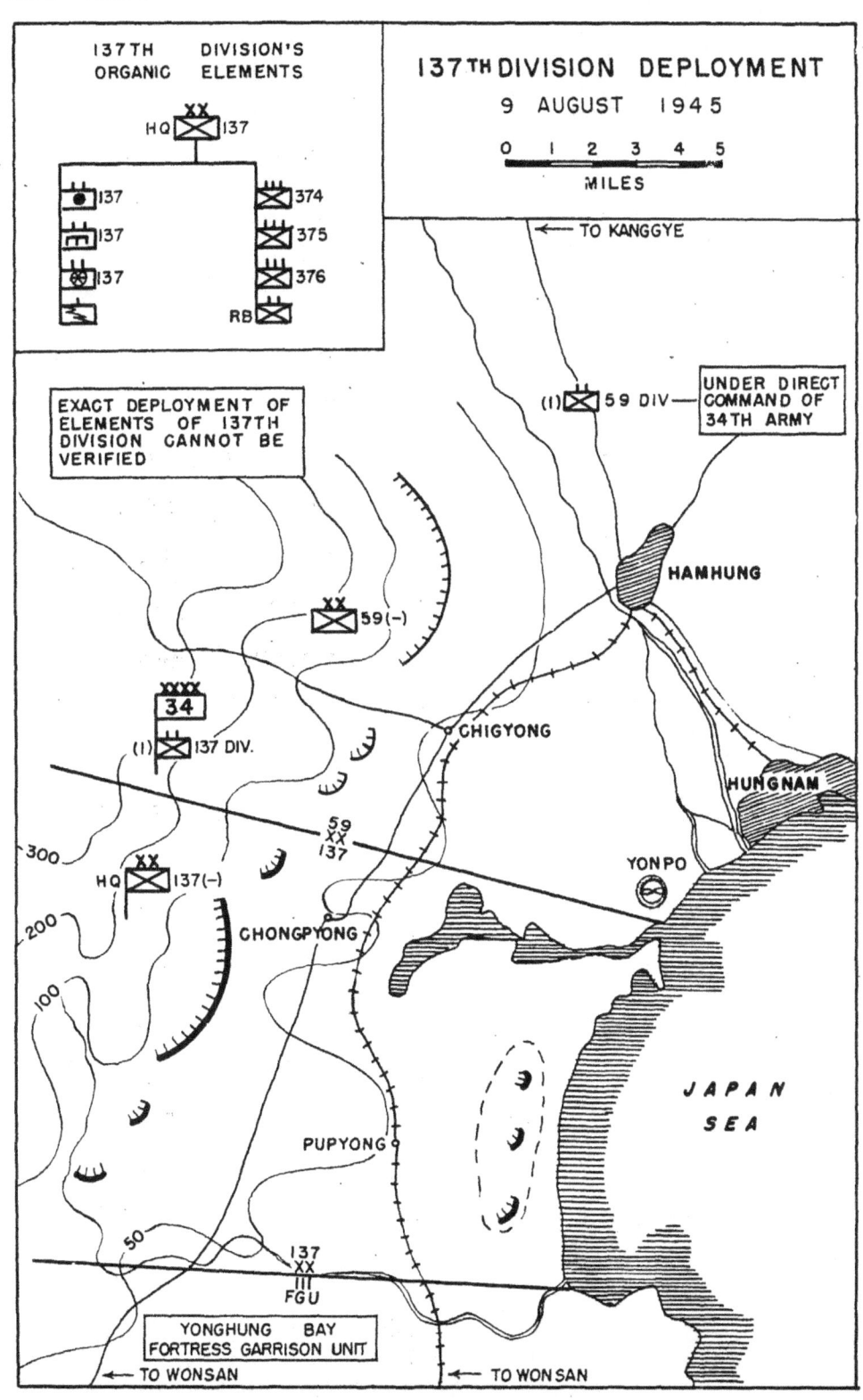

received consisted only of rifles and light and heavy machine guns. Artillery guns and other equipment, though requisitioned and en route to the divisions, were never received. The division had hardly any fortification materials and camping equipment, and in the midst of training had to rush supply personnel to Antung to get some. The only items the division was issued at Antung, however, were one saw per battalion and one axe per company. In addition, there was an acute shortage of explosives for close-quarter operations. Aside from the shortages of materiel, moreover, there was a scarcity of food and provisions. Although the division submitted frequent requests to the Army, it received very little, and at the end of the war had only a two-day supply on hand. The fact that only three trucks were available for transport increased the division's apprehension as regards re-supply. Furthermore, locally obtainable foodstuffs were inferior.

As the right-wing unit of Thirty-fourth Army, the division was deployed in the hilly area west of Chongpyong and Pupyong, facing generally east. On its left was the 59th Division. (See Map No 1)

Situation Immediately Prior to Hostilities

Thanks to the efforts of the Nanam Divisional District Unit, the quality of the training of junior officers and men given by that Unit was generally satisfactory. Section chiefs of division headquarters, however, were all well advanced in years. Infantry regimental commanders, moreover, were not too young, and it was feared that despite their wealth of experience in regimental duties their performance on the battlefield would be unsatisfactory. As a matter of fact, since nearly all officers had previously been deferred from military service and were relatively old, it was feared that very few members of the division were in condition to perform military duties satisfactorily.

Division efforts to unify its components into one combat team and to carry out training were hindered by the lack of essential items of equipment. However, in unifying and training the division, relatively rapid progress was made in a short period, through the vigorous efforts of unit commanders. Also contributing to this progress was the absence of problems of military discipline (despite the fact that many Korean soldiers were in the division), and also the low rate of injury and sickness.

Signal communication with Army headquarters, and through it with the Yonghung Fortress Garrison Unit, was maintained by wire and wireless telegraph and was generally good, but with 59th Division no communications could be established mainly because of the confusion following the occupation of positions. Within the division's operational zone, where the terrain was difficult and the units widely dispersed, there was an inadequate quantity of wire and wireless telegraph equipment, and the division had to supplement it by inaugurating a visual signal communications net.

End of the War and Negotiations with the Soviets

The surrender of Japan and the termination of the war were a great shock to the troops of all units. Fortunately, there was no chaos or disorder among the troops.

In accordance with a series of orders from the Army, the division began making preparations to assemble, first, in the Chongpyong-Pupyong area, then along the railroad leading to Yonghung, later again in the Chongpyong-Pupyong area, and finally in the Chongpyong-Yonghung area. These changing orders resulted from the conflict between Japanese and Soviet views as to where Japanese troops should assemble. (See Monograph No 155-O)

Assembly in Pyongyang

Meanwhile, with the end of war, the division was assigned directly to the Seventeenth Area Army. It was ordered to send its main body to Pyongyang for the maintenance of peace and order, and to dispatch one regiment to Wonsan to protect Japanese residents. For the latter mission, the division selected the 375th Regiment, but while this unit was being transported by rail to Wonsan, word was received that that city was already occupied by elements of the Soviet Army. The 375th Regiment was therefore ordered to turn back and join the division's main body at Pyongyang. It arrived just prior to the occupation of the Pyongyang airfield by the Soviet Army, and was the last division element to reach Pyongyang, except for an element of division headquarters which, travelling in five trucks, had difficulty negotiating the precipitous Nangnim Mountain Range of Korea.

Through the good offices of the Pyongyang Divisional District Unit, the division, immediately upon arrival at Pyongyang, was provided billets either at the military barracks or at the middle schools there. Having only a two-day supply of provisions, the division sought immediate replenishment from the local air branch depot and ordnance branch depot. At the same time it submitted requisitions to the Seventeenth Area Army, and as a result was authorized to obtain a supply of provisions from stocks at Susaek. However, because the railway to Susaek had been severed by the Soviet Army, the division finally ended up obtaining provisions from the Pyongyang Divisional District Unit Headquarters.

Cease-fire negotiations were conducted between the commander of the Pyongyang Divisional District and Lieutenant Colonel Rakon of the Soviet Army shortly after the latter's arrival at the Pyongyang airfield. Later, when Soviet Army Headquarters arrived, all Japanese units were ordered to assemble in the Chuul area. There, one regiment was quartered at the Mitsui Airplane Factory, some units at the primary school; others had to bivouac. Later some units were provided quarters in the barracks formerly used by infantry noncommissioned officer candidates, while division headquarters moved to the building of the Ordnance and Intendance Departments of the Divisional District. Later, a third change in billeting arrangements in Chuul was made: officers were interned in the Migundang Barracks; men in the Samhamni Barracks. All arms, ammunition, and other material were confiscated, including a huge quantity of clothing and provisions which the Japanese had earlier distributed among Koreans.

The Soviet occupation force in Pyongyang consisted of military police, motor transport, antiaircraft artillery, and air units. The occupation force took a generally conciliatory attitude toward Japanese troops and residents. However, the Soviets released imprisoned Koreans and manipulated them from behind the scenes, so that the Japanese were oppressed by them. Moreover, further oppression came from the Korean Public Peace Maintenance Society at Pyongyang. Not infrequently, hooligan Koreans and Soviet soldiers drove Japanese out of their homes, searched and looted their houses, and assaulted them. Moreover, Japanese civilian refugees from eastern Manchuria who fled to Pyongyang and tended to congregate in the girls high school were ill-fed and ill-clothed, but Soviet authorities did not accord them any positive relief. Again and again, Japanese resident's associations appealed to Soviet and Korean authorities. What small help was given was barely enough for these refugees to keep alive.

In the meantime,[51] Major General Ihara, chief of staff of

---

51. The author of this monograph was unable to give more specific dates or hours.

Seventeenth Area Army, arrived at Pyongyang from Seoul by air for conferences with Soviet authorities. Although the Divisional District had negotiated with the Soviets in matters relating to the cease-fire and disarmament, and continued to negotiate regarding certain local matters, General Ihara opened negotiations relative to measures to be taken after the cease fire and disarmament had been effected. These included the protection of Japanese residents and the maintenance of public peace. Although negotiations conducted by both General Ihara and the commander of the Divisional District proceeded smoothly, the Soviet authorities were deceitful and unfaithful from the beginning to the end. Moreover, they created unnecessary hardships by issuing directives on the spur of the moment.

In some cases, unruly behavior on the part of Japanese soldiers resulted from Soviet orders to separate them from officers and noncommissioned officers. The most flagrant of these occurred at the Samhamni Barracks where the disorder was beyond description. Soldiers scattered their weapons, vehicles, clothing, and medical supplies along a road near the barracks for a distance of about one "ri" (about 3.927 kilometers), and set fire to them. Soviet officers and men, as well as Koreans, were observed in search of valuables among the smoldering remains.[52]

---

52. Much of this monograph, although prepared by a former colonel, was written in unmilitary language. At this particular point in the narrative, the author, apparently attempting to give his monograph a dramatic touch, wrote: "I was reminded of Napoleon's retreat from Moscow."

After the cease-fire, Kwantung Army ordered the release of all officers drafted in Manchuria. Although most units in Manchuria complied, the division, most of whose officers were in this category, did not receive word of this order until a withdrawing unit arrived at Pyongyang. The division released some officers to return to Manchuria, but only in exceptional cases. However, in accordance with an order from Seventeenth Area Army, it sent some officers to Pyongyang as city police assistants, authorizing them to return to Manchuria as occasion permitted. However, almost all of them were arrested by the Korean Public Peace Maintenance Society at Pyongyang and sent back to the barracks in Chuul. Some had been arrested while on their way to Pyongyang to serve as city police assistants and, because they were disguised as soldiers, were returned to enlisted barracks.

Meanwhile, Soviet authorities conducted frequent searches for Japanese in the vicinity of Pyongyang, and arrested many. On the other hand, many escaped.

Officers interned at the Migundang Officers' Internment Camp near Pyongyang were from the following units: Pyongyang Divisional District Unit, military affairs departments, military police units, military hospitals, ordnance branch depots, air depots of the western district of North Korea as far as Antung, several naval officers who had supervised coal mines under the navy's jurisdiction, the 137th Division, Supply Command and Fortification Corps of

Kwantung Army, air units, airfield units, police officials, provincial governors, and one infantry regiment of the 120th Division. Some of these officers were taken from the camp and imprisoned by Soviet authorities. While these officers were interned, Soviet officers frequently looted their barracks, taking such items as boots, watches, razors, and other personal belongings, on the pretext of inspection.

Monograph No 155-Q

CHAPTER XVII

The Nanam Divisional District Unit[53]

Organization and Missions

The origin of the Nanam Divisional District Unit is traceable to the 19th Depot (Training) Division, which at Nanam had been responsible for training recruits for tactical commands. When this training division itself was reorganized in March 1945 into the 79th Infantry Division, its training center was left in the hands of small units, actually training cadres. Seventeenth Area Army was confronted with organizing into one command not only these small training units but also the numerous nearby garrison units that were responsible for guarding important installations such as railroad stations and power stations. The number of these garrison units had increased with the rise of tension in Manchuria and Korea.

On 20 April Seventeenth Area Army ordered the new 79th Division to organize the Nanam Divisional District Unit, not only with existing units but also with new ones yet to be formed. Thus the components of the Nanam Unit had two types of missions--those of training and of maintaining peace and order--which were to be assumed by the

---

53. This chapter was assembled by the First Demobilization Bureau from various sources in its possession.

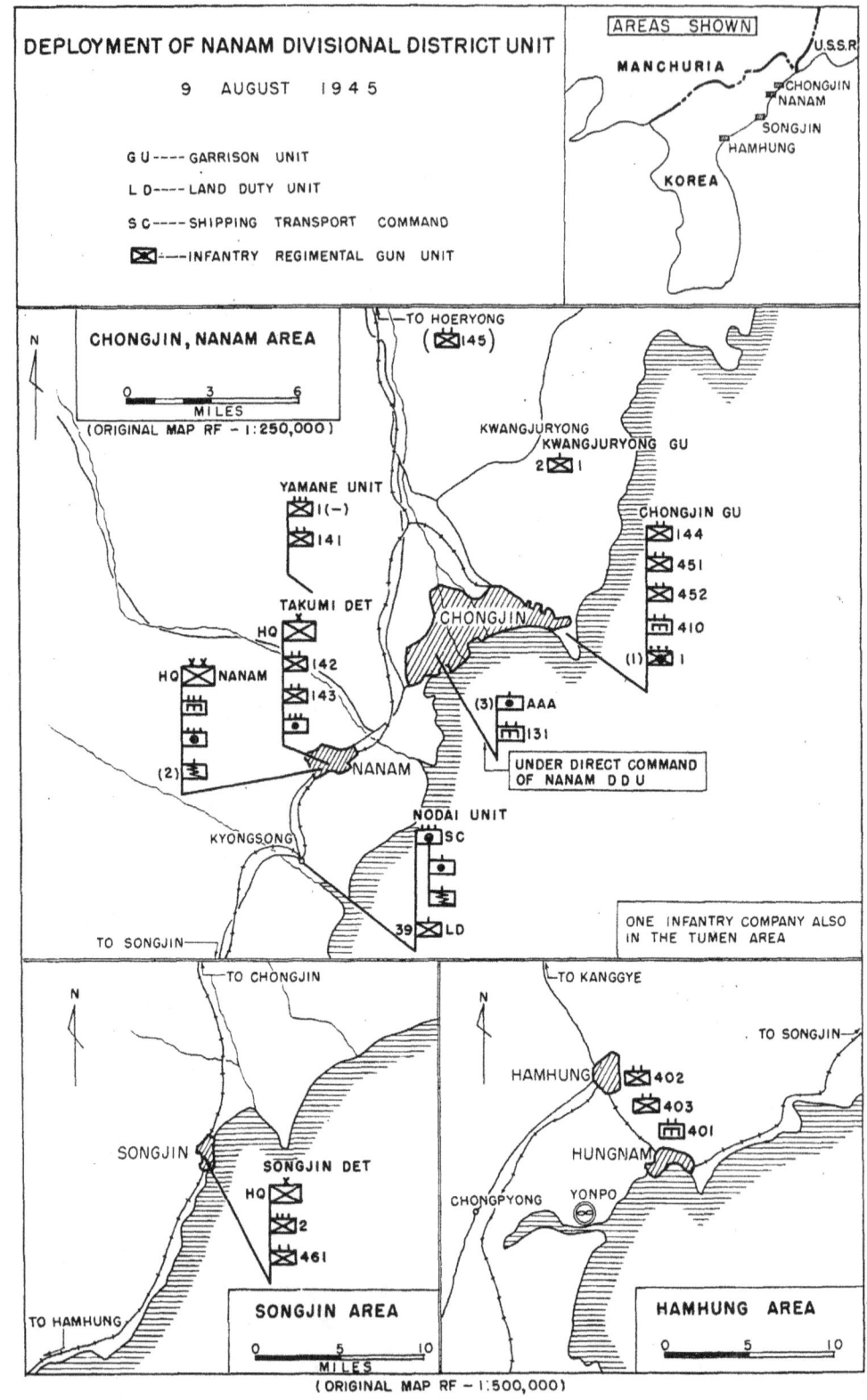

Nanam Unit itself as its principal functions. Other divisional district units in Korea had substantially the same missions.

The commander of the Nanam Divisional District Unit was Lieutenant General Sokichi Nishiwaki. His chief of staff was Colonel Yutaka Shirakawa. Although the Nanam Unit was approximately division size, though not structurally, the wide dispersal of its components gave it less unity than that expected in a division. The strength of training elements was approximately 10,426, that of guard units about 8,841, while that of tactical units was about 1,500.

Because of the wide dispersal of units, General Nishiwaki organized most of his command into two sub-districts, the Nanam Sub-district Command under Major General Hiroshi Takumi, and the Hamhung Sub-district Command under Major General Yoshisada Imaizumi. Each sub-district was further subdivided and these subdivisions assumed the name either of its commander or of the town near which it was located. (See Map No 1)

The main training elements of the Nanam Unit were the 1st and 2d Infantry Depot Units, the artillery, engineer, transport units (all structurally regiments), and signal unit (structurally a company). The guard units were of two classifications, those that had been in existence at the time of the Nanam Unit's organization, and those newly organized. Of the former there were five—the 141st through 145th Guard Battalions; of the latter there were eleven—the 401st through 403d, the 405th, the 408th through 410th, the 451st and 452d, and the 461st and 462d Specially Established Guard Battalions.[54]

General Takumi had in his Nanam Sub-district Command five detachments: his own, the (Colonel) Yamane Detachment, the Chongjin Garrison Unit, the (Colonel) Nodai Detachment, and the Kwangjuryong Garrison Unit. General Imaizumi had two detachments in his Hamhung Sub-district Command. Besides his own at Songin, he had a Hamhung-Hungnam Guard Detachment stationed between those two towns.

The tactical units, all of which were retained under the direct command of the Nanam Unit headquarters, consisted of the 65th Independent AAA Battery, the 2d Battery of the 85th Independent AAA Battalion, one battery of the 46th Independent AAA Battalion, and the 131st Independent Engineer Battalion. The logistical units were also retained under the direct command of the headquarters. Principal among these was the North Korea Branch of the 1st Shipping Transport Command which was responsible for coastal shipping operations; it had signal and depot elements for its support, and artillery elements for its defense. Other logistical units were: the 39th Land Duty Unit, the 37th Air Signal Unit, and an element of the Signal Unit of Imperial General Headquarters.

---

54. "Specially established" actually means "especially established to meet the emergency." Personnel in these units were of lower quality than the average, and were obtained principally when the bottom of the barrel was being scraped during the mass-mobilization of July 1945. Most of its members had previously been deferred.

Assignment and Missions

Since the Nanam Unit was essentially a non-tactical command--although it was given several tactical units--it was initially assigned to the Korea Administrative Defense Army rather than to the Seventeenth Area Army.[55] These two armies had joint jurisdiction in Korea, the former over civilian defense, the latter over operational preparations; both were commanded by Lieutenant General Yoshio Kozuki.

Under the Kwantung Army commander's authority to issue orders to General Kozuki's commands in matters relating to operational preparations, Thirty-fourth Army in early August notified the Nanam Unit to be prepared to assume two operational missions. (For administrative matters, the Nanam Unit remained under the jurisdiction of the Korea Administrative Defense Army). These missions were to prevent an enemy amphibious landing in the Chongjin area, and to check any enemy attempts to make an overland drive in the area between Chongjin and Hongwon. Ever since the main body of the 79th Division had departed the Nanam area in June and its headquarters in late July, such operational missions had been anticipated. Although the 137th Division was then being organized in this area, it was not to complete its organization until a few days before

---

55. For a record of the Korea Army (Seventeenth Area Army and Korea Administrative Defense Army) see Monograph No 22.

MONOGRAPH NO. 155-Q
MAP NO. 2

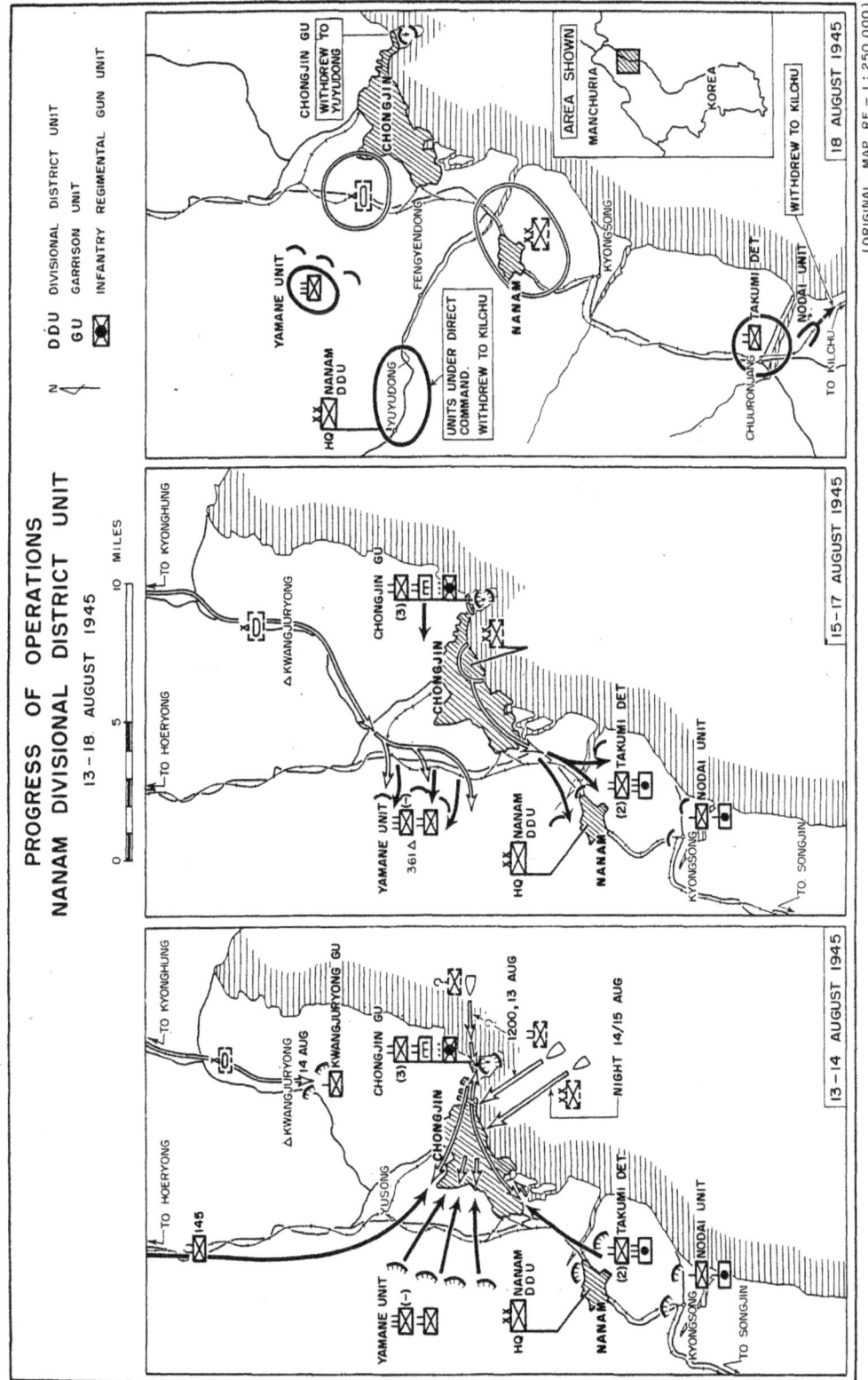

the outbreak of hostilities, and in any event was scheduled for deployment elsewhere.

General Nishiwaki, with a view to guarding the Chongjin area against Soviet invasion, ordered his Chongjin Garrison Unit to occupy previously constructed positions on the Chongjin Peninsula, the Yamane Detachment to occupy the sector about five miles west of Chongjin, and the Takumi Detachment to defend Nanam by deploying elements both east and west of the city. He also ordered the Kwangjuryong Garrison Unit, which consisted mainly of the 2d Company of the 1st Infantry Depot Unit, to defend Kwangjuryong Pass. At the same time he deployed the Nodai Detachment at Kyongsong, and ordered General Imaizumi's Sub-district Command to defend Songjin, Hamhung, and Hungnam. Headquarters remained at Nanam.

Opening of Hostilities   (See Map No 2)

On 9 August Soviet forces were reported to be attacking along various fronts of Manchuria and to have crossed into Korea near Kyonghung.[56] It was not until the 13th, however, that they engaged elements of the Nanam Divisional District Unit. The initial attack took the form of an amphibious assault at Chongjin.

---

56. On the 10th the Nanam Divisional District was placed directly under Thirty-fourth Army, but it is uncertain as to whether it ever received this order. However, at the time it was given operational missions, it was informed that in the event of hostilities it would be assigned to Thirty-fourth Army. (The same order assigned Seventeenth Area Army to Kwantung Army, and the Thirty-fourth Army to Seventeenth Area Army.)

At noon of 13 August the Soviets put ashore approximately 600 men on the beaches of Chongjin harbor.[57] This assault was supported by another landing, presumably by a company size unit, north of the Chongjin peninsula. These two landings placed the enemy at both sides of the peninsula's neck.

The Chongjin garrison, whose old 75-mm mountain guns had previously attacked the landing craft, immediately engaged the enemy. At the same time the Yamane and Takumi Detachments left their defense positions, respectively west and south of Chongjin, and hurried towards the city, and the 145th Guard Battalion, under orders of the Nanam Unit Headquarters, departed Hoeryong and hastened to reinforce the left flank of the Yamane Detachment.

After landing, the enemy quickly began to attack the Chongjin peninsula's defenses from the rear, meanwhile attempting to join forces across the peninsula's neck. After joining forces the enemy left small elements on the peninsula to wipe out remaining resistance, and began advancing his main body westward toward Yusong and southward

---

57. According to an article printed in a Japanese magazine on the eighth anniversary of the Soviet invasion of Manchuria, this landing (as well as the one at Najin on the 10th) was supported by the Soviet Pacific Fleet which was based at Vladivostok and commanded by Admiral Yumasheyev. This fleet consisted of one cruiser, eight destroyers, ninety submarines, and sixty torpedo boats. Simultaneous with the land invasion of Manchuria this fleet moved to disrupt Kwantung Army's maritime transportation. (<u>Asiatic Mainland Affairs</u> pp 39-40, 1 Aug 53, published in Tokyo, Japan, by the Asiatic Mainland Research Institute which is composed largely of ex-military men. A translation of this article is in the files of MHS, HQ AFFE)

to Chongjin city. Meanwhile, one enemy element that had succeeded in advancing to the southern part of Chongjin was encountered by the Takumi Detachment and was annihilated by it.

By daybreak of the 14th the enemy had formed a front near the perimeter of the city. The Yamane and Takumi Detachments pressed against this front and, fighting in the streets, they succeeding in breaking through at various places, but were unable to reach the north side of Chongjin.

At midnight of 14 August, the enemy landed a division size force at Chongjin harbor. In view of this major landing, General Nishiwaki ordered the Yamane and Takumi Detachments to disengage the enemy and return to their original defense positions.

In the northernmost positions of the Nanam Unit, meanwhile, the Kwangjuryong Garrison Unit on the 14th reported that it was being confronted by an enemy armored force of about brigade size which presumably had entered Korea near Kyonghung on the 9th. Its subsequent actions were not learned.

Nanam Divisional District Headquarters had lost contact with higher headquarters due to the severance of communications, and was unaware of the Imperial Rescript of 15 August. Its force continued to engage the enemy from the 16th to the 18th and by holding previously prepared defense positions, it checked the enemy's southward advance. On the morning of 18 August, General Nishiwaki decided to move his troops to the vicinity of Kilchu, about sixty miles south of Chongjin. At about 1800 hours, while en route, a staff officer of the Korea Administrative Defense Army joined the retreating columns, bringing word of the cease-fire order.

Losses sustained during the initial phases of operations totalled about 110 killed, and during operations from defensive positions about 117 killed.

End of Hostilities

On the morning of 19 August, General Nishiwaki, accompanied by his chief of staff, Colonel Shirakawa, met with a Soviet division commander at Nanam. As a result of this conference a formal cease-fire agreement was reached.

The next day the Chongjin Garrison Unit was disarmed at Yuyudong, Fengyendong, and Chuuronjang, and later was assembled at the Nanam Drill Grounds. On the 22d the unit was marched to Komusan, arriving on the 22d. Quarters were provided in the dormitory of the cement plant or in the semi-cave shelters which had been built around the primary school.

The Songjin Detachment and the Hamhung Guard Unit were disarmed at their positions. The Songjin Detachment moved to Nanam to join the main force of the Divisional District, and then, in compliance with a Soviet Army directive, moved to Hamhung.

Personnel of the Nanam Divisional District Unit interned at Komusan numbered 5,700, including 669 Korean soldiers; those of Kwantung Army units about 800. All these personnel were organized into six labor battalions, each consisting of 1,000 men, and were sent to Soviet territory beginning in October. About 500 men, considered surplus to the labor battalions, were moved to the Puryong Internment Camp.

Monograph No. 155 - Table No. 1

Actual Strength of Kwantung Army Components at Outbreak of Hostilities (August 1945) and KIA Estimates*

Units	Actual Strength	KIA (%)
Kwantung Army		
GHQ	3,308	-
125th Div	11,450	-
Kwantung Army Supply Department	73,093	185
Directly assigned units	77,182	527
Total:	165,033	712 (0.4%)
First Area Army		
HQ	741	1
122d Div	16,027	49
128th Div	12,634	1,095
134th Div	14,056	471
139th Div	9,793	20
132d IMB	5,545	725
Directly assigned units	24,650	320
Total:	83,446	2,681 (3.2%)
Third Army		
HQ	968	-
79th Div	15,633	142
112d Div	15,068	930
127th Div	12,839	853
Najin FGU	1,280	136
Directly assigned units	17,152	375
Total:	62,940	2,436 (3.9%)
Fifth Army		
HQ	800	10
124th Div	14,824	2,297
126th Div	16,613	1,857
135th Div	14,228	1,631
15th BGU	1,700	1,400
Directly assigned units	27,606	2,196
Total:	75,771	9,391 (12.4%)
First Area Army Total:	222,157	14,508 (6.5%)
Third Area Army		
HQ	1,660	-
138th Div	8,810	-
79th IMB	6,772	-
134th IMB	4,448	-
Directly assigned units	20,788	157
Total:	42,478	157 (0.4%)
Thirtieth Army		
HQ	610	-
39th Div	16,274	1
107th Div	14,070	1,380

(Cont'd)

117th Div	13,694	150
148th Div	9,828	16
133d IMB	4,898	-
9th Tk Brig	2,281	-
Directly assigned units	7,748	-
Total:	69,403	1,547 (2.2%)
Forty-fourth Army		
HQ	400	-
63d Div	10,499	-
108th Div	18,141	110
136th Div	13,559	-
130th Div	7,400	-
1st Tk Brig	5,371	-
Directly assigned units	13,720	170
Total:	69,090	280 (0.4%)
Third Area Army Total:	180,971	1,984 (1.1%)
Fourth Army		
HQ	928	-
119th Div	18,721	1,253
123d Div	17,764	879
149th Div	12,100	-
80th IMB	7,068	1,077
131st IMB	4,797	3
135th IMB	4,138	228
136th IMB	4,318	-
Directly assigned units	25,630	-
Total:	95,464	3,440 (3.6%)
Thirty-fourth Army		
HQ	650	-
59th Div	14,916	-
137th Div	9,806	-
Nanam DDU	19,267	745
Directly assigned units	5,465	-
Total:	50,104	745 (1.5%)
Grand Total:	713,729	21,389 (2.9%)

* These data were furnished by the 1st Demobilization Bureau and in some instance differ from the figures given by authors of sub-monographs.

LEGEND

Div ...... Infantry Division
IMB ...... Independent Mixed Brigade
FGU ...... Fortress Garrison Unit
BGU ...... Border Garrison Unit
DDU ...... Divisional District Unit

Monograph No. 155 - Appendix No. I

Major Tactical Ground Units of Japanese Army Up to 1945

LEGEND

Div .... Infantry Division
Konoye Div .. Imperial Guard Infantry Division
Brig .... Independent Mixed Brigade
Inf Brig .... Independent Infantry Brigade
Guard Brig .. Guard Infantry Brigade
TKD .... Tank Division
TKB .... Tank Brigade
Zone .... Operational Zone
* .... Annihilated

First General Army (Cmdr: General Marshal Gen Sugiyama)
(Zone: East Homeland)

11th Area Army
(6 divs, 2 brigs)
- 72d Div
- 142d Div
- 157th Div
- 222d Div
- 308th Div
- 322d Div
- 95th Brig
- 113th Brig

12th Area Army
(21 divs, 13 brigs)
- 1st Konoye Div
- 3d Konoye Div
- 44th Div
- 81st Div
- 84th Div
- 93d Div
- 140th Div
- 147th Div
- 151st Div
- 152d Div
- 201st Div
- 202d Div
- 209th Div
- 214th Div
- 221st Div
- 234th Div
- 316th Div
- 321st Div
- 354th Div
- 1st TKD
- 4th TKD
- 66th Brig
- 67th Brig
- 96th Brig
- 114th Brig
- 115th Brig
- 116th Brig
- 117th Brig
- 1st Guard Brig
- 2d Guard Brig
- 3d Guard Brig
- 2d TKB
- 3d TKB
- 7th TKB

13th Area Army
(6 divs, 4 brigs)
- 73d Div
- 143d Div
- 153d Div
- 224th Div
- 229th Div
- 355th Div
- 97th Brig
- 119th Brig
- 120th Brig
- 8th TKB

(Cont'd)

Total of First General Army (33 divisions, 19 brigades)

Second General Army (Cmdr: General Marshal Shunroku Hata)
(Zone: West and South Homeland)

15th Area Army (8 divs, 3 brigs)	11th Div 144th Div 155th Div 205th Div 225th Div 230th Div 231st Div 344th Div	121st Brig 123d Brig 124th Brig
16th Area Army (14 divs, 11 brigs)	25th Div 57th Div 77th Div 86th Div 145th Div 146th Div 154th Div 156th Div 206th Div 212th Div 216th Div 303d Div 312th Div 351st Div	64th Brig 98th Brig 107th Brig 108th Brig 109th Brig 122d Brig 125th Brig 126th Brig 4th TKB 5th TKB 6th TKB

Total of Second General Army (22 divisions, 14 brigades)

Fifth Area Army (Cmdr: Lt. General Kiichiro Higuchi)
(Zone: Hokkaido, Sakhalin, Kuriles and Aleutians)

(5 divs, 2 brigs)	7th Div 42d Div 88th Div 89th Div 91st Div	101st Brig 129th Brig

Tenth Area Army (Cmdr: General Rikichi Ando)
(Zone: Formosa and Okinawa)

(8 divs, 11 brigs)	9th Div 12th Div 24th Div* 28th Div 62d Div* 66th Div 71st Div	44th Brig* 45th Brig 59th Brig 60th Brig 61st Brig 75th Brig 76th Brig

(Cont'd)

	90th Div	100th Brig 102d Brig 103d Brig 112th Brig

Ogasawara Group (Cmdr: Lt. General Yoshio Tachibana)
(Zone: Bonin Island)

(1 div)	109th Div	

Kwantung Army (Cmdr: General Otozo Yamada)
(Zone: Manchuria and Korea)

1st Area Army (10 divs, 1 brig)	79th Div 112th Div 122d Div 124th Div 126th Div 127th Div 128th Div 134th Div 135th Div 139th Div	132d Brig
3d Area Army (9 divs, 5 brigs)	39th Div 63d Div 107th Div 108th Div 117th Div 125th Div 136th Div 138th Div 148th Div	79th Brig 130th Brig 134th Brig 1st TKB 9th TKB
17th Area Army (7 divs, 2 brigs)	96th Div 111st Div 120th Div 121st Div 150th Div 160th Div 320th Div	108th Brig 127th Brig
4th Area Army (3 divs, 4 brigs)	119th Div 123d Div 149th Div	80th Brig 131st Brig 135th Brig 136th Brig
34th Area Army (2 divs, 1 brig)	59th Div 137th Div	133d Brig

Total of Kwantung Army
(31 divs, 13 brigs)

(Cont'd)

China Expeditionary Army (Cmdr: General Yasuji Okamura)
(Zone: China)

North China Area Army (6 divs, 11 brigs)	47th Div 110th Div 114th Div 115th Div 168th Div 3d TKD	1st Brig 2d Brig 3d Brig 5th Brig 8th Brig 9th Brig 4th Cav Brig 1st Inf Brig 2d Inf Brig 10th Inf Brig 14th Inf Brig
6th Area Army (5 divs, 14 brigs)	58th Div 64th Div 68th Div 116th Div 132th Div	17th Brig 32d Brig 81st Brig 82d Brig 83d Brig 84th Brig 85th Brig 86th Brig 87th Brig 88th Brig 5th Inf Brig 7th Inf Brig 11th Inf Brig 12th Inf Brig
13th Area Army (5 divs, 3 brigs)	60th Div 61st Div 65th Div 69th Div 161st Div	90th Brig 92d Brig 6th Inf Brig
6th Area Army (2 divs, 3 brigs)	70th Div 133d Div	62d Brig 89th Brig 91st Brig
23d Area Army (3 divs, 3 brigs)	104th Div 129th Div 130th Div	23d Brig 8d Inf Brig 13th Inf Brig
Direct Commands (6 divs)	3d Div 13th Div 27th Div 34th Div 40th Div 131st Div	

Total of China Expeditionary Army
(27 divisions, 34 brigades)

(Cont'd)

Southern Army (Cmdr: General Marshal Juichi Terauchi)
(Zone: South-western Area and Area North of Australia)

Army	Divisions	Brigades
Burma Area Army (7 divs, 3 brigs)	18th Div 31st Div 33d Div 49th Div 53d Div 54th Div 56th Div	24th Brig 72d Brig 105th Brig
7th Area Army (5 divs, 8 brigs)	2d Konoye Div 37th Div 46th Div 48th Div 94th Div	25th Brig 26th Brig 27th Brig 28th Brig 35th Brig 36th Brig 37th Brig 70th Brig
14th Area Army (13 divs, 4 brigs)	1st Div 8th Div 10th Div 16th Div 19th Div 23d Div 26th Div 30th Div 100th Div 102d Div 103d Div 105th Div 2d TKD	54th Brig 55th Brig 58th Brig 68th Brig
18th Area Army (3 divs, 1 brig)	4th Div 15th Div 22d Div	29th Brig
2d Army (4 divs, 2 brigs)	5th Div 32d Div 35th Div 36th Div	57th Brig 128th Brig
18th Army (3 divs)	20th Div 41st Div 51st Div	
37th Army (2 brigs)		56th Brig 71st Brig
38th Army (3 divs, 1 brig)	2d Div 21st Div 55th Div	34th Brig

(Cont'd)

Direct Commands (1 div, 2 brigs)	14th Div	49th Brig 53d Brig

Total of Southern Army
(39 divisions, 23 brigades)

Eighth Area Army (Cmdr: General Hitoshi Imamura)
              (Zone: Solomon Islands)

(3 divs, 4 brigs)	6th Div 17th Div 38th Div	38th Brig 39th Brig 40th Brig 65th Brig

Thirty-first Army (Cmdr: Lt. General Toshisaburo Mugikura)
              (Zone: Central Pacific Area)

(3 divs, 5 brigs)	29th Div* 43d Div* 52d Div	47th Brig* 48th Brig* 50th Brig 51st Brig 52d Brig

Grand Total: 172 divisions, 125 brigades

Monograph No. 155 - Appendix IIa

Conditions in USSR Internment Camp at RADA for Japanese POWs

Camp Facilities:

This camp was opened on 15 November 1945, and accommodated about 6,800 POWs, mostly officers. Quarters were of wood construction; some semi-cave quarters were also used. Heating was done by Piechka stoves. No electricity. POWs were well treated compared with other internment camps, since most of internees were officers. The camp closed on 25 August 1946. Most of the officers were transferred to Erabka Internment Camp. 300 men were sent near Tambov to work on farms.

Use of POW Labor:

8 hours per day
- Lumbering
- Transporting logs
- Farming
- Road construction
- Factory work

Daily Rations (three meals):

Stipulated amount*
- Rice .... 300 gr
- Other grains .... 100 gr
- Bread .... 300 gr
- Meat .... 75 gr
- Fish .... 80 gr
- Sugar .... 30 gr
- Salt .... 30 gr
- Vegetables .... 600 gr
- Butter .... 20 gr
- Oil .... 5 gr

(* Stipulated amount was never provided)

Allowances:

15 rubles per month for field grade officers.
10 rubles for company grade officers.

- Clothing .... Insufficient
- Blankets 2
- Toilet paper .... None
- Towels .... None
- Soap .... 400 gr/month
- Matches .... 1 bx/month
- Tabacco .... 15 gr/day
- Tea .... 3 gr/day

Medical Facilities:

Health Office:
- Army Doctors (Soviet) 20
- (Japanese) .. 20
- Nurses 40
- Medical aid men 20

Medical supplies: Insufficient and low grade
Patients (average per month): Approx. 300
Bath: Once a week

Sources:

This data was compiled from information obtained by the Demobilization Bureau from repatriates.

Monograph No. 155 - Appendix IIb

Conditions in USSR Internment Camp at VALESKY for Japanese POWs

Camp Facilities:
  Camp population: Unknown
  Quarters: Wood construction. A few quarters had individual beds, but most were double-decked.
  Heaters: Piechka and other type stoves.

Use of POW Labor:
  On the basis of a monthly physical examination, all personnel were classified as to the volume of work they could perform.

POWs	Hours	
1st grade	8 hrs/day	Weak POWs were excused from work.
2d grade	8 hrs/day	Hospitalized patients were given
3d grade	Approx. 6 hrs/day	rest and recuperation.

  Lumbering, farming, and factory work. (One day off per week.)
  Excused from outdoor labor when temperature was 25 degrees below zero.

Daily Rations (three meals):
  Rice .... 200 gr   Fish .... 150 gr
  Other grains .... 250 gr   (Patients .... 200 gr)
  Black bread .... 350 gr   Sugar -- EM .... 18 gr
    (White bread for patients)   Officers ..... 30 gr
  Meat .... 50 gr   Salt .... 5 gr
    (Patients .... 100 gr)   Vegetables .... 800 gr
                                        Oil .... 20 gr
  Butter, cheese, and fruit were occasionally provided patients.

Allowances:
  Monthly wage, estimated in July 1947, was based on 8 hrs/day:
  Odd jobs .... 18.20 rubles   General labor .... 24.83 rubles
  Light work .... 21.45 rubles

Clothing:
  Coat & trouser 1   Gloves, shoes ..... 1 pair each
  Shirt, cap, overcoat .... 1 each   Pillow and case ... 1
  Socks 2
  During winter, headgear, gloves, and overcoats were issued.

Market prices of commodities:
  Black bread (1 kg) 3.2 rubles   Wrist watch .... 300 rubles
  Soap 5   "   Shoes 40   "
  Vodka (1 litre) ...115   Boots 80   "
  Wool serge suit .. 120

Medical Facilities
  Health Office: Attended by Japanese and Soviet Army doctors and medical aid men. Seriously ill patients were hospitalized in Soviet hospitals and were given same treatment as Soviet patients.

Sources:
  Data obtained from Prisoner's Story in Siberia by Mr. Yasuyo Kurihara, a former private, unit unknown. The author was a pro-communist, a member of the so-called "Democratic Group" and "Culture Committee" of the internment camp.
  Source of information is not considered very reliable.

Monograph No. 155 – Appendix IIc

Conditions in USSR Internment Camp at MORSHANSK No. 64 for Japanese POWs

Camp Facilities:
No. of Japanese POWs: Officers: 2,000, enlisted men: 800
Majority of the internees consisted of personnel from Kwantung Army Headquarters, units in southern Manchuria, and air force personnel. (Approx. 7,000 German POWs were also interned in this camp.)
Quarters: Wood construction. Beds were double-decked.

Use of POW Labor:
Classification of workers established by monthly physical examinations:
POWs
1st grade) Suitable for   3d grade ... Light work
2d grade) hard labor   4th grade ... No labor
Reclamation of gas pipes, lumbering, work in tabacco factory, and miscellaneous work.

Daily Rations (three meals):
Regular amount based on orders of USSR Domestic Affairs Office

	Officers	EM		Officers	EM
Rice	100 gr	100 gr	Vegetables	600 gr	800 gr
Other grains	300 gr	350 gr	Oil	25 gr	7 gr
Black bread	300 gr	350 gr	Salt	30 gr	30 gr
Meat with bones	75 gr	50 gr	Sugar	30 gr	18 gr
Fish	80 gr	100 gr	Soy bean paste	50 gr	30 gr

Allowances: -- Data not available

Medical Facilities:
Health Office: Japanese physician (Lt Col) examined all POWs and was supervised by a Soviet physician (female captain). Hospital patients were classified as 1) bed patients, 2) those excused from all work, 3) those permitted to perform light work, and 4) those fit for any type of work.
Bath: Once a week

Punishment Regulations:
Recalcitrants were 1) placed in a detention camp, or 2) given "company" punishment (reduced rations or hard labor), or 3) placed in penitentiary.

Correspondence:
Around May of 1946, one postcard was provided for each ten POWs; only 50 characters were permitted to be written on each card. Japanese "Kana" (not "Kanji") had to be used to facilitate censorship. No replies to these cards were ever received. Later each POW was given an individual postcard, and gradually they began to receive replies from relatives in Japan.

Source:
Date obtained from Till the Day of Repatriation by Mr. Seiichi Aziki, former officer, assigned to a unit formerly located in Mukden.
Source of information is fairly reliable.

Monograph No. 155 - Appendix IIIa

List of Commanders in Kwantung Army
(Early 1943)

Kwantung Army, General Yoshijiro Umezu

    Kwantung Defense Army, Lt Gen Bin Kinoshita

    29th Division, Lt Gen Toshimichi Uemura

    Mechanized Army, Lt Gen Shin Yoshida
        1st Tank Division, Lt Gen Toshimoto Hoshino
        2d Tank Division, Lt Gen Tasuku Okada

    Second Air Army, Lt Gen Ritsudo Suzuki
        2d Air Division, Lt Gen Kumaichi Teramoto
        4th Air Division, Lt Gen Ryosuke Nakanishi

    First Area Army, General Tomoyuki Yamashita
        10th Division, Lt Gen Jiro Sogawa

    Second Army, Lt Gen Yoshio Kozuki
        71st Division, Lt Gen Noboru Toyama

    Third Army, Lt Gen Eitaro Uchiyama
        9th Division, Lt Gen Mamoru Hara
        12th Division, Lt Gen Takazo Numata

    Fifth Army, Lt Gen Jo Iimura
        11th Division, Lt Gen Takeshi Takamori
        24th Division, Lt Gen Hiroshi Nemoto

    Twentieth Army, Lt Gen Kameji Seki
        8th Division, Lt Gen Shizuo Yokoyama
        25th Division, Lt Gen Yaezo Akashiba

    Third Area Army, General Korechika Anami
        14th Division, Lt Gen Kengo Noda
        28th Division, Lt Gen Teizo Ishiguro

    Fourth Army, Lt Gen Tatsumi Kusaba
        1st Division, Lt Gen Mitsuo Nakazawa
        57th Division, Lt Gen Sanetaka Kusumoto

    Sixth Army, Lt Gen Seiichi Kita
        23d Division, Lt Gen Genshichi Oikawa

List of Commanders in Kwantung Army
(Early 1944)

Kwantung Army, General Yoshijiro Umezu

    Kwantung Defense Army, Lt Gen Shin Yoshida

    27th Division, Lt Gen Yoshiharu Takeshita

    29th Division, Lt Gen Takeshi Takashina

    Second Air Army, Lt Gen Torashiro Kawabe
        2d Air Division, Lt Gen Masao Yamase
        4th Air Division, Lt Gen Yoshitaro Sakaguchi

    First Area Army, General Tomoyuki Yamashita
        1st Tank Division, Lt Gen Toshimoto Hoshino
        2d Tank Division, Lt Gen Tasuku Okada

    Third Army, Lt Gen Eitaro Uchiyama
        9th Division, Lt Gen Mamoru Hara
        12th Division, Lt Gen Hidezo Hitomi
        71st Division, Lt Gen Noboru Toyama

    Fifth Army, Lt Gen Toshimichi Uemura
        11th Division, Lt Gen Takashi Takamori
        24th Division, Lt Gen Hiroshi Nemoto

    Twentieth Army, Lt Gen Masaki Honda
        8th Division, Lt Gen Shizuo Yokoyama
        25th Division, Lt Gen Reizo Kato

    Third Area Army, General Naosaburo Okabe
        14th Division, Lt Gen Sadae Inoue
        28th Division, Lt Gen Senichi Kushibuchi

    Fourth Army, Lt Gen Tatsumi Kusaba
        1st Division, Lt Gen Mitsuo Nakazawa
        57th Division, Lt Gen Mikio Uemura

    Sixth Army, Lt Gen Jiro Sogawa
        23d Division, Lt Gen Fukutaro Nishiyama

(Cont'd) Monograph No. 155 - Appendix IIIc

List of Commanders in Kwantung Army
(31 July 1945)

Kwantung Army, General Otozo Yamada

    Fourth Army, Lt Gen Mikio Uemura
        119th Division, Lt Gen Kiyonobu Shiozawa
        123d Division, Lt Gen Teijiro Kitazawa
        149th Division, Lt Gen Toichi Sasaki

    Thirty-fourth Army, Lt Gen Senichi Kushibuchi
        59th Division, Lt Gen Shigeru Fujita
        137th Division, Lt Gen Yoshisuke Akiyama

    First Area Army, General Seiichi Kita
        122d Division, Lt Gen Tadashi Akashika
        134th Division, Lt Gen Jin Izeki
        139th Division, Lt Gen Kyoji Tominaga

    Third Army, Lt Gen Keisaku Murakami
        79th Division, Lt Gen Teisho Ota
        112th Division, Lt Gen Jikizo Nakamura
        127th Division, Lt Gen Ryutaro Koga
        128th Division, Lt Gen Yoshishige Mizuhara

    Fifth Army, Lt Gen Noritsune Shimizu
        124th Division, Lt Gen Masatake Shiina
        126th Division, Lt Gen Kazuhiko Nomizo
        135th Division, Lt Gen Yoichi Hitomi

    Third Area Army, General Jun Ushiroku
        108th Division, Lt Gen Torajiro Iwai
        136th Division, Lt Gen Toru Nakayama

    Thirtieth Army, Lt Gen Shojiro Iida
        39th Division, Lt Gen Shinnosuke Sasa
        125th Division, Lt Gen Tatsuo Imari
        138th Division, Lt Gen Tsutomu Yamamoto
        148th Division, Lt Gen Motohiro Suemitsu

    Forty-fourth Army, Lt Gen Yoshio Hongo
        63d Division, Lt Gen Kenichi Kishikawa
        107th Division, Lt Gen Koichi Abe
        117th Division, Lt Gen Hiraku Suzuki

    Seventeenth Area Army,* Lt Gen Yoshio Kozuki
        120th Division, Lt Gen Shinichi Yanagawa
        150th Division, Lt Gen Giichiro Mishima
        160th Division, Lt Gen Masao Yamawaki
        320th Division, Lt Gen Kinzaburo Yasumi

    Fifty-eighth Army, Lt Gen Sahiju Nagatsu
        96th Division, Lt Gen Mamoru Iinuma
        111th Division, Lt Gen Tamio Iwasaki
        121st Division, Lt Gen Yoshito Masai

* Assigned to Kwantung Army on 10 August 1945

Monograph No. 155
Appendix No. IV, Chart 1

JAPANESE CASUALTIES

(All figures represent the best estimates that can be made by the Japanese Welfare Ministry from incomplete data and unverified sources)

	Mobilized	Overseas	Homeland	Killed or Missing	Total Repatriated[1]
Army	6,939,101	3,100,000	2,400,000	1,439,101	(Breakdown not available)
Navy	2,119,710	400,000	1,300,000	419,710	
Civilians	(Not applicable)	3,100,000	(Not applicable)	658,595	
Total	9,058,811	6,600,000	3,700,000	2,517,406	6,249,286

1. Data compiled in May 1950. (See Chart 2)

Monograph No. 155 - Appendix No. IV Chart 2

FIGURES ON JAPANESE REPATRIATES

(All figures represent the best estimates that can be made by the Japanese Welfare Ministry from incomplete data and unverified sources)

Number of Japanese Overseas at End of War		Repatriated[1]				Unrepatriated
		Army	Navy	Civilians	Total	
USSR Adm Area[2]	Siberia (after war)[3]	700,000	448,135	4,237	17,984	470,356	229,644
	Kwantung Territory	225,954	10,449	468	215,037	225,954	0
	North Korea	322,546	25,151	236	297,159	322,546	0
	Karafuto, Chishima	372,016	15,958	26	276,606	292,590	79,426
China Adm Area	China Proper	1,501,265				1,501,265	0
	Manchuria	1,105,837				1,045,525	60,312
	N. French Indo-China	32,037				32,037	0
South Korea[4]		595,479				595,479	0
Formosa[4]		479,339				479,339	0
Hong-Kong		19,222				19,222	0
Okinawa		69,375				69,375	0
Iki, Tsushima		62,389				62,389	0
Central Pacific[5]		130,906				130,906	0
Philippines		132,917				132,917	0
Dutch East Indies		15,590				15,590	0
South East Asia[6]		710,727				710,727	0
Hawaii		3,592				3,592	0
New Zealand		797				797	0
Australia		138,680				138,680	0
Total		6,618,688				6,249,286	369,402[7]

1. Data compiled in May 1950.

2. USSR Administration Area
   Total captured 1,620,516
   Repatriated 1,311,446
   Unrepatriated 309,070

3. Figures in this column exclude killed or missing. (See Chart 1)

4. Although Koreans and Formosans were considered Japanese citizens, these figures exclude them regardless of where they were. (both military personnel and civilians)

5. Indicates Guam, Saipan, Tinian, etc.

6. Indicates South French Indo-China, Malaya (including Singapore).

7. The Japanese Welfare Ministry estimated that 252,811 died in captivity as of 1 May 1954.

INDEX

AAA
   Battalions, Independent
      46th: 259; 85th: 259
   Battery, Independent
      65th: 259
   Regiment: 26th: 13, 40
   Units
      Hsingking: 13, 40; 4th: 33
Abe, Maj, Takeo: 192, 214
Acheng: 187, 233
Aihun (Aigun): 63, 65, 103, 183, 185, 187, 195, 196n, 197, 201, 202, 206-209, 211, 214, 216-17, 219-21, New: 221
Air Army
   Second Headquarters: 13
Air Officers School: 71
Akikusa, Maj Gen: 186-87
Akiyama, Lt Gen, Yoshisuke (Cmdr 137th Div): 248
Amphibious tank: 101
Amur River: 64, 172-76, 181, 183, 192, 195-96, 196n, 198, 204-05, 207-08, 220
Angangchi: 190, 236
Antitank Battalion
   29th Ind: 81, 84, 102, 138-39
Area Armies
   First: 1
   Third: 1-17, 47, 50-54, 65, 68-69, 87, 89, 95, 101, 106, 109, 147, 152, 154-55, 158, 167-68, 185
      cease-fire orders: 110
      components: 3
      delaying operational plan: 4, 5, 8
      demobilization order: 54, 113
      fortification plan for Mukden (Nago plan): 168
      Gen, Ushiroku's view: 6
      general officers taken away: 117
      Move of Hq from Tsitsihar to Mukden: 80-81, 145, 172
      new zone assigned: 2
      orders to 44th Army on 10 Aug: 103
      plan to move to redoubt area: 109
      rejects 108th Div's suggestion: 154-55
      responsibility for provinces: 1
   Sixth: 237
   Seventeenth: 178, 237, 239, 251-52, 254-55, 257, 260
   Korea Army reorganized: 241
   Korea Administrative Defense Army: 241, 260, 264
   North China: 128, 137, 138n, 155-56, 159-60
Armies (See also Kwantung and Kwantung Defense Armies)
   Third: 84
   Fourth: 1, 62, 65, 85, 90, 172-191, 193, 196, 199, 205, 266, 228
      cease-fire orders: 184, 186
      controversy on disposition of Aihun Unit: 206
      fortifications for delaying plan: 175
      general officers taken away: 187
      Hq move to Harbin: 182, 231
      Hq move to Tsitsihar: 172-173, 195, 202
      recommends 123d Div counter-offensive: 208
      redeployment to Meihokou: 185-86
      reorganization of: 178
      return order to Harbin: 186
      surrender negotiations: 233
   Fifth: 188
   Twelfth: 137

Thirtieth: 1-17, 52, 70, 99, 103
  activation: 3
  as a redoubt defense force: 185
  cease-fire orders: 16, 42
  deployments of units: 10
  Headquarters at Hsinking: 13
  Headquarters at Meihokou: 11
  Headquarters at Yenchi: 9
  order of battle: 7
  orders of 10 Aug: 38
  organization of Hq: 6
Thirty-fourth: 237-247, 260
  cease-fire negotiations at Yenchi: 243
  cease-fire orders: 243
  components: 238
  disposition of divisions: 240
  Hq at Hamhung: 238
  operational missions: 239
  responsibility zone: 242
  under Seventeenth Area Army's control: 241, 261n
Forty-fourth: 1, 78-127, 138-39, 147
  boundary change: 14
  cease-fire orders: 110, 112, 125, 184
  chief of staff meeting: 93, 95
  disposition of units: 82
  Hq at Liaoyuan: 81, 85;
    departs Liaoyuan: 108
  operational plan: 85-86
  order of battle: 81, 84
  orders of 10 August: 104
  origin of Headquarters: 78
  withdrawal to Mukden: 25, 109
  zone: 2, 8
Army, General
  China Expeditionary: 148, 156n, 160, 237
Army Hospitals: Arshaan: 82; Haicheng: 163; 2d Hailar: 82, 111; Jehol: 156; Mutanchiang: 188; Paichengtzu: 82, 111; Port Arthur: 163; 36th Field: 69
Artillery Battalions, Independent
  7th: 7, 10; 10th: 227, 231; 11th: 238; 14th: 82; 21st: 7, 10
Artillery Battery
  6th Ind Heavy: 98, 111
Artillery Command
  8th: 62
Artillery Regiments: 1st Heavy: 7, 10; 17th Heavy: 82, 84, 111; 19th Heavy: 7, 10; 30th Heavy: 82, 98, 111; 39th: 20; 108th: 146, 157; 123d: 192; 125th: 67; 136th: 166; 148th: 37, 40; 149th: 226, 231
  Mutanchiang Heavy: 238
Battalions (See Artillery, Infantry, Motor, Tank and Transport Battalions)
Blagoveshchensk: 58, 177
Blittora, Maj Gen, Soviet Army: 116, 120
Bombing by US. aircraft: 78
Border
  Inner Mongolia: 154
  Manchurian-Korea: 172, 185
  Mongolian-Manchurian: 14
  Outer Mongolia: 177, 181
Border Garrison Units
  4th: 62; 5th: 63, 178; 6th: 63-64, 178, 183, 196, 219; 7th: 63; 13th: 63
Borzya: 177
Brigades (See also Infantry, Tank Brigades) 1st Mobile: 47
Cavalry Regiment
  171st: 143, 145
Cease-fire orders
  Imperial General Headquarters: 112
  Kwantung Army: 72
  Third Area Army: 53, 110
  Thirtieth Army: 16
    countermanding of: 42
  Thirty-fourth Army: 243
  Forty-fourth Army: 110, 112, 125, 184

39th Div: 26; 108th Div: 160;
117th Div: 140; 123d Div: 212;
125th Div: 72; 136th Div: 170;
137th Div: 251; 138th Div: 53;
148th Div: 42; 149th Div: 232
135th Ind Mixed Brig: 224
Nanam Divisional District Unit: 264
Continuation of fighting after,
135th Ind Mixed Brig: 184, 214, 224
Nanam Divisional District Unit: 263
Cease-fire negotiations
Kwantung Army: 115
Third Area Army: 116-17
Fourth Army: 186
Forty-fourth Army: 116
Chalaitochi: 112
Chalantun: 177, 187
Changpaishan (Paitaoshan): 21, 65, 68
Changchun (Hsinking): 5, 13
Changtu: 14, 111
Chaoshui: 220, 223, 225
Chaotung: 232
Chaoyangchen: 20, 47, 50
Chengchiawopeng: 211
Chiamussu: 109n
Chian: 66, 73
Chiang Kai-shek: 160
Chientao Province: 6
Chienkuo University: 17, 33
Chihfeng: 79, 144, 146-47, 151-52
Chiko: 183, 195-97, 204-05, 207, 209-10
China
air attack from: 88
Central: 84
Eighth Route Army (Chinese Communist): 78, 83, 144-50, 154-55, 159, 164-65
guerrilla tactics in North: 94
Nationalist Government of: 124-25
North: 83, 113, 132, 134
units from: 9
Chinese
Communist: 2, 76, 79, 128, 132, 142, 144, 146-47, 160
intelligence network: 147
Nationalist forces: 2, 165
offensive in August: 148
underground activities in Jehol: 149
Chinchou Province: 1, 154
Chinchuan: 5, 8
Chinhsi: 144
Chinhsien: 77, 113-14, 124, 143-44, 150, 152, 154-60, 164-65
Chinglung: 144, 159
Chingyuan: 5, 50
Chiyoda Park: 119
Chongjin: 243, 260-64
Chongpyong: 246, 249, 251
Chushchakov, Gen, Soviet Army: 245
Chuul: 252-53, 255
Chuuronjang: 264
Dairen: 163
bombed by US planes: 78
Conference: 4 (See Kwantung Army)
Port Arthur-area: 89
special service agency: 109n
Dairen-Hsinking Railway (See Railway)
Demobilization Bureau: 48, 219, 225, 257
Demobilization instruction: 54, 72 (See Kwantung and Third Area Armies)
Depot Units
19th Depot Division: 257
1st Infantry: 261
2d Infantry: 258
Desert: 100, 131, 173
District Defense Command
Central: 87n
Hsinking: 17, 33
Pinchiang Province: 87n, 182
Southwest: 87n, 147, 149
Tsitsihar: 228-29, 232
Western: 87
Divisions (See Infantry, Tank

divisions)
Eighth Route Army (See China)
Eiko: 238 (See Yonghung)
Engineer Regiments
   39th: 20, 25; 40th Ind: 42; 123d 192; 148th: 42; 149th: 226
Engineer Unit
   2d Headquarters: 7
     from China: 11, 118
   40th Ind: 7
   131st Ind Battalion: 259
Erabka (USSR): 234 (See Internment Camps; Appendix No. II)
Erhchan: 174-75, 183, 185, 200-01, 206, 214, 216, 218, 220 222-25
Estimation of Soviet forces on 14 June: 3
Facheng College: 33
Faku: 114
Fanchiatun: 17, 44
Fapiehla: 63-64
Far East: 145
Fenchiahu: 228
Fengcheng: 5, 109
Fengtien Province: 1, 9
Field Hospital (See Army Hospital)
Flag
   Chinese Nationalist: 125
   Korean national: 126
   red: 186
Flood: 101, 102
Freight Depots
   Field: 85
   Jehol Branch: 156
French Indo-China: 6
Fouhsin: 144, 146, 155-57, 59
Fujita, Col, Sanehiko: 62-63, 66, 68, 72-73, 77
Fukunaga, Col: 27
Fulaerhchi: 230-32
Fulungchuan: 37
Fushun: 9-10, 50, 52-60
   bandits in: 126
   Coal Mine Co: 58-59, 122-23
Garrison Units (See also Border Garrison Units)
   1st Special: 117, 119
   9th Independent: 142
   74th L of C: 226
   Chongjin: 259, 261-62, 264
   Kwangjuryong: 259, 261, 263
   Kwantung Territory: 248
   Yonghung Bay Fortress: 238-39, 250
Genda, Mr, Matsuzo: 113
Germany, surrender of: 79
Gilchin: 177
Goto, Col, Sampei: 192
Goto Unit: 74-75
Great Wall: 79, 142, 144, 146-52, 159-61
Guard Battalions
   141st-145th: 258
   401st-403d, 405th, 408th-410th, 451st-452d, 461st-462d Special Established: 259
Guard Units (See also Special Guard)
   3d Special: 179, 202-03; 76th L of C: 178; 101st: 32-33; 102d: 179; 104th: 178; Fushun: 55; Hamhung: 264; Manchukuoan Imperial Palace: 45; Penchihu: 166
Guerrilla warfare: 86-88, 93-96, 124, 128, 132-34, 142, 144, 155, 164-65, 218
   anti-guerrilla operations: 128
   maneuvers of: 94, 132
   special service agency: 109
   tactics: 131
Haicheng: 162-64, 171, 145
Hailar: 7, 84-85, 101, 103, 109n, 174-77, 181, 183n, 184-87, 230-31, 235
Hailin: 187, 233, 236
Hailung: 4, 10, 18-20, 24
Hamada, Maj Gen, Junosuke (Cmdr 135th Brig): 220
Hamhung: 237, 239-40, 244-46, 261, 264
Hamyong
   Namdo Province: 242

Pukto Province: 240, 242
Hanamiyama: 197
Hankow: 18, 237-38
Harada, Maj: 171
Harbin: 32, 48, 58, 87, 164, 174, 181, 185, 187, 189-90, 216-17, 233-35
Hasegawa, Capt, Yoshio: 192
Hashiba, Col: 135-36
Heiho: 58, 64, 101, 109n, 173, 196, 226
    Province: 62, 173, 192, 218
Hengtaohotzu: 187, 189, 191, 233
Hirama, Maj: 209; Unit: 210-11
Hirano, Maj Gen: 118
Hirata, Maj, Bunichi: 62-63
Hirokawa, Maj, Fumio: 192
Hirose, Maj, Shinkichi: 7
Hoeryong: 262
Homan Dam: 33
Ho-Muhsia, Lt Gen, Manchukuoan Army: 147, 165
Honan Province: 137
Hongo, Lt Gen, Yoshio (Cmdr 44th Army): 81
Hongwon: 260
Hopei Province: 128
Hospitals (See Army Hospitals)
Hsian: 10, 19-20, 22, 26, 29
    deputy governor of prefecture: 23-24
    head of Railway Station: 22-23
Hsifengkou: 151
Hsiheiho: 63-64
Hsinhsiang: 83, 137
Hsingan: 79-80, 84, 86, 90, 104-06, 108, 109n
    East: 1, 173
    General Province: 89, 122
    Mountain Range: 158, 173-74
    North: 173
    South: 1, 87
    West: 1, 87, 123
Hsinganling: 79, 104
Hsinglung (Hsiaying): 144
Hsinkai River: 106

Hsinking: 4-6, 10-15, 17, 20, 22-24, 27, 29, 31-32, 36-37, 39-46, 48, 58, 87-88, 99, 101, 103-04, 107-08, 140-41, 182, 218, 237
    Kwantung Army conference: 3
    Defense District: 17, 33
    Garrison area: 20, 45
    special municipality: 13n
    148th Div's Command Post: 39
Hsinmin: 101, 111-112, 168, 170
Hsinpin: 5
Hsintun: 55-57
Hsunho: 197, 209-10
Hsunpila River: 204, 210
Huaite: 17, 41, 44
Huangpao: 168
Huanjen: 5, 66, 73, 76, 109
Hulan: 190
Hulutao: 144
Hunchun: 11, 38
Hungnam: 246, 261
    Korean Nitrogen Co: 246
Hupeh Province: 137-38
Hutou: 101, 103
Ihara, Maj Gen: 253-54
Ihsien: 156-57, 159
Iida, Lt Gen, Shojiro (Cmdr 30th Army): 6-7, 10, 39
Ijichi, Col, Sueharu: 167
Imada, Col, Shigeru: 68, 74-75
Imaizumi, Maj Gen, Yoshisada: 258-59, 261
Imari, Lt Gen, Tatsuo (Cmdr 125th Div): 62, 62n, 63, 66, 68, 70-71
Imperial General Headquarters
    30 July order: 7
    defense plan of west and south Manchuria: 80
Imperial Rescript: 16, 16n, 26, 71-73, 158, 170, 182, 212, 243, 263
Independent Mixed Brigades
    Hara Unit, 8th: 148; 15th: 128; 78th: 192, 195; 80th: 183n, 185; 130th: 103, 111, defense of

Mukden: 109; 131st: 87, 179, 182, 185; 133d: 13, 40, 43, 238; 134th: 69, 74; 135th: 63, 179, 183, 196–97, 203, 206, 211, 213, 219–225; cease-fire orders: 224; components: 219; fighting until 20th: 224

Infantry Divisions
  39th: 7–8, 10, 12–14, 18–31, 38, 44
    trfd fr China: 17
    move to Hsinking: 21
  57th: 63–64
  59th: 239–240, 249–250
    trfd fr China: 238
  63d: 48, 80–81, 85, 94, 102–04, 106–08, 110–11, 114, 128–136, 138, 148, 156n
    arrived in Manchuria: 83, 130
    assigned to Forty-fourth Army: 130
    composition of: 128–29
    defense of Mukden: 109, 134
    garrison duty in China: 128–29
    trfd fr China: 134
  79th: 242, 248, 257, 260
  107th: 8, 14, 41, 78–83, 87, 90, 92–95, 98, 101, 103, 111, 123
    assigned to Thirtieth Army: 104–06
  108th: 2, 4, 79, 83, 103, 111, 113, 142–165, 168
    assembly of: 157
    assigned to Forty-fourth Army: 109, 155
    combat effectiveness of: 153
    composition of: 142
    move to Liaoyang: 158–59
    operational mission: 147
    Southwest Defense Command: 147
    withdrawal to Fouhsin-Chinhsin line: 155
  117th: 8, 14, 41, 43–44, 80–81, 90, 93, 102–03, 137–41
    assigned to Forty-fourth Army: 137
    assigned to Thirtieth Army: 104, 106–07, 139
    cease-fire orders: 140
    composition of: 84–86, 137
    missions in China: 137
    trfd fr China: 83, 137–38
  119th: 180, 183n
    withdrawal to Wunoerh: 185
  120th: 256
  123d: 64, 180, 184, 192–218, 220, 223–24
    cease-fire orders: 212
    components of: 192
    controversy on disposition of Aihun Unit: 206
    estimate of Soviet: 204–05
    new operational plan: 197–98
    surrender negotiations: 213
    trfd to Soviet Territory: 217
  125th: 7–8, 10, 12, 38, 62–77, 178, 193
    activation: 62
    attached to Kwantung Army: 69
    cease-fire orders: 72
    missions in Tunghua: 68
    reorganization in July: 67
    trfd to Tunghua: 65–66, 196, 200
  136th: 103, 111, 155–56, 166–71
    activation: 166
    components of: 166
    defense of Mukden: 109, 167
    defend Penchihu sector: 169
  137th: 238–40, 248–256
    activation: 239, 248, 260
    assigned to Seventeenth Area Army: 251
    cease-fire negotiations: 254
    cease-fire orders: 251
    deployment: 249
  138th: 7–8, 10, 47–61
    activation: 47
    assigned to Third Area Army: 52
    cease-fire orders: 53
    demobilized drafted men: 53

disarmament: 55
formation of Hq: 48
move to Fushun: 52
148th: 7-8, 10, 12, 15, 17, 32-46, 38, 41, 45, 87
  activation: 32
  controversy re defense of Hsinking: 35, 169n
149th: 179, 185, 187, 226-236
  components of: 226
  defense plan of Tsitsihar city: 228
  move to Harbin: 182, 232
Nanam Divisional District Unit: 240, 243-44, 248-49, 257-265
  cease-fire negotiations: 264
  cease-fire order on 18 Aug: 264
  components of: 257
  Soviet landings: 262
  under Thirty-fourth Army's tactical command: 242, 261n
Pyongyang Divisional District Unit: 252, 254-55
  cease-fire negotiations: 252

Infantry Brigades
  66th: 130; 67th: 131; 87th: 137-38, 138n, 140; 88th: 137-38

Infantry Regiments
  231st: 14, 17, 20, 22-24, 27; 232d: 20, 22-24, 27; 233d: 20, 23-24, 27; 240th: 144, 148-49, 156, 159-61; 241st: 144-46, 148-50, 153, 155, 157, 159-60; 242d: 144, 149, 152, 157, 159; 268th: 192, 197; 269th: 192, 196-97, 204, 208-209, 212; 270th: 192, 197; 274th: 63-65, 226-27, 229; 275th: 63-67, 70, 73-74; 276th: 64, 67, 74; 276th: 64, 67, 74; 371st: 166, 169; 372d: 163, 166, 168, 171; 373d: 166; 375th: 251; 383d: 36, 40; 384th: 37, 40, 42; 385th: 37, 40, 42; 386th: 226-27; 387th: 266, 230-31; 388th: 67, 74

Infantry Battalions
  67th: 135; 77th: 134; 203d: 137; 204th: 138n, 141; 205th: 138n; 206th: 138n, 139; 388th: 139; 389th: 137; Magara, 63d Div: 148, 157; Oda, 63d Div: 148, 157
Innami, Col, Kiyoshi: 226
Inoue, Lt Gen: 77
Inoue, Lt Col: 164
Intelligence: 95, 96, 100, 147, 153, 176
  Special Department: 71
  Special Unit: 203-04, 209, 211-12; 604th: 69
Intendance Duty Unit: 65
Internal Peoples' Commissariat: 216
Internment Camps: 234n
  at Chongpyong: 246
  at Erabka (USSR): 234, (See also App II)
  at Haicheng: 162
  at Hailin: 187-88, 233-34
  at Hsinking: 45
  at Komusan: 264
  at Migundang: 253, 255
  at Morshansk (USSR): 58, 171
  at Mukden: 57, 121
  at Mutanchiang: 234
  at Nanling: 45
  at Peiling: 57, 121-22, 135, 171
  at Puryong: 265
  at Rada (Lada) (USSR): 234
  at Samhamni: 253
  at Sunwu: 216, 224
Ioi, Lieutenant: 161
Irie, Major: 43
Ishikawa, 1st Lt: 160
Itung River: 15, 37, 42-43
Iwai, Lt Gen, Torajiro (Cmdr 108th Div): 143, 147-48, 154
Japanese
  refugees: 58, 189, 233, 235, 253
  residents: 5-6, 31, 53, 58, 76, 122, 161, 188, 198, 217, 221, 224, 235, 247, 251, 254
  residents association: 189, 231
Jehol: 1, 2, 78-79, 83, 87, 89,

142n, 143-46, 150-52, 154-55, 159-61, 164-65
Jeshui: 145-46, 149-50
Kadota, Col: 73
Kaifeng: 18
Kailu: 83, 85, 102, 108, 131, 134
Kaitung: 138-39
Kaiyuan: 18, 20, 22-24, 29, 84, 98, 111
Kaneko, Col, Kenjiro: 172
Kanggye: 240
Mannan: 232
Karymskaya (USSR): 99
Kashimadai: 197
Kashimoto, Capt, Yoshinari: 192
Katayama, Staff Officer: 213
Kato, Maj Gen, Michio: 7
Kato, Maj, Takeo: 78
Kawase, Chief of Police Affairs Agency: 77
Khabarovsk (USSR): 187, 233
KIA figures: 225
Kilchu: 263
Kinoshita, Col: 47, 132
Kishikawa, Lt Gen, Kenichi (Cmdr 63d Div): 132
Kishitani, Mr: 165
Kitazawa, Lt Gen, Teijiro (Cmdr 123d Div): 192
Kojinyama: 197
Komusan: 244, 264
Kondo, Capt, Toyonobu: 63, 68, 74
Korea: 66, 238-242, 246-47
  latitude 38 degrees: 244
  northern: 237-41, 255
  southern: 241
Korean: 31, 44, 109n, 125-26, 190, 203, 218, 253-54
  attacks on Japanese: 216
  imprisoned Koreans released by Soviet: 253
  in Tunghua: 77
  oppression of Japanese: 247
  Public Peace Maintenance Society at Pyongyang: 253, 255
  soldiers released from duty: 233
  soldiers serving in Japanese units: 190, 250, 264
  flight to rear areas: 236
Kozuki, Lt Gen, Yoshio (Cmdr 17th Area Army): 260
Kuangtoushan: 147
Kuchengtzu: 171
Kungchuling: 16-17, 19-20, 22, 24, 27-28, 33, 43-44, 141
Kungyuan: 166-68
Kupeikou: 144, 151
Kurautsvenko, Gen Soviet Army: 56
Kushantzu: 70
Kushibuchi, Lt Gen, Senichi (Cmdr 34th Army): 237
Kuwa, Lt Col, Masahiko: 1n, 7, 10, 16-17
Kwangjuryong: 259, 261
Kwantung Army
  strength in August 1945: Table No 1
  boundary change with China Expeditionary Army: 155
  cease-fire orders: 72
  Command Post at Tunghua: 71
  control of Seventeenth Area Army: 242, 261n
  decision to organize 122d to 128th divisions: 62
  defense of major cities: 9
  defense positions at Wunoerh: 174
  delaying operational plan: 1, 3-4, 154, 172, 219
  demobilization of forces: 72, 255
  guerrilla warfare training: 94-95
  last defense line: 66
  officers of Hq: 58
  Rear Command Post: 12
  re-disposition of major subordinate commands: 172
  responsibilities in Northern Korea: 241
  weakest part of defense system: 79

Kwantung Defense Army: 2, 79-81, 84, 89, 142
   move to Mukden from Hsinking: 78
   redesignation as Forty-fourth Army: 2, 81, 147
   reorganization into tactical command: 80
Kyonghung: 261, 263
Kyongsong: 261
Labor battalions: 30, 46, 57, 135, 156, 160, 163-64, 171, 188, 234, 265
   construction units: 217
Land Development Groups: 164, 189, 217, 230, 235; Korean: 236
Land Duty Companies
   39th: 259; 88th: 69, 74
Laohokou: 138
Liao River: 25, 26, 101
Liaoyang: 109, 111, 113, 122-23, 158-59, 161-62, 164, 168, 171
Liaoyuan: 25, 27-28, 41, 81, 83, 85-86, 89, 96, 104, 107-08, 112, 130; Prefecture: 87; Training Unit: 94
Lichiatun: 187, 233
Lichuan (Tuchuan): 102, 105, 107-08, 111, 139
Linchiang: 66, 69, 77
Lingyuan: 145, 150, 157
Linhsi: 79, 89, 144, 146, 152, 154, 160
Liuchiachangtzu: 161
Liuho: 5, 8, 10, 50, 69
Lungchiang Province: 1, 87, 173
Lupei: 14
Lytton Commission: 142
Machida, Lt Col, Kensuke: 192
Maeda, Capt: 159-60
Maki, Col: 205
Malanyu: 15, 160
Manchouli: 58, 99, 101, 173-74, 177, 181, 183n, 184-85, 226
Manchoutun: 64

Manchukuo
   independence proclamation: 142
Manchukuoan
   Army
      1st Division: 165
      along the Great Wall: 79
      danger of revolt in Chinhsien: 113, 124
      First Army District: 113
      Fifth Army District: 147, 156, 165
      in Chilin: 49
      in Forty-fourth Army zone: 88, 96, 101
      in Harbin: 49
      in Hsingan: 79
      in Hsinking: 36
      in Tunghua: 73, 77
      Japanese officers assigned to: 124, 165
      Military Academy Cadet Unit: 37, 40, 45
      in Fushun: 59
      ordnance depot: 66, 68
      raiders: 31
      rebel forces: 27
      rebels in Mukden: 58
      regiment in 123d Div sector: 218
      revolt: 15, 125, 165, 218
      revolt at Harbin, Hulan, Shuangcheng and Angangchi: 190
      tactical unit: 124
      troops desertion: 124-25
      units in 149th Div sector: 228-30, 235
   Emperor (Manchukuoan)
      arrest at Mukden: 77, 116
      flight to Tasutzukou: 77
      sent to Soviet by air: 116
   Government: 5, 13, 42, 97, 231, 235
      agencies cooperate with Fourth Army: 189
      Japanese officials: 218

    officers not loyal to
        Japan: 123
    senior officers: 46
  Imperial Palace: 41
    Guard Unit: 45
  Military police: 45
  Officers School: 15
Manchurian
  attitude toward the Soviets: 60
  Aviation Co: 33
  Electric Industry Co: 113
  looting by mobsters: 162
  military personnel: 231
  Motion Picture Co: 45
  police: 124, 125, 148, 176, 190, 228, 230, 236
    in Tunghua: 77
  public sentiment: 97, 190
  revolts: 159-60
  rioters: 161, 164, 218
  South Arsenal: 120-21
  South Railway Co: 93, 113
  Telegraph and Telephone Co: 93, 113, 152
Maritime Province: 246
Maruoka, Lt Col, Shigeo: 32, 38-39
Mass-mobilization during July: 48, 65, 67, 122, 166, 239, 248, 259n
Matsumoto, Mr: 218
Matsumura, Maj Gen, Tomokatsu: 17, 71, 80
Mechanized force (Soviet)
  crossed the western border: 38
  on western front: 15
  reached the Dairen-Hsinking Railway: 44
Meihokou: 5, 10-14, 19, 34, 38-39, 70, 185
Mengchiatun: 16, 39
  ordnance depot: 17
Midori Kosaku: 96
Migundang: 253
Mihara, Col, Shichiro: 248
Military Police Units
  at Hsingan: 106
  MP commandant in Hsinking: 107
Minagawa, Mr: 148
Mitano, Maj, Toru: 64, 68
Miyagishi, Col: 63
Miyata, Lt Col: 80
Mixed Brigades (See Independent Mixed Brigades)
Mizunuma, Capt: 156, 168
Mojuhin, Lt Gen, Soviet
  Second Army: 214
Mongolia: 2, 7, 9, 95, 97, 99-100, 142, 144, 146, 154-55, 160, 173, 177
  spies from: 89
  Soviet forces in: 145
Mongolian: 109n, 124
  Army: 79
  Cavalry: 102
  Officers School: 106
  Outer Mongolian Army: 160
  rebellion of Army: 105
  revolt: 124
Mori, Maj: 224
Morshansk (USSR): 58, 171
Moscow (USSR): 171, 234, 254
Motor Battalion
  27th Ind Hv: 7, 10
Mukden: 4-12, 25, 28, 32-34, 50, 55, 57-60, 65-66, 77, 80-81, 103-05, 107-09, 110-12, 114, 116, 121-22, 125, 134-35, 145, 152, 155-56, 156n, 157, 164-65, 169, 172
  bandits in: 126
  Incident: 142
  public disorder in: 119
Muleng: 103
Murakami, Lt Gen, Keisaku (Cmdr 3d Army): 6
Murakami, Maj: 208
  Unit: 210-11
Mutanchiang: 11, 38, 101, 109n, 164, 188-89, 236
Nagai, Lt Col, Sen: 68, 74-75
Nago Plan: 168-69
Najin: 242, 262n
Nakajima, Lt Gen, Yokichi: 52

Nakamura, 2d Lt: 224
Nakayama, Lt Gen, Toru (Cmdr 136th Div): 166
Nanam: 244, 248, 257, 260-61
Nangnim Mountain Range: 252
Nanling: 45-46
Nantsamuhuote: 10
Nanyan Hill: 204, 210
Napoleon: 254
Naval Fuel Depot Unit: 55
Nencheng: 174, 176, 182, 184, 220, 222, 232
Nenchiang River: 230
Neutrality Pact between Japan and Soviet Russia: 205
Niimi, Maj Gen: 75
Nikaido, Lt Col, Kensuke: 166
Nishiwaki, Lt Gen, Sokichi (Cmdr Nanam Divisional District Unit): 258, 261, 263-64
Nodai, Col: 259, 261
Nohara, Lt Col: 16n
Noho: 226-27
Nungan: 41
  vice-governor of Prefecture: 37
Okano, Col, Kaoru: 68, 74
Okinawa
  annihilation of the Japanese: 79
Ogawa, 1st Lt, Toshio: 68, 74-75
Ogi, Col, Hiroshi: 237, 243
Oguchi, Maj, Shizuo: 18
Omori, Col: 119
Onishi, Lt, Tomiji: 12
Ordnance Depots: 18th Field: 204; 19th Field: 82; Fourth Army: 195
Ordnance Duty Units: 65, 68, 192
Ota, Col, Kiichi: 192
Otpor (USSR): 177
Outer Mongolian Army: 2 (See also Mongolia)
Oyuerh River: 210
Pacific war: 124
Paichengtzu: 41, 44, 84, 86, 93, 104
Pailing: 90, 104, 106, 111
Paishihlatzu: 64

Palikangtzu: 228
Pamiencheng: 27, 84
Panshih: 47
Paoting: 128-29
Peian: 173-74, 177, 187, 196, 211, 216-17, 226-27
Peichen: 160
Peiling: 57-58, 111, 121-22, 125, 135, 171
Peipiao: 160
Peiping: 128-29
Penchihu: 5, 8, 78, 122, 166-68
  Steel Works: 169
Piehla River: 221, 224
Pinchiang Province: 173
  governor of: 186
  Provincial Government: 189
Pinganchen: 140
Pingchuan: 144, 147, 150, 159
Pingchuang: Map No 1-2, sub-monograph I (108th Div)
Pingfang: 186
Pokotu: 174-75, 177
Poli: 165
Port Arthur: 89, 163
Prisoners of War, Japanese: 244
  Explanation of Status: 114-15
  Treatment in USSR: App II
Pupyong: 245, 249, 251
Puryong: 265
Pyongan
  Namdo Province: 242, 244
  Pukto Province: 242, 244
Pyongyang: 240, 244, 251-55
Rada (Lada) (USSR): 234
Raiding battalions
  of 107th Div: 98; of 108th Div: 143, 146, 157, 160; of 123th Div: 192; of 136th Div: 166, 168; of 149th Div: 226; Chart No 1, Submonograph B
Raiding Units
  2d: 81, 84, 108, 112; 12th: 179; Aritomi: 168; in Harbin: 182
Railway
  Antung-Mukden: 5
  Arshaan-Talai: 91

Borzya (USSR)-Tamsag: 177
Chilin-Mukden: 5, 47, 50
Dairen-Hsinking: 4-6, 11, 14, 17, 20-21, 24, 26, 34, 38, 79, 168, 172
Dairen-Mukden: 145
Hankow-Peiping: 238
Harbin-Mutanchiang: 191
Heiho-Sunwu-Peian: 195
Hsinking-Mukden: 2
Hsinking-Tumen: 172
Jehol: 150
Liaoyuan-Tungliao: 81, 83, 86, 131
Mukden-Shanhaikwan: 158
Noho-Tsitsihar-Chiangchiao: 230
Paichengtzu-Arshaan: 90, 104, 106
Peiping-Mukden: 238
South Manchurian: 25
Ssupingchieh-Taonan: 81 84, 86, 123
Ssupingchieh-Tsitsihar: 91
Strategic Trans-Manchurian: 174
Tamsag (Outer Mongolia): 95
Tungliao-Tahushan: 131
Trans-Siberian (USSR): 176-77
Railway Force
  Chinhsien Branch: 91, 104, 107, 159
  Continental: 91, 104, 159
  Hamhung Branch: 249
  Tsitsihar Branch: 91, 104, 107
Rakon, Lt Col, Soviet Army: 252
Reconnaissance Regiment
  57th: 64-65
Redoubt areas: 4n, 185
  Fengcheng and Huanjen: 109
  Penchihu sector: 169
  Tunghua: 5, 8, 71, 154
Regiments (See Artillery, Infantry, Tank Regiments)
Road
  Aihun-Erhchan-Nencheng-Tsitsihar: 200, 218
  Apaka-Linhsi-Chihfeng axis: 145
  Chilalin-Hailar: 102
  East Uchumuchin-Lichuan: 102
  Heiho-Erhchan-Nencheng-Tsitsihar axis: 174
  Heiho-Peian axis: 174
  Kailu-Changwu-Hsinmin-Mukden: 107
  Liaoyuan-Paichengtzu: 92
  Manchouli-Hailar: 102
  Manchouli-Hailar-Wunoerh-Pokotu axis: 174
  Shengwutun-Sunwu: 210-11
  Ssupingchieh-Liaoyuan-Tungliao: 92
  Sunwu-Hsunho: 209
  Sunwu-Peian-Harbin: 204
  Pingchuan-Kuangtoushan axis: 149
  Tungliao-Kailu: 85, 92
Road Construction Unit
  47th Field: 42, 85, 90, 111
Sakamoto, Col: 43
Samhamni: 253-54
Sanho: 109n, 183, 185
Sanhochiao: 149
Sankuoshan: 102
Santaoka: 183
Sasa, Lt Gen, Shinnosuke (Cmdr 39th Div): 18
Sasaki, Lt Gen, Toichi (Cmdr 149th Div): 229, 232
Sato, Col, Sadaji: 47n, 128
Sato, Maj, Yutaka: 142, 161-62
Sea Duty Company: 41st: 82, 99
Segawa, Col, Masao: 63, 68
Sejima, Lt Col: 71
Seoul: 237, 240, 254
Shanchengchen: 4, 50, 52
Shanghai: 126
Shanhaikwan: 144, 149, 152, 155
Shanshenfu: 64-65, 178, 220, 222
Shengwutun: 63, 183-85, 195, 197, 202, 204, 207-10, 216
Shenwutun: 62-64, 195-96
Shihjen: 69, 73
Shihmen: 129
Shii, Maj: 116

Shimizu, Capt, Goichi: 192
Shipping Transport Command
   1st: 259
Shirakawa, Col, Yutaka: 258, 264
Shoji, Maj Gen, Sen: 138
Shuangcheng: 190
Shunteh: 128
Siaokan: 18
Siberia: 77, 173
Signal Regiment
   31st: 84, 92, 99, 111
Signal Unit, Kwantung Army: 92
Sokolov, Col, Soviet Army: 30
Songin: 259, 261
Soviet
   army forces arrive in Mukden:
     55, 58, 114, 117, 120, 125,
     135
   army forces reached Liaoyuan:
     112, 162
   attitude of officers: 56
   bombing of Manchuria: 51, 220,
     230
   crossing of the Amur River:
     183, 207, 221
   disarmament by: 74
   entry into the war: 50, 90,
     100-01, 155, 167, 180-81,
     205
   estimate of strength: 99
   forces in Mongolia: 145
   forces to Far East: 145, 176
   gunboats on the Amur: 223
   invasion of Korea: 261-62
   operations against: 142
   Pacific Fleet: 262n
   released imprisoned Koreans: 253
   surprise attack at Manchouli:
     184
   threat of invasion: 79
   trickery of: 119
   Twenty-fifth Army: 243, 245
   underground forces: 51
   weakness in air power: 51
   weapons surrendered to: 74
Special Service Agency: 69, 109n;
   Apaka: 163; Hailar: 177; Harbin:
96, 186; Heiho: 202; Hsingan:
   96, 108, 112, 114; Sunwu: 177
Ssuchan: 218
Ssuping Province: 24
   deputy governor of: 24-25,
     31, 87
Ssupingchieh: 8, 11-14, 17-31,
   38, 40, 85, 98, 103, 105, 123
Suehiro, Col, Isamu: 16n, 157
Suemitsu, Lt Gen, Motohiro (Cmdr
   148th Div): 17, 32-33, 38, 45
Sugata, Maj, Masami: 219
Sugawara, Mr: 77
Sugihara, Unit cmdr: 74-75
Suichung: 78, 144
Suihua: 58
Suiyang: 11, 38
Sungari River: 33
Sunwu: 62, 64, 172, 174-77, 180,
   184, 186-87, 192-93, 195-99,
   203, 207-10, 212-14, 216-17,
   220, 222-24
Supply Depot
   19th Field: 85, 90
Susaek: 252
Suzuki, Lt Gen, Hiraku (Cmdr 117th
   Div): 138-39
Tachengtzu: 155
Taian: 226-27
Tailai Prefecture: 87
Takahashi, Mr: 77
Takebayashi, Col: 118
Takenaka: 74-75
Takeda, Lt Col, Prince Tsunenori: 80
Takeda, Maj Gen, Seiichi: 118
Takumi, Maj Gen, Hiroshi: 258-59,
   261-63
Talai: 140
Tali Lake: 155
Tambov (USSR): 234
Tambovka (USSR): 177
Tamsag: 95, 177
Tamura, Col: 246
Tanaka, Maj, Koreshige: 202
Tank Division: 1st: 62
Tank Brigades
   1st: 103, 111, defense of

Mukden: 109
  9th Ind: 81, 98, 103
Tank Regiment
  35th: 13, 40-41, 43
Taoan (Paichengtzu): 41, 44, 84, 86, 93, 104
Taonan: 14, 41, 79, 81, 84-86, 102, 105-06, 138-40
Tasutzukou: 77
Tatung School: 17
Telegraph News Service: 72
Tepossu: 82
Tiehhsi: 114
Tiehling: 52, 111
Tientsin: 126, 140
Togwon: 246
Tsitsihar: 6, 80, 82-85, 172, 174, 176-78, 181-82, 184, 187, 189, 226-27, 229-30, 232, 235
  Mayor of: 231
Tukoutzu: 222-23
Tungan: 62, 109n
Tungfeng: 10, 13, 20, 26, 29
Tunghua: 1, 4, 6, 8, 10, 12-13, 34, 69, 76-77, 50, 65-66, 69-71, 73-75, 77, 110, 123, 154, 178
  Iron Foundry: 66-67
Tungken River: 204
Tungkou: 18, 20
Tungliao: 14, 79, 81, 83, 85-86, 93, 101, 106, 112, 114, 130-31, 158
Tungling: 60, 111, 120, 134
Tungning: 101
Transport Battalions
  53d Ind: 69, 74
  82d Ind Motor: 178
  112th Ind Motor: 82
Transport Companies
  73d Ind: 85, 111
  277th Motor: 151, 156
Transport Regiments
  108th: 157; 123d: 192, 214; 125th: 67; 136th: 166; 148th: 38; 149th: 226

Transport Unit: 65
Tsuchida, Col, Yutaka: 192
Tsuchiya, Maj Gen: 232
Tsutsui, Maj, Yoshio: 137
Tsuyuki, Maj, Jinzo: 192
Uchumuchin: 102 (See Road)
Uemura, Lt Gen, Mikio (Cmdr 4th Army): 173
Ulan Bator: 164
Umenoya Hotel: 11, 38
Umezu, Gen, Yoshijiro (Chief, Imperial GHQ): 4
United States
  possible invasion of Korea by forces of: 89
Ushiroku, Gen, Jun (Cmdr 3d Area Army): 5, 5n, 113
  opinions of decisive battle: 6
Vacuum zone: 79
Vladivostok (USSR): 164, 262n
Wang, Gen, Manchukuoan Army: 113
Wangchiatun: 228
Washington D.C.: 13n
Wenkuantun: 120
White Russian: 109n, 125-26
  Bureau: 127
Wonsan: 240, 244, 246, 251
Wuchakou: 14, 41, 79-80, 82-83, 85-86, 90, 98, 123, 230
Wunoerh: 174-75, 185-86
Yalu River: 66
Yamada, Gen Otozo (Cmdr, Kwantung Army): 13
  arrival at Tunghua: 71
  return to Hsinking from Tunghua: 16, 71
Yamagishi, Maj, Takeshi: 7, 12, 43
Yamaguchi, Col: 39
Yamamoto, Lt Gen, Tsutomu (Cmdr 138th Div): 49-50, 52
Yamamoto, 1st Lt: 68, 74-75
Yamamoto, Kazuo: 74-75
Yamanaka, Col, Takasuke: 192
Yamane, Col: 259, 261-63
Yamato Hotel: 187
Yang, Governer of Tunghua

Province: 77
Yangmulin: 27, 30
Yehpaishou: 146, 150-53
Yellow River: 137
Yenchi: 6-7, 9-10, 13, 19, 109n
   conference: 243-45
Yingcheng: 18
Yingkou: 146
Yokoyama, Maj, Akizo: 68, 74-75
Yonghung: 238-39, 251
Yonpo: 246
Yoshikawa, Col, Takeshi: 7, 39
Yoshioka, Lt Gen, Manchukuoan
   Army, Yasunao: 116
Yoshitake, Maj Gen: 137, 138n
   Detachment: 137, 138n
Yumasheyev, Admiral, Soviet: 262n
Yusong: 262
Yuyudong: 264
Zabaikal (USSR): 17
   Soviet Area Army: 99

www.ingramcontent.com/pod-product-compliance
Lightning Source LLC
Chambersburg PA
CBHW082026300426
44117CB00015B/2364